T0305085

# Makeshift Work in a Changing Labour Market

# Makeshift Work in a Changing Labour Market

The Swedish Model in the Post-Financial Crisis Era

*Edited by*

## Christina Garsten

*Professor in Social Anthropology, Department of Social Anthropology and Score (Stockholm Centre for Organizational Research), Stockholm University, Sweden*

## Jessica Lindvert

*Associate Professor in Political Science, National Agency for Education, Sweden*

## Renita Thedvall

*Associate Professor in Social Anthropology, Score (Stockholm Centre for Organizational Research), Stockholm University, Sweden*

Cheltenham, UK • Northampton, MA, USA

Published by
Edward Elgar Publishing Limited
The Lypiatts
15 Lansdown Road
Cheltenham
Glos GL50 2JA
UK

Edward Elgar Publishing, Inc.
William Pratt House
9 Dewey Court
Northampton
Massachusetts 01060
USA

A catalogue record for this book
is available from the British Library

Library of Congress Control Number: 2014950857

This book is available electronically in the **Elgar**online
Business subject collection
DOI 10.4337/9781783479740

ISBN 978 1 78347 973 3 (cased)
ISBN 978 1 78347 974 0 (eBook)

Typeset by Columns Design XML Ltd, Reading
Printed and bound in Great Britain by T.J. International Ltd, Padstow

# Contents

# Contributors

**Matilda Ardenfors** is a political scientist with an interest in the design and implementation of policy, in particular the relation between policy for growth and labour market policy. She is currently working as a management consultant at Ramböll Management Consulting, a consultancy operating in northern Europe. She is head of a department working mainly in the field of growth and innovation policy towards the public sector.

**Ilinca Benson** is Research Director at the Centre for Business and Policy Studies in Stockholm. She holds a PhD in Business Administration from Stockholm School of Economics. Her dissertation thesis dealt with transition in the labour market and the role of outplacement agencies.

**Erik Berntson** is Associate Professor and Senior Lecturer in Work and Organizational Psychology at the Department of Psychology at Stockholm University. His research concerns work and organizational psychology in general – how individuals act, react and perceive their working life. Also, how the labour market changes and how these changes affect working life in general and the individual in particular is of interest. Specifically, he has focused on the concept of employability from a psychological perspective, where he has investigated both what determines employability and what the consequences of being employable are.

**Christina Garsten** is Professor at the Department of Social Anthropology, Stockholm University, and Chair of the Executive Board of Score (Stockholm Centre for Organizational Research). She recently joined Copenhagen Business School as Professor of Globalization and Organization. She researches globalization processes in corporations and markets. Her current project is on the role of think tanks in setting agendas for global governance. Earlier works have focused on transnational organizational culture, on organizational visions of transparency and accountability for transnational trade, and on policy changes towards flexibility and employability in work life.

**Marie Hjalmarsson** holds a PhD in Education and is Senior Lecturer at the Department of Nursing, Health and Culture and the Chair of the

Board of Education at University West, Sweden. Her research focuses on working life with a special interest in learning and how it can be studied and understood in different ways. She is currently focusing on competence and inter-professional learning in welfare professions, as well as the shifting strategies for work life integrated learning in higher education institutions. Her earlier works have focused on power and resistance in caring professions, and on gender in relation to competence and professional identity.

**Jessica Lindvert** is Associate Professor in Political Science with an interest in governance, comparative politics and process tracing. She currently holds a position as Director of Education at the Swedish National Agency for Education.

**Gunilla Olofsdotter** holds a PhD in Sociology and is based in the field of work life studies. She has a particular interest in examining the consequences of flexibility for individuals and work organizations. Earlier works have focused on research on temporary agency work, critical management studies of welfare projects and gender mainstreaming of public organizations. She is currently involved in a research project on labour market migration from Sweden to Norway mediated by temporary work agencies in cooperation with researchers from Work Research Institute in Oslo and Oslo University.

**Julia Peralta** holds a PhD in Economic History and is an Assistant Professor at the School of Health and Medical Sciences at Örebro University. Her research deals with global economic problems and the construction of normality/anomaly, more specifically, on social policy, the emergence of the welfare state, medical history and economic development. Her earlier work focused on the 1990s as a period of economic crisis and mass unemployment. A point of departure for Peralta's research is that definitions of social problems are complex processes of social construction where notions of unemployment are understood and conceptualized differently over time. Frames of interpretation are seen to contribute to the construction and/or (re)production of categories of unemployed within the context of active Swedish labour market policies.

**Ida Seing** has a PhD in medical science with a background in political science. She is a researcher at the Department of Medical and Health Sciences, Linköping University. She conducts research on the organization of social activation policies in local practice. Her dissertation project puts focus on the Swedish social security system by analysing welfare state actors' and employers' role in the return to work process of workers on sick-leave. Her research interests include social and labour market policies and work life issues.

**Renita Thedvall** is Associate Professor in Social Anthropology, Director of Studies at the Department of Social Anthropology and Deputy Director of Score (Stockholm Centre for Organizational Research) at Stockholm University. She is based in the field of policy and organizational anthropology. Earlier works have focused on how policies around quality in work and fair trade are developed, shaped and framed via indicators and standards. Currently, she is working on how the management model Lean is negotiated, discussed and implemented and how it operates in public preschools.

**Lars Walter** is Senior Lecturer at the School of Business, Economics and Law, University of Gothenburg. His research focuses on the organization and practices of labour markets and the intersection between labour markets and the organization of work and employment. Some of his recent publications are: 'The role of organizational objects in construction projects: The case of the collapse and restoration of the Tjörn Bridge' in *Construction Management and Economics* (2014) together with Alexander Styhre; 'Objects-in-use and organizing in action nets: A case of an infusion' in *Journal of Management Inquiry* (2013) together with Kajsa Lindberg; and *Assembling Health Care Organizations: Practice, Materiality and Institutions* (Palgrave Macmillan 2012) together with Kajsa Lindberg and Alexander Styhre.

# Acknowledgements

Few things in society engage us as much as work does. Work is the subject of our daydreams and visions for the future when we are young; work engages our endeavours as adults. It provides a platform for community, as well as the opportunity to shape our identity. But work can also be something that shuts people out from community and participation and from shaping our own future. No wonder work is so central to politicians, scientists and bureaucrats as well as to people in general.

This book is the result of several years of research about the changes that have shaped the Swedish labour market over the last couple of decades. It has grown out of research projects and the research environment that constitutes Score (Stockholm Centre for Organizational Research) at Stockholm University and Stockholm School of Economics. The research projects that are relevant here are particularly: The politics and practices of capability: Lifelong learning for all in a knowledge-intense work life? (supported by the Swedish Research Council); and the research programme Organizing Markets (funded by the Swedish Foundation for Humanities and Social Sciences).

Our ambition has been to highlight what we have seen as key trends in the transformation of the Swedish labour market and discuss these with researchers with similar interests from other universities and disciplines. Our hope is that the book will serve both as a source of information for those interested in work and labour, as well as an inspiration for further reflection and discussion on the dynamics of the Swedish model.

We have had great pleasure in each other's and the authors' views and perspectives during the writing process. Colleagues at Score have also contributed valuable insights and constructive suggestions. We would like to extend a warm thanks to all research colleagues who contributed to the creation of this book.

Stockholm, October 2014
Christina Garsten, Jessica Lindvert and Renita Thedvall

# 1. Introduction: makeshift work in a global labour market

## Christina Garsten, Jessica Lindvert and Renita Thedvall

In the contemporary world, labour markets and the everyday lives of work are being radically transformed. The guiding ideals for how labour markets should be organized are strongly influenced by fluctuations in the economy and by the direction of ideological winds. In this way, the labour market represents a good indicator for broader changes occurring in society. In 2007, the collapse of the financial market in the US had repercussions all over the world. Many countries fell into recession, the effects of which were dire and immediate, both in the financial world and in the manufacturing industry. Entire regions across the world were soon faced with the threat of mass unemployment. People who had never before had cause to worry about what it might mean to lose their jobs entered the ranks of the unemployed for the first time. For some, redundancy notices came quickly and seemingly without warning; for others, they were more expected. The crisis hit some parts of society hard, resulting in unemployment levels we had not seen since the beginning of the 1990s. A large part of the world is now getting used to unemployment numbers that were recently seen to be unacceptable.

After this economic slump, the labour market has become a tougher, more competitive place than it has been for many years. Already with the crisis of the 1990s the labour markets of the Western world underwent significant changes and a different labour market emerged. The neoliberal political ideas of free markets, free trade and emphasis on individual entrepreneurial capabilities and skills as an ideal for organizing society and the labour market slowly gained ground (Harvey 2005; Peck 2010). Twenty years later this ideal had become naturalized as a policy formula for solving problems with unemployment and social exclusion in many countries formerly guided by other ideals, such as an active labour market policy with the goal of protection and full employment rather than workfarism and activation (Daguerre 2007; Larsson, Letell and Thörn 2012; Rogowski, Salais and Whiteside 2012).

The mobility of finance capitalism challenges the capacity of nation states to control transnational corporations by way of political action and legislation. As corporations go global, they are contesting national regulations of workers' rights and human rights, operating across seemingly liminal regulatory spaces. With the limited capacity of nation states and international institutions to oversee the extent to which globalizing corporations are adhering to legal frameworks, work conditions are increasingly subject to voluntary regulations operating at transnational levels. New regimes of accountability aiming to institute ethics and social responsibility in organizational practice are being circulated globally (see, for example, Dolan and Rajak 2011; Scherer, Palazzo and Matten 2009).

With local economies being increasingly tied to global financial flows, national labour markets are as well drawn into the wider circuits of economic activity. In the words of Harper and Lawson (2003: xvi): 'There is no greater issue in the current configuration of work than globalization.' The increased global interconnectedness of markets has had a significant impact on the shaping of national labour markets. As noted by Dicken (2004: 538), 'a whole set of interconnected processes operates simultaneously to produce the changing map of employment, its reverse image, unemployment, and the increasingly uneven map of income.' Similarly, as stated by Scholte (2005: 222), '[a]ccelerated globalization has affected not only the opportunities of waged employment, but also the conditions of work.' In a general sense, globalization processes put downward pressures on benefits, wages and safeguards, particularly for unskilled and semi-skilled labour. In the search for new markets and profitable production arrangements, corporations are outsourcing and externalizing their operations across great distances. Globalization moves jobs such as software development, customer services and assembly work to different places in the world depending on proficiency, wage levels and production costs.

Globalization has been a key force in the displacement of Fordist models of work and production and a concomitant decline of the Fordist social contract (Sholte 2000: 222–3). This move places the worker more clearly at the mercy of market demands and fluctuations, and under more fickle labour contracts. This development, Sholte notes, has affected the North particularly strongly, altering expectations of social provisions, benefits, rights and duties of workers. Flexibilization has contributed to the deregulation of the Swedish labour market, and to the advancement of short-term or contingent contracts (see for example Aronsson 2001;

Furåker, Håkansson and Karlsson 2007; Håkansson, Isidorsson and Kantelius 2013). The advancement of the notion of 'employability' (see Garsten and Jacobsson 2004; McQuaid and Lindsay 2005; Peck and Theodore 2000), pushed by large-scale organizations such as the EU and the OECD, has further fuelled flexibilization, through an accent on the capacity and agency of individuals to create their own job opportunities and careers. In a similar way, notions of 'entrepreneurship' and 'lifelong learning' highlight the readiness for change and for learning-to-learn anew that are deemed necessary in the competitive global labour market (see Weinert et al. 2001). Buzzwords such as these, however fluid and polyvalent, offer a sense of direction to what might otherwise be experienced as the opportunistic and chance-like movements of contemporary capitalism.

Despite its powerful homogenizing force, globalization is not a single unified process or phenomenon, but a complex assemblage of interrelated processes. Globalization does not occur in the same way everywhere. Rather, large-scale processes interact with particular national institutional structures, policies and systems of meaning to articulate quite specific outcomes. In this sense, large-scale economic developments do not involve the stamping of identical imprints across the world, but their outcomes are contingent processes, which depend on their interactions with locally specific circumstances. Accordingly, the world of work is 'creolized' in particular ways, reflecting dynamic interactions of global influence and local cultural specificities (cf. Hannerz 1987). We thus need to be wary about generalizing too fervently about the implications of globalization on local or national labour markets and work practices. Whilst national labour markets are undoubtedly becoming increasingly drawn into transnational circuits, there is still a degree to which they are *inter*national in character, rather than globalized. National regulatory frameworks, conventions and traditions tend to retain some of their influence. Neoliberal ideals have had different impacts in state politics around the globe, mixing with other ideals and translating differently into differing political and organizational contexts (Bonoli and Natali 2012; Ong 2006).

Still, market-based solutions to labour market policy have influenced the welfare state politics of Sweden and have gained a strong hold as an organizing principle and ideal model for social life. The Swedish welfare state has been increasingly hollowed out and mass unemployment has become a reality in what used to be seen as a model case for a full employment society.[1] Social insurance entitlement levels and services have been reduced and subject to increasing sanctions. This is indicative of an increasingly neoliberal direction in labour market policy. This book is about the sway of global market ideals and neoliberal politics into the Swedish labour market.[2] It describes how the Swedish labour market is guided by a market- and bureaucratic logic that is manifested in both the organization of the labour market and in the shaping of the human being as an actor in the labour market.

## TRANSNATIONAL IDEALS AND LABOUR MARKET MODELLING

In Sweden, and in other parts of the world guided by social-democratic welfare ideals, there has been a reorganization of the public sector from decommodification and removal of services from the market towards market-based solutions (Blomqvist 1996; Brunsson and Hägg 1992) and labour market deregulation (Blomqvist 2004; Garsten 2008). At the same time, social and employment policy in the EU have shifted focus from full employment and social protection towards promotion, activation and social investment (Daguerre 2007, Rogowski, Salais and Whiteside 2012, Larsson, Letell and Thörn 2012). This increased focus on workfare and activation connotes a particular way of governing human beings, replete with assumptions of individual agency, responsibility, and capacity to solve unemployment by the help of personal coaches and individualized incentives to work (Garsten, Hollertz and Jacobsson 2013). Responsibility is removed from the state and placed on the individual.

Depending on one's viewpoint, these changes may be seen in the light of a 'social investment perspective' or a 'labour market deregulation at the margins' perspective (Bonoli and Natali 2012). The social investment perspective argues that states have moved away both from the Keynesian ideal and the neoliberal ideal towards a focus on social cohesion with maximized return on social expenditures (OECD 1997; Jenson 2010). It is understood that the best way to maximize return is by investment in children and human capital, and to encourage people to change their paths. Jenson writes: 'There is now some consensus around descriptions of a shared package of policy design that is child-centred as well as employment friendly, and focused on investment in human capital as well as on breaking the intergenerational cycle of disadvantage' (2012: 23). In this perspective, focus is placed on the social costs of unemployment benefits and social protection schemes and employment are promoted through, for example, in-work benefits to create incentives to work (Jenson 2012). The labour market deregulation at the margin perspective points towards the divided labour market consisting of core employees and flexible employees, for which the degree of social protection is to the disadvantage of the latter group (Bergström and Storrie 2003; Garsten 2008). In this perspective, focus is placed on the changes and deregulation of laws and the organization of the labour market, with a view to its human and social implications.

In our view, the social investment perspective does not move away from neoliberal ideals and market-based solutions, as proposed by Jenson. The social investment perspective and the labour market deregulation at the margin perspective both focus on the neoliberal market with its emphasis on cost effectiveness, individual responsibility and deregulation of social protection in the labour market, albeit with very different points of departure. What these two differing perspectives make clear is that there is no convergence towards a neoliberal orthodoxy in any generalized sense of the term (Bonoli and Natali 2012; Scharpf and Schmidt 2000). The Swedish labour market is one example of how these ideals are played out, and how they are intertwined.

## AUDIT CULTURES IN THE LABOUR MARKET

At the same time as the market logic works as a guiding principle for how to organize labour markets and labour market policies, they are also permeated by a bureaucratic logic where work practices, employment measures, workers and unemployed alike are classified and made measurable to show performance; by scholars understood as the bureaucratic heart of neoliberalism (Power 1997; Rose and Miller 1992; Shore and Wright 2000). A useful concept pertaining to these processes is the notion of *management bureaucracy* (Hall 2008). Hall describes management bureaucracy as a way to capture the market and client ideals with the advancement of 'audit society' (Power 1997) and increased bureaucratization. Garsten and Jacobsson (2013) argue that these bureaucratic 'techniques of legibility' allow for an organizational 'reading' and processing of individuals and work practices in the labour market. Through the usage of routines, typologies, diplomas and certifications the strengths and weaknesses of individuals and work processes are made legible, and the bureaucratic apparatus enhances its governing functions. Legibility thus makes individuals and work practices 'process-able' (ibid.).

Techniques of legibility are closely related to the bureaucratization processes guiding the audit society (Power 1997) or audit cultures (Strathern 2000a), which entail that both individuals and organizations are becoming subject to increased scrutiny and control. The need for auditing is based on a lack of trust in the process (Power 1997) and a tendency to place trust in the seeming objectivity and political neutrality of numbers (Strathern 2000a). Indicators are used as instruments to guide and govern. The use of statistics then becomes a way of governing by numbers (Miller 2001). That which is 'political' moves from the realm of interests and values into the realm of technologies such as indexes, indicators and statistics.

In audit cultures, the organizing of labour market policy and work practices in public organizations has been dominated by the management techniques of New Public Management (NPM) (Hood 1991; Sahlin-Andersson 2001; Shore and Wright 2000). In its general form, NPM is based on the conception that goals must be set and then evaluated by results, in the form of indicators and statistics, to be able to hold someone accountable. The results are then often 'benchmarked', with 'best practices' and 'good examples' produced and presented. These management techniques derive their direction to a large extent from the management ideal of transparency, of making things or processes visible (see, for example, Garsten and Lindh de Montoya 2008; Hood and Heald 2006).

The notion of 'transparency' suggests that regulation may in part be accomplished by way of revelation (Florini 2003). The idea is that by making information about policy-making processes, decision-making, environmental and labour practices or budgets accessible to the public, and to international and transnational organizations, governments and corporations are forced to be accountable and trustworthy. Transparency, then, gives the impression of being all good and neutral. However, there is nothing innocent about the idea of transparency (Strathern 2000b). Much may be hidden behind the 'veil of transparency' and what is made transparent is a matter of choice (West and Sanders 2003: 26). Still, the management ideal of transparency works as a regulatory mechanism, giving weight to audit procedures and techniques of legibility in the management of individuals and work practices in the labour market.

## MAKESHIFT WORKERS: EXPECTATIONS AND OBLIGATIONS IN THE CONTEMPORARY LABOUR MARKET

As a consequence of new political ideals, ever more responsibility is placed on individuals to make themselves employable in order to fit the demands of the labour market (Garsten and Jacobsson 2004; Larsson, Letell and Thörn 2012). This applies in particular to people who are looking for work, but also to those who already have a job. The ideal employee is 'the enterprising self' (Miller and Rose 1995), capable of carving out his or her niche in the labour market. People are encouraged to be creative and autonomous, crafters of their own success. Ideally, they should be imaginative and responsible, but also risk-taking, open to change, hard-working, self-reliant, optimistic and self-assured (Heelas 1991; Ho 2009; Martin 1997; Thedvall 2004). Quite simply, the individual is expected to be entrepreneurial. This is thus a different type of idealized citizen than that encouraged in industrial society's 'organizational man' (Whyte 2002). The contemporary ideal is a person who jumps from job to job and welcomes change, who takes responsibility for both her or his work and career, someone who is imaginative, self-assured and optimistic: the flexible and employable person (Barley and Kunda 2001; Garsten 2008; Garsten and Jacobsson 2004).

The norm of the enterprising, entrepreneurial worker goes hand in hand with the notion that people's knowledge and skills often have a 'best-before' date. And the wheels are spinning faster and faster. The average period of employment at each employer is becoming briefer, the 'best-before' date of education and training becoming shorter, employment contracts becoming less fixed, project-based employment more common, and career paths less and less standardized (Augustsson and Sandberg 2004; Beck 1992; Bosco 1997; Hansen and Orbán 2002; Sabel and Zeitlin 1997). In today's work life, learning has also come to be seen as a fixed point of reference from which people can navigate (Raelin 2008, OECD 1996). Since the late 1990s, lifelong learning has outcompeted all other terms in the field to the extent that we can talk about a discursive or policy epidemic (Jarvis 2007; Nicoll 2006). In December 2006, the European Commission and the European Council also issued a recommendation on lifelong learning. The background to this initiative was that the education systems of most of the member countries still targeted young people, the participation of adults in learning and education was not increasing fast enough, and that low-skilled people educated themselves only to a much lesser extent. The EU hereby underlined the importance for member states to create functioning infrastructures for adult learning (European Commission 2000, 2006). In the EU, learning has also come to replace education in many contexts (European Commission 2006). This signals not only a linguistic change, but a different way of thinking, acting and organizing, where focus is placed on people's capacity for individual learning, rather than on the provisions of the educational system or on the labour market system.

Sweden exemplifies well the wider trends of these ideals as the all-encompassing solution for labour market efficiency.

## SWEDISH FRICTIONS: TOWARDS A MAKESHIFT IDEOLOGY

For the most part of the late twentieth century, the Swedish labour market was guided by ideals of full employment and active labour market policy (cf. Furåker and Blomsterberg 2002; Ohlsson and Olofsson 1998). Historically, these ambitions were articulated in the Swedish model, which combines key economic and political objectives into a shared theoretical framework, within which an active labour market policy plays a decisive role. Active labour market policy in this approach focused on labour market training programmes of the unemployed to fit the demands of the labour market. In this approach, social security was also seen as a precondition for economic development. The community's acceptance of economic change was thought to be based on employees' perceptions of enjoying some degree of social security. This is still the case, but the very idea of what social security means has shifted towards more of a makeshift ideology.

This makeshift ideology emphasizes in a nutshell the principle of exchangeability of people. The employment situation is characterized by a continued and constant exchange situation where the performance of employees is continuously under the microscope, and investigated with various performance instruments to ensure and make clear that the exchange takes place in the most economically rational way. As a whole, the new labour market entails a challenge – not only for the unemployed, but also for those who already have jobs. Being employable is today essential, regardless of whether one has a job or not. The exchange process itself has thus come into greater focus for the cadre of organizations that support the Swedish labour market.

The makeshift ideology has particular organizational manifestations. The Public Employment Service in Sweden has, for example, undergone a radical reorganization (for details see Chapter 2). In 1993, the state monopoly on employment services ended and there is now a range of actors other than the state engaging in employment services. These new rules have cleared the way for a brokering market. Temporary staffing agencies in the labour market have grown strong (see, for example, Bergström et al. 2007; Håkansson and Isidorsson 2004; Koene et al. 2014). Coaching firms are another group of private actors that in various ways mediate, or prepare people for employment (Benson 2008). The Swedish state and the Public Employment Services have instead taken on a more controlling role, making sure that the unemployed follow labour market regulations for receiving unemployment benefits.

For the unemployed, labour market policy and regulations have an increased focus on workfare and activation with an enhanced emphasis on matching, supply and demand, and competition rather than labour market training programmes and skills development. Activation in Sweden has, over the last decades, and even more so during the conservative alliance government in the period 2006–2014, shifted towards individualized solutions such as job coaching and the Job and Development Programme (Garsten, Hollertz and Jacobsson 2013). In relation to these changes, the social security of persons has become increasingly connected to their ability to work. Stricter eligibility criteria for unemployment insurance have been introduced, requirements on occupational and geographical mobility increased, participation in active measures no longer qualifies for a new benefit period, a time limit for unemployment insurance has been introduced (300 days; 450 days for parents with children in the household under 18) as well as sanctions for non-acceptance of an assignment to a programme or an 'appropriate job' (Bengtsson and Jacobsson 2013; Garsten, Hollertz and Jacobsson 2013). Furthermore, Sweden has implemented strong activation principles, not only in unemployment insurance but also in health insurance, and introduced new requirements in order to qualify for social assistance (Bengtsson and Jacobsson 2013; Björnberg 2012; Garsten, Hollertz and Jacobsson 2013).

The above themes are developed in the chapters of this book, and a number of concrete examples from the labour market in Sweden are given. In Part I, we discuss the changes in the Swedish labour market from an organizational perspective. The focus here is on how the infrastructure for employment services has changed, how governance of today's employment services differs from that of the past, and how people who work as counsellors, employment officers and career coaches view their task, and how lifelong learning is used as an organizational tool. In Part II of the book, we relate all of this to the perspective of the human being.

## A MARKET FOR MEDIATING EMPLOYMENT TAKES SHAPE

In the first part of the book (chapters 2–7), we describe what the market for employment services looks like, the various functions of the different actors, and how these functions differ from one another.

In Chapter 2, Jessica Lindvert describes how government influence over the labour market and employment services has changed. The Public

Employment Service is now only one of many actors in a growing employment services market (though it remains a controlling body for the unemployment insurance fund). The Public Employment Service no longer holds the unique status as an employment agency it used to hold. In today's labour market, we can distinguish at least four types of employment brokering agencies whose activities are primarily aimed at getting people into employment: a first group is made up of the established government agencies, such as the Public Employment Service and the Social Insurance Agency (*Försäkringskassan*). A second group comprises staffing agencies and insurance companies, and a third group consists of stakeholders, like union organizations and employer associations that collaborate by way of so-called employment security councils. A fourth group are the in-house actors, consisting of 'employer rings' set up between companies or in larger company groups via job exchange centres or transition units (Bäckström 2006).

Another new development is the sorting of jobseekers into different categories, divided up among different employment services actors. For its part, the Public Employment Service increasingly works with job-seekers furthest from the labour market, such as new immigrants, people on long-term sick leave, youths and people with disabilities. This is a part of the Public Employment Service's political mandate (SFS 2007:1030). On the private side of employment services, agencies tend to specialize in different occupational categories and industries. For example, there are currently staffing firms that specialize in health care, sales and marketing, higher education, or in ethnic and cultural expertise. Here, a market based on a logic of differentiation is emerging, where specialist skills and expertise is considered to facilitate the mediation of employment (Garsten and Jacobsson, 2013).

In chapters 3, 4 and 5 we show how the Public Employment Service organizes itself in the employment services market. In Chapter 4, Julia Peralta points out significant differences between the tasks of the placement officers (employment officers) and the counsellors. The division of roles is based on a division between, on the one hand, jobseekers defined as 'self-reliant', where the work of the case officer is concentrated on matching jobseekers to employers and, on the other hand, groups defined as problematic, where the activities have to a greater extent to do with activation. The role of the placement officer is to maintain a good reputation outwardly, with employers, companies and society at large. Similarly to how brokers pack and sell products, placement officers work to match 'suitable' jobseekers to employers and companies; here, it is a matter of a speedy process where things move very quickly. In cases where the Public Employment Service's job is to mediate work rapidly, the placement officer plays a central role.

The Public Employment Service's second main group, the counsellors, act increasingly as therapists for people further removed from the labour market and where they, through conversation with the jobseeker, try to find paths to activity. It is more common for the counsellors to see their work as a calling, and the educational backgrounds of these case officers are often in health care, behavioural therapy or education. The task of the counsellor is similar to that of a priest or therapist as a spiritual caregiver. In cases where the task relates to activating and helping weaker groups, the counsellors take a dominant role and their work is focused on helping the jobseekers to understand what they want.

Chapters 3–5 also discuss how and with what ambition employment officers classify and categorize people. In Chapter 4, Lars Walter describes how the jobseekers must learn what it means to be a jobseeker, in accordance with the demands placed on them by the Public Employment Service. Walter describes a process of gradual adaptation to the expectations expressed by case officers and to the structures that apply. In the introductory phase, the jobseeker has a relatively high degree of autonomy. If a person registers as a jobseeker, follows the rules and maintains contact with the Public Employment Service, that person may choose to present him- or herself and seek the jobs that he or she wishes. In a second phase, when an action plan is drawn up, the relationship changes in that the job search builds more on the idea of jointly formulated goals and strategies. In this phase, the Public Employment Service is responsible for monitoring compliance and has a greater ability to initiate sanctions. When a jobseeker, in a third phase, loses her unemployment insurance and becomes registered in the job and development programme, individual autonomy is further reduced in that the jobseeker's situation is even more tightly regulated, managed and controlled. Thus, the descriptions used in the classification become more than just descriptions; they become an expression of governance and control.

In Chapter 5, Ida Seing looks at the processes of coding jobseekers with reduced work capacity done by the Public Employment Service. In this way, the jobseekers are sorted into different groups that are targeted by different intervention packages. The Public Employment Service's prioritizing of the so-called weak groups is expressed, among other ways, in the rapid increase in the number of people with disabilities registered since the beginning of the 1990s. One of the government's interim targets includes that employment levels for people with disabilities should in the long term reflect their representation in the population as a whole. The target group's employment level should also increase more rapidly than the rest of the labour force (Prop. 2007/08:1, Expenditure Area 13).

A second trend that we draw attention to involves the Public Employment Service's increasingly audit- and assessment-related methods for administrating the flow of people from unemployment into new jobs (chapters 3–5). It is through these methods that labour market policy is turned into action. The work of coupling jobseekers' experience and knowledge to a standardized taxonomy involves certain experiences being routinely defined as important and others as less so. By extension, the taxonomy means that a norm is established for what is desirable. The growing emphasis on the case officer's controlling function demonstrates the increased importance placed on legalities and equal treatment of jobseekers, and increased efficiency in the handling of jobseekers.

Yet another change investigated here is that more initiatives towards cooperation are now taken between government agencies, municipalities, companies and other organizations. When it comes to work-related rehabilitation, one often looks for common solutions whereby different organizations are responsible for different parts of the process, for instance, for counselling, investigations, rehabilitation and preparatory measures. For example, in 2008, the Public Employment Service and the Social Insurance Agency entered into more extensive cooperation in the area of rehabilitation. The Public Employment Service also works with other so-called complementary actors, such as private job coaches.

Today, staffing firms are established employment brokering agencies, both in recruitment services and in terms of contracting and temporary staffing. In Chapter 6, Gunilla Olofsdotter shows how staffing firms learn to handle competition and relations with client companies. The penetration rate of staffing agencies (i.e. how large a percentage of the employed population that work for staffing agencies) in the Swedish labour market was estimated to be 1.5 per cent in 2013 (scb.se/aku), showing a strong growth rate during the years of the financial crisis, since 2009. There is reason to believe that the actual number is even higher. Many jobseekers pass through a staffing agency during the course of a year, without being directly employed by them. Another reason why the penetration rate may presumably be somewhat higher is the fact that the number of employed includes not only people who are actually working, but also people enrolled in labour market measures. Gunilla Olofsdotter describes how staffing firms have become actors to reckon with in both temporary staffing and long-term recruitment of labour, and how their clients must learn how best to make use of them. A market has emerged in the competition between staffing agencies and the job opportunities offered by client organizations. Temporary staffing also lays bare certain tensions and imbalances in the labour market. The mobile work lives of contracted consultants, with short-term social relations and high demands on adaptability, are up against the norm of traditional permanent employment and the desire for long-term employment at a single workplace. The presence of staffing agencies, at first perceived as an exception, and in certain cases as a threat to established norms, is now an accepted feature of the labour market.

In Chapter 7, Ilinca Benson addresses the development and normative message of transition agreements. Almost half of all employees in Sweden are covered by transition agreements. In order to meet the growing demand for this type of protection in working life, an actual market for transition services has emerged, with commercial actors, government actors and other stakeholders. Benson shows that the transition programmes offered in the transition agreements differ in some respects, but that they often contain some form of assessment of the unemployed person's prospects of getting a job, starting a business, or in some other way becoming a member of the working population. The programmes often contain counselling on how to look for a job and an action plan. Transition actors see looking for work as a skill that needs to be taught, and which is best achieved through personalized advice or coaching. Benson highlights that this trend implies that market logic increasingly forms the basis, or is at least held up as an ideal, for social relations between actors in the labour market. This means a shift in norms – from employment security to employability. Employment security is based on a worker's relationship to an employer – where the security lies in the employment relationship. Employability, on the other hand, is based on the employee's perceived value in the labour market. This in turn entails that a job in itself does not guarantee security – it is instead a matter of ensuring that one remains attractive and in demand in the market.

And last but not least, we want to emphasize the tendency towards the increasing responsibility placed on the individual in searching for a new job. For example, the Public Employment Service has introduced individual action plans where the jobseeker and the public employment officer together draw up a plan for how the jobseeker is going to find employment. The individual action plan has become an important tool in the public employment officer's everyday work (see Chapter 3 by Lars Walter). If we turn our gaze to recent reforms, we see that the Public Employment Service has been working to redirect its arsenal of measures from conversion of people's skills (fitting the labour market) by training and practice to a focus on the individual's ability to transform her- or himself to become employable. The recipe of the day calls for providing support to those who have recently become unemployed – entirely in line with the general trend towards an increased focus on the individual's responsibility and ability to take initiative. Increased emphasis is placed on the case officer as an assessor or verifier of which jobseekers are employable, to what extent a jobseeker is employable, and the extent to which a jobseeker qualifies for unemployment insurance. This discussion leads us to the second part of the book.

## THE HUMAN DIMENSION IN A CHANGING LABOUR MARKET

In the second part of the book, chapters 8–12, we describe the contemporary labour market from the perspective of the human being. Today's labour market places demands on people to be able to take initiative, to plan, to organize and to perform complex work tasks (Boud and Garrick 1999; Thång 2006). 'Career School' sections in daily papers inform people how they can show that they are 'right for the job' or how to 'spring clean' their CVs. In today's labour market, a person can sell him- or herself as a worker in a market, as a competent market actor (Benson 2008). It is quite simply a matter of making oneself employable. Catchwords in today's labour market are for employees to be flexible, independent and accountable. One theme addressed in the book is what the demands for industrious, entrepreneurial people mean for the employee?

An important platform for understanding the individual's conditions is the organizational change that has taken place in the labour market and in the organization of work. Temporary employment positions are now more commonplace than they were in the beginning of the 1990s.[3] Flexibility in the labour market to a certain extent requires more mobile actors, with transferable skills, that can fit together like Lego pieces in a complex organizational game. From an employer's perspective, it is also easier to make changes to the staffing structure and to assemble a workforce according to the business's needs. With a more varied selection of organizations offering employment services, staffing solutions, skills development and rehabilitation, the relations individuals have to these organizations also become different. People's sense of belonging to an organization changes, as contracts become more transient.

In Chapter 8, Erik Berntson discusses the 'new' psychological contract that is governed by catchwords such as exchange, flexibility and development and what it means to 'feel employable'. Perceived employability has become central for an individual's health and well-being, but also for how he or she operates in the workplace. Perceiving oneself as employable is a way to gain control over one's own work life, it provides scope to act both externally, by being able to change jobs, and internally, by signalling that one believes in one's own worth. Regardless of whether the individual actually changes jobs or not, the perception of being employable itself is a way to cope with a flexible work environment. For the individual, this means a lifelong commitment to improving one's employability, which in practice means lifelong learning.

Yet another trend addressed in this part of the book is the need for individuals to showcase knowledge and skills to be viable in the labour market. In order to get a job, it is important that relevant knowledge be documented in the form of transcripts, diplomas, certifications or authorizations (Garsten et al. 2006). In Chapter 10, Renita Thedvall discusses the focus on evidence-based practice in social work, implying that the decisions of social workers must increasingly be based on scientifically proven knowledge. There must be visible evidence that an intervention works. Experience-based knowledge, which is harder to verbalize, is given less space. This has also had consequences for how social workers perform their work. Demands to make one's knowledge visible have meant an increase in social workers' administrative burden, as the time it takes to conduct investigations has increased (Thedvall and Rossi 2009). This trend has led to a change in how individuals learn their jobs at the social services office. More emphasis is being put on formal, standardized courses in evidence-based methods. It is formal, visible and articulated knowledge that dominates skills development in the social services office.

The idea that knowledge and skills must be made visible is also found in other areas of social care, such as home help services. In Chapter 9, Marie Hjalmarsson shows how attempts to rationalize home help and make it more effective led to an attempt to make the work practices of home help personnel visible. One instrument used by the municipality was to equip home help workers with handheld computers that they used to record the tasks they performed. However, since the computers only highlight work that counts as direct care, and not relational work, this creates challenges and tensions for home help workers. It is above all the elements in between, or 'indefinable time', that are problematic – since it is impossible to register and visibilize such work practices, and thus to demonstrate their value. When this indefinable time is removed from the workday, home help workers develop yet another experience-based skill – that of learning to balance their loyalties to the care recipients, their workmates and the employer, meaning that they break certain rules put in place in the name of rationalization, but not others. This they do in order to continue to carry out their work satisfactorily. The micro-management of services that the care recipient has been granted makes these conflicting loyalties tangible and contributes to the renewed importance of the workers' 'balancing skill'.

In Chapter 11, Matilda Ardenfors and Jessica Lindvert illuminate the difference between formal access to skills training in working life and the ability to take advantage of it. Even if skills development is offered – on paper – in the workplace, there are a number of factors that prevent people from taking advantage of it. The study, which looks at the Swedish Police, Social Services, the automotive industry and the food industry, shows that access to professional development is dependent on where in the organization a person works, whether that person works in production or in an administrative capacity. Occupational groups whose work demands post-secondary education (policing, social services and administrative positions in the noted industries) generally have access to a larger range of formal professional development in the workplace than others. This study shows that there are a number of key factors that prevent employees from taking advantage of the training opportunities offered. For example, in many organizations, there are strong norms about collegiality and a reluctance to let the work team down. A lack of influence over work shifts as well as an inability to predict them also affects employees' actual possibilities of taking part in skills development. The same applies to the ability to take part in training programmes outside regular work hours, a difficult equation not least for workers with young children. In addition, many also have doubts about whether the skills development offered can increase their employability outside the current work organization. As a whole, it appears that professional development in the workplace remains a resource primarily for employees who already have the key to lifelong learning and who already learned, during their education years, to seek out knowledge and learn new things. For others, the offer of professional development remains an offer that is not realized (see, for example, Lindvert and Jambrén 2005; Garsten et al. 2006; Thedvall and Rossi 2009).

These chapters raise the question of whether lifelong learning with its positive connotations is perceived as an offer with no strings attached? Or should lifelong learning be seen instead as a decree that the self-regulating individual has become responsible for? Is lifelong learning changing to become more a demand than an option in the eyes of employees? And what type of knowledge – experience-based, tacit knowledge or standardized and textualized knowledge – is it that is encouraged? With these chapters in hand, Christina Garsten discusses these issues in a concluding chapter, focusing on the trend towards exchangeability, measurability and accountability. In this final chapter, she argues that the normalizing practices that characterize the organization of the labour market reinforce the notion that the labour market is in some respects a market. These normative practices contribute to shaping human beings as a labour force and as a commodity in the labour market, and also shape the actors involved in employment services into market actors.

Work is a cornerstone of people's individual and social development, as well as of the economy. How the mediation of employment is organized is a question that affects all agencies in society and has great significance for how working life is shaped. When the labour is reorganized, there is reason for us to contemplate the ensuing effects on individuals as well as on society as a whole. What are the practices that govern the brokering of labour? What assumptions do they build on? What normative messages are being conveyed to people in search of job opportunities? Sweden, with its long history of active labour policy and strong regulations, provides a poignant illustration of the transnational influences of changing policy ideals. It is with these questions that we embark on a quest to understand the new job market.

## NOTES

1. Unemployment in Sweden in December 2007 was 5.6%, in the same period 2009 8.6%, and in 2013 7.5% (*Arbetskraftsundersökningar*, AKU, www. scb.se).
2. Research underpinning this book was made possible by different sources of funding (see each chapter for details). The synthetic work was realized by a research programme grant from The Swedish Foundation for Humanities and Social Sciences, *Organizing Markets*, coordinated by Nils Brunsson.
3. According to Statistics Sweden's labour surveys (*Arbetskraftsundersökningar*, AKU, www.scb.se), fixed term employees made up 14.1% of the total number of employed persons aged 16–64 for the second quarter of 2010, compared to 10.5% for the same period in 1993.

## REFERENCES

Aronsson, Gunnar (2001), 'A new employment contract', *Scandinavian Journal of Work, Environment & Health*, 27(6), 361–4.
Augustsson, Fredrik and Åke Sandberg (2004), 'Time for competence? Competence development among interactive media workers', in Christina Garsten and Kerstin Jacobsson (eds), *Learning to be Employable: New agendas on work, responsibility and learning in a globalizing world*. Basingstoke: Palgrave Macmillan, pp. 210–30.

Bäckström, Henrik (2006), *Omställningssystemets agenter och försäkringar på den svenska arbetsmarknaden. Bemanningsföretag, försäkringsbolag, myndigheter och trygghetsråd i helig allians?* Report 2006:4. Stockholm: National Institute for Working Life.

Barley, Stephen R. and Gideon Kunda (2001), 'Bringing work back in', *Organization Science*, 12(1), 76–95.

Beck, Ulrich (1992), *Risk Society: Towards a new modernity*. London: Sage.

Bengtsson, Mattias and Kerstin Jacobsson (2013), 'The end of the universal welfare state? Activation and social protection in a new century in Sweden'. Draft paper.

Benson, Ilinca (2008), *Organisering av övergångar på arbetsmarknaden. En studie av omställningsprogram*. Stockholm: Economic Research Institute (EFI), Stockholm School of Economics.

Bergström, Ola and Donald Storrie (eds) (2003), *Contingent Employment in Europe and the United States*. Cheltenham and Northampton, MA: Edward Elgar.

Bergström, Ola, Kristina Håkansson, Tommy Isidorsson and Lars Walter (eds) (2007), *Den nya arbetsmarknaden – Bemanningsbranschens etablering i Sverige*. Lund: Academia Adacta AB.

Björnberg, Ulla (2012), 'Social policy reforms in Sweden: New perspectives on rights and obligations', in Bengt Larsson, Martin Letell and Håkan Thörn (eds), *Transformations of the Swedish Welfare State: From social engineering to governance?* Houndmills, Basingstoke: Palgrave Macmillan.

Blomqvist, Christine (1996), *I marknadens namn. Mångtydiga reformer i svenska kommuner*. Stockholm: Nerenius and Santérus förlag.

Blomqvist, Paula (2004), 'The choice revolution: Privatization of Swedish Social Services in the 1990s', *Social Policy & Administration*, 38(2), 171–93.

Bonoli, Giuliano and David Natali (eds) (2012), *The Politics of the New Welfare State*. Oxford: Oxford University Press.

Bosco, Andrew (1997), 'Putting Europe into the systems: A review of social protection issues', in E. Gabaglio and R. Hoffman (eds), *European Trade Union Yearbook 1997*. Brussels: ETUI.

Boud, David and John Garrick (1999), *Understanding Learning at Work*. London: Routledge.

Brunsson, Nils and Ingemund Hägg (1992), *Marknadens makt*. Stockholm: SNS förlag.

Daguerre, Anne (2007), *Active Labour Market Policies and Welfare Reform. Europe and the US in comparative perspective*. Basingstoke: Palgrave Macmillan.

Dicken, Peter (2004/2003), *Global Shift: Reshaping the global economic map in the 21st century*. London: Sage.

Dolan, Catherine and Dina Rajak (2011), 'Introduction: Ethnographies of corporate ethicizing', *Focaal – Journal of Global and Historical Anthropology*, 60, 3–8.

European Commission (2000), *A Memorandum on Lifelong Learning*. SEC 1832.

European Commission (2006), *Adult Learning: It is never too late to learn*. Communication from the Commission 2006, 614.

Florini, Anne (2003), *The Coming Democracy: New rules for running a new world*. London: Island Press.

Furuåker, Bengt and Marianne Blomsterberg (2002), 'Arbetsmarknadspolitik', in Lars H. Hansen and Pal Orban (eds), *Arbetslivet*. Lund: Studentlitteratur.

Furåker, Bengt, Kristina Håkansson and Jan Ch. Karlsson (eds) (2007), *Flexibility and Stability in Working Life*. Basingstoke: Palgrave Macmillan.

Garsten, Christina (1999a), 'Betwixt and between: Temporary employees as liminal subjects in flexible organizations', *Organization Studies*, 20(4), 601–17.

Garsten, Christina (1999b), 'Loose links and tight attachments: Modes of employment and meaning-making in a changing labor market', in Richard A. Goodman (ed.), *Modern Organizations and Emerging Conundrums*. Lanham, MD: New Lexington Press.

Garsten, Christina (2008), *Workplace Vagabonds: Career and community in changing worlds of work*. Basingstoke: Palgrave Macmillan.

Garsten, Christina and Kerstin Jacobsson (eds) (2004), *Learning to be Employable: New agendas on work, responsibility and learning in a globalizing world*. Basingstoke: Palgrave Macmillan.

Garsten, Christina and Kerstin Jacobsson (2013), 'Sorting people in and out: The plasticity of the categories of employability, work capacity and disability as technologies of government', *Ephemera. Theory and Politics in Organizations*, 13(4), 825–50.

Garsten, Christina and Monica Lindh de Montoya (eds) (2008), *Transparency in a New Global Order: Unveiling organizational visions*. Cheltenham and Northampton, MA: Edward Elgar.

Garsten, Christina, Katarina Hollertz and Kerstin Jacobsson (2013), 'Local worlds of activation. The diverse pathways of three Swedish municipalities'. Paper presented the ESPAnet-conference in Poznan, 5–7 September 2013. Session 9: The local welfare state.

Garsten, Christina, Niklas Jambrén, Jessica Lindvert and Renita Thedvall (2006), *From Employment to the Development of Workers' Capabilities: Mobility, learning and responsibility in Swedish worklife*. Report for the European Commission.

Hall, Patrik (2008), *Managmentbyråkrati. Organisationspolitisk makt i svensk offentlig förvaltning*. Malmö: Liber.

Hannerz, Ulf (1987), 'The world in creolization', *Africa*, 57, 547–59.

Hansen, Lars H. and Pál Orbán (2002), *Arbetslivet*, Lund: Studentlitteratur.

Harper, Douglas and Helen M. Lawson (eds) (2003), *The Cultural Study of Work*. Lanham, MD: Rowman & Littlefield.

Harvey, David (2005), *A Brief History of Neoliberalism*. Oxford: Oxford University Press.

Heelas, Paul (1991), 'Cults for capitalism. Self religion, magic and the empowerment of business', in Peter Gee and John Fulton (eds), *Religion and Power, Decline and Growth*, London: British Sociological Association, pp. 28–42.

Ho, Karen (2009), *Liquidated: An Ethnography of Wall Street*. London: Duke University Press.

Hood, Christopher (1991), 'A Public Management for all seasons?', *Public Administration*, 69(1), 3–19.

Hood, Christopher and David Heald (eds) (2006), *Transparency: The key to better governance?* Oxford: Oxford University Press.

Håkansson, Kristina and Tommy Isidorsson (2004), 'Hyresarbetskraft. Användning av inhyrd arbetskraft på den svenska arbetsmarknaden', *Arbetsmarknad and Arbetsliv*, 10, 187–205.

Håkansson, Kristina, Tommy Isidorsson and Hannes Kantelius (2013), 'Stable flexibility: Strategic long term use of temporary agency workers in Sweden', *International Journal of Action Research*, 9(3), 278–95.

Jarvis, Peter (2007), *Globalisation, Lifelong Learning and the Learning Society: Sociological perspectives.* London: Routledge.

Jenson, Jane (2010), 'Diffusing ideas after neo-liberalism: The social investment perspective in Europe and Latin America', *Global Social Policy*, 10, 59–84.

Jenson, Jane (2012), 'A new politics for the social investment perspective: Objectives, instruments, and areas of intervention in welfare regimes', in Bonoli, Giuliano and David Natali (eds), *The Politics of the New Welfare State.* Oxford: Oxford University Press, pp. 21–44.

Koene, Bas, Christina Garsten and Nathalie Galais (eds) (2014), *Management and Organization of Temporary Agency Work.* London: Routledge.

Larsson, Bengt, Martin Letell and Håkan Thörn (eds) (2012), *Transformations of the Swedish Welfare State. From social engineering to governance?* Basingstoke: Palgrave Macmillan.

Lindvert, Jessica and Niklas Jambrén (2005), *Landet lagom i 2000-talet. Arbete, lärande och socialt ansvar i politik och praktik.* Score Working Paper Series 2005, 4.

Martin, Emily (1997), 'Managing Americans: Policy and changes in the meanings of work and the self', in Cris Shore and Susan Wright (eds), *Anthropology of Policy. Critical perspectives on governance and power.* London: Routledge, pp. 239–57.

McQuaid, Ronald W. and Colin Lindsay (2005), 'The concept of employability', *Urban Studies*, 42(2), 197–219.

Miller, Peter (2001), 'Governing by numbers: Why calculative practices matter', *Social Research*, 68(2), 379–95.

Miller, Peter and Nikolas Rose (1995), 'Production, identity, and democracy', *Theory and Society*, 24(3), 427–67.

Nicoll, Kathrine (2006), *Flexibility and Lifelong Learning: Policy, discourse, politics.* London: Routledge.

OECD (1996), *Lifelong Learning for All: Meeting of the Education Committee at Ministerial Level.* Paris: OECD.

OECD (1997), *Beyond 2000. The new social policy agenda*, OECD Working Papers, V. Paris: OECD.

Ohlsson, Rolf and Jonas Olofsson (1998), *Arbetslöshetens dilemma: motsättningar och samförstånd i svensk arbetslöshetsdebatt under två hundra år.* Stockholm: SNS.

Ong, Aihwa (2006), *Neoliberalism as Exception. Mutations in citizenship and sovereignty.* Durham, NC: Duke University Press.

Peck, Jamie (2010), *Constructions of Neoliberal Reason.* Oxford: Oxford University Press.

Peck, Jamie and Nik Theodore (2000), 'Beyond "employability"', *Cambridge Journal of Economics*, 24, 729–49.

Power, Michael (1997), *The Audit Society: Rituals of Verification*. Oxford: Oxford University Press.

Prop. 2007/08:1 *Budgetpropositionen för 2008*.

Raelin, Joseph A. (2008), *Work-based Learning: Bridging knowledge and action in the workplace*. San Francisco, CA: Jossey-Bass.

Rogowski, Ralf, Robert Salais and Noel Whiteside (2012), *Transforming European Employment Policy. Labour market transitions and the promotion of capability*. Cheltenham and Northampton, MA: Edward Elgar.

Rose, Nicholas and Peter Miller (1992), 'Political power beyond the state: Problematics of government', *British Journal of Sociology*, 43(2), 173–205.

Sabel, Charles and Jonathan Zeitlin (eds) (1997), *World of Possibilities: Flexibility and mass production in western industrialization*. Cambridge: Cambridge University Press.

Sahlin-Andersson, Kerstin (2001), 'National, international and transnational constructions of New Public Management', in Tom Christensen and Per Lægreid (eds), *New Public Management: The transformation of ideas and practice*. Aldershot: Ashgate.

Scharpf, Fritz W. and Vivien A. Schmidt (2000), *Welfare and Work in the Open Economy Volume I: From vulnerability to competitiveness in comparative perspective*. Oxford: Oxford University Press.

Scherer, Andreas Georg, Guido Palazzo and Dirk Matten (2009), 'Introduction to the special issue: Globalization as a challenge for business responsibilities', *Business Ethics*, 19(3), 327–47.

Scholte, Jan Aart (2005/2000), *Globalization: A critical introduction*. Basingstoke: Palgrave Macmillan.

SFS 2007:1030, *Förordning med instruktion för Arbetsförmedlingen*, Swedish Code of Statutes.

Shore, Cris and Susan Wright (2000), 'Coercive accountability: The rise of audit culture in higher education', in Marilyn Strathern (ed.), *Audit Cultures: Anthropological studies in accountability, ethics and the academy*. London: Routledge, pp. 57–89.

Strathern, Marilyn (ed.) (2000a), *Audit Cultures. Anthropological studies in accountability, ethics and the academy*. London: Routledge.

Strathern, Marilyn (2000b), 'The tyranny of transparency', *British Educational Research Journal*, 26(3), 309–21.

Thång, Per-Olof (2006), 'Arbetslivspedagogik', in Jan Holmer and Birger Simonson (eds), *Forskning om arbetslivet*. Lund: Studentlitteratur.

Thedvall, Renita (2004), 'Do it yourself: Making up the self-employed individual in the Swedish Public Employment Service', in Christina Garsten and Kerstin Jacobsson (eds), *Learning to be Employable: New agendas on work, responsibility and learning in a globalizing world*. Basingstoke: Palgrave Macmillan, pp. 131–51.

Thedvall, Renita and Nina Rossi (2009), *Lärandets praktik inom socialtjänsten och livsmedelsindustrin*. Score Working Paper Series 2009, 5.

Weinert, Patricia, Michèle Baukens, Patrick Bollérot, Marina Pineschi-Gapènne and Ulrich Walwei (2001), *Employability. From theory to practice*. New Brunswick, N.J.: Transaction.

West, Harry G. and Todd Sanders (eds) (2003), *Transparency and Conspiracy: Ethnographies of suspicion in the new world order*. Durham, NC: Duke University Press.

Whyte, William H. (2002/1956), *The Organization Man*. Philadelphia, PA: University of Pennsylvania Press.

# PART I

A market to mediate employment takes shape

# 2. A policy for the new job market

## Jessica Lindvert

The conditions for people in today's new job market are different from those of yesteryear. In descriptions of the new market, one commonly hears expressions like *individualization*, *marketization*, or that people must increase their own *employability* – expressions that all stress a process of change from one situation to another. The thought behind this chapter is to provide an overview of how public sector activities in the area of labour market are organized, which ideas have dominated, and which actors have been influential during the past 50 years.[1] I begin by discussing the characteristic features of active labour market policy from historical and international standpoints. A second section addresses the Public Employment Service specifically, focusing on how it is organized and how its assignments are formulated. I then conclude with a discussion of how the power over labour market policies has changed in that employers and unions have lost influence and auditing bodies have become the new holders of power (see also Lindvert 2006).

## ACTIVE LABOUR MARKET POLICY

An active labour market policy aims to stimulate people to be mobile, through matching or labour market training. It differs from passive labour market policy, which is purely monetary support paid to the individual, such as unemployment insurance benefits and social assistance. The metaphor of the *wings of security* (*vingarnas trygghet*) used to be a concept for the active variety of labour market policy, where an individual's security is safeguarded by active measures such as moving allowance, labour market training and opportunities for retraining. This is a form of security that exists within the framework of the labour market as a whole, not security associated with a particular employment position, referred to in Sweden as 'shell' security (*snäckskalets trygghet*).

The active Swedish stance is often also connected to the work strategy (*arbetslinjen*) (or, the work and skills strategy, *arbets-och kompetenslinjen*). The work strategy has for many years been a fundamental concept in the making of active labour market policy. It is controversial and has held different meanings through different time periods: at times the strategy's elements of obligation have been stressed, and at times its elements relating to rights (Junestav 2004). During the crisis years of the 1990s, the work strategy was often discussed in terms of a right: the sizable public investments made to activate the population in labour market measures were, for example, legitimized by rhetoric such as 'the work strategy is holding firm' and 'no one should be left out' (Lindvert 2006).

It is obvious that the debate climate is different today. The work strategy has been a key concept in the political rhetoric of Sweden's recent conservative alliance government (2006–2014) – who advocate that it must be worthwhile to be gainfully employed. The obligations and disciplining elements have gained prominence. The work strategy is used to legitimize the fact that compensation levels for unemployment insurance benefits have been reduced and sickness benefits made less generous. The stress is now on the individual's obligation to look for work, to not take sick leave, to show up for work (see, for example, Allians för Sverige 2006; Dagens Nyheter 2009). Even in the EU employment policy debate, the concept plays a central role, where activation is an important economic concept, the meaning of which relates to obligations. Using activation in this way signals a shift in Europe's employment policies towards putting the interests of employers and companies first. Here, activation occurs according to the employer's terms, not the employee's (Salais and Villeneuve 2004).

### Active Labour Market Policy in International Comparison

Swedish labour market policy is increasingly being aligned with the EU's market-oriented employment policies. Historically, however, the Swedish version of labour market policy has differed considerably from the policies pursued in countries such as the US or the UK, or in other parts of Europe, outside Scandinavia. In welfare policy contexts, Sweden is usually classified as a social democratic welfare model that differs from the liberal welfare model (and the conservative model). In the social democratic model, it is traditionally the state that constitutes the key basis for citizens' social security. The social democratic welfare model is characterized by a large public sector, publicly administrated general social security systems, a general pension system, health insurance, employment insurance and parental insurance. In the liberal model, the market is the main source of welfare, and distributes the resources, social services and insurance coverage. In the case of the latter, the state lies 'low and flat', and public social policy is limited to the very poorest (Esping-Andersen 1999).

If we look at labour market policy specifically, the Swedish system (along with the other Nordic countries) has been described as intervening or institutional. Here, the state has been allowed to intervene and regulate the supply and demand in the labour market; the labour market is considered to work best when government actors and market actors work together. A central point of the Swedish version has also been that unemployed individuals should be offered support, training and practical experience from the Public Employment Service in order to increase their prospects for future employment (not just unemployment insurance benefits or social assistance). The active labour market policy in Sweden thus differs from labour market policy in liberal countries where government involvement has long been minimal (see, for example, Van der Berg et al. 1997).

## Changes in Labour Market Policy over Time

Active labour market policy has its roots in a political economic action programme developed by Swedish Trade Union Confederation (LO) economists Gösta Rehn and Rudolf Meidner in the late 1940s.[2] The programme, referred to in the vernacular as 'the Swedish model', received international attention for its ambition of combining economic and social objectives (capitalism and socialism, if you will). A central idea of the programme was to accelerate the growth of business and industry. Through government intervention, the goal was to weed out inefficient companies and be able to move resources to where the conditions for growth were better. However, this strategy proved to need supplementing in order to support those who lost their jobs. A stronger social safety net was introduced to persuade individuals to move to other regions or retrain themselves for more successful industries. And it was through this combination of priorities that active labour market policy in its modern guise came to be – as a concession to create more secure conditions for people affected by these rationalizations (Ohlsson and Olofsson 1998).

Observing the changes over time, we see that in the 1950s, labour market policy consisted of measures aimed at 'equipping' selected groups (usually men working in industry) to meet the needs of business and industry. The number of people in such programmes increased from about 500 a year in the early 1950s, to over 30 000 a year at the beginning of the 1970s (Ohlsson and Olofsson 1998: 142). The increase can be explained in part by the fact that the Swedish economy was in an expansive phase, and in part by a change in strategy regarding how to reduce unemployment. From the 1950s, public employment services and training were no longer drawn in when the economy was booming and unemployment fell. Government continued to invest in labour market measures even when the demand for labour was great. In the 1970s, investments in active labour market policy programmes were substantial, above all now because of expansion to the public sector in connection with women entering the workforce. Ideas of equality and justice also gained a foothold at that time and contributed to giving previously overlooked groups, such as older individuals and people with physical and mental disabilities, an opportunity to enter the workforce.[3]

In the 1980s, there was a shift, and public labour market policy began to show a greater interest in the needs of companies. Efforts went into adapting the supply of labour to the employers' demands, in the form of labour market training in certain occupational areas where workers were in short supply. So-called city and special public employment services were also introduced at that time. The work of public employment officers came to a large degree to be governed by what jobs were available, and employers could turn to special contact people at the Public Employment Service. In the middle of the decade, labour market training also gained a more independent position; in 1985, a separate authority was established (AMU, which has since evolved into today's state-owned labour market and staffing service Lernia), with the National Labour Market Administration thereby taking on the role of purchaser of education and training.

The final decade of the 1900s was characterized by a serious downturn in the economy, leading to mass unemployment and skyrocketing costs for labour market measures. Despite the financial problems of the state, however, the government chose to invest in keeping people in labour market programmes, even if the quality was extremely poor. The number of people taking part in labour market interventions more than doubled during the crisis years. The task of Public Employment Service offices became less about matching people to jobs and preparing them for the labour market, and more about preventing widespread social exclusion (Lindvert 2006, Chapter 3). During these years, labour market policy also received harsh criticism. The volume-oriented intervention programmes faced strong criticism from auditors, politicians, researchers and social commentators. One of labour market policy's core activities, labour market training, was subject to especially stinging critique. Up until the 1980s, economists had shown that labour market training had had a positive effect on an individual's likelihood of finding future employment. In the 1990s, however, the effects of training proved less favourable. In some cases, participation in training programmes was judged to have direct negative consequences (Calmfors et al. 2002). In defence of the politicians responsible, it is often cited that they succeeded at least on one important point: in not creating acceptance of unemployment as a lifestyle.

## THE PUBLIC EMPLOYMENT SERVICE'S ORGANIZATION AND ASSIGNMENT

In recent years, substantial administrative changes have occurred at the Public Employment Service. In 2008, the National Labour Market Administration (*Arbetsmarknadsverket,* AMV) changed its name to the Public Employment Service (*Arbetsförmedlingen*). In connection with this, a restructuring of the organization began, meaning that three agencies were merged to form one. The Labour Market Administration had formerly been organized as three separate authorities. Centrally, there was the National Labour Market Board (*Arbetsmarknadsstyrelsen*); at the regional level were the county labour boards (authorities with limited responsibilities); and at the local level there were the Public Employment Service offices.[4] By way of the reorganization, the county labour boards were closed down and replaced by four centrally governed by market regions (north, south, east and west), and some 70 so-called labour market areas were established at the local level (and may include one or more public employment service offices). Today, the name Public Employment Service (*Arbetsförmedlingen*) applies to the entire authority. It is doubtful whether the closing of the county labour boards resulted in a centralization in the true sense of the word, however, since the regional (i.e. county) authorities had never been particularly influential. The agency's power has always been at the national level (Lindvert 2006).[5]

### The Public Employment Service's Assignment Today

Today, the Public Employment Service covers all of Sweden, with approximately 12 500 employees. Most of these, about 10 000, work as case officers at the various employment offices. There are three ways to access the Public Employment Service's services: the internet, customer services line, or visits in person to a local employment office. The Public Employment Service also provides counselling and work-related rehabilitation, and directs people to labour market programmes (more about these can be found in chapters 3–5). The Public Employment Service also has the task of ensuring that people receiving unemployment benefits are at the disposal of the labour market. In this context, the agency is an overseeing body that makes sure that the people receiving unemployment insurance benefits actively engage in seeking work, and accept job offers that are reasonable considering their previous work experience and training.

The Public Employment Service's assignment is set out by the Swedish Riksdag (parliament) and the Swedish Government, and articulated in the Ordinance with Instruction for the Public Employment Service (SFS 2007:1030). This long-term instruction is clarified on an annual basis in the budget bill and in the government's appropriation directive to the Public Employment Service. The current instruction (SFS 2007:1030) explicates the Public Employment Service's assignment as being to improve how the labour market functions, primarily by effectively 'matching' those who are seeking employment to those seeking labour, with priority given to those furthest from the labour market, and to contribute to a steady increase in employment over the long term.

The agency's activities themselves should in turn be designed such that they fulfil a number of goals. They should be performed in an efficient and uniform manner within the regulatory framework, should be designed such that jobseekers and employers have access to similar services everywhere in the country, should be adapted to the varying needs and conditions in different parts of the country, should lead to increased geographical and occupational mobility, should be adapted to the individual's requirements and conditions, should not distort competition or contribute to job opportunities being forced out, and should be designed such that they increase diversity and counteract discrimination in working life.

The Public Employment Service shall in addition ensure that unemployment insurance works as a transition insurance, bring in complementary actors to quickly and efficiently get jobseekers working, actively procure information on job vacancies, and follow up and evaluate the impact of the agency's activities and labour market measures on the workings of the labour market, conduct assessments of the labour market situation to provide the necessary basis for future labour market policy, and assist government agencies and others who conduct evaluations and follow-up in the Public Employment Service's field of activity.

As a whole, there has for many years been a wide range of tasks and objectives covered in the Public Employment Service's governing documents. The focus, however, has shifted considerably in recent years. One change is that the market-oriented elements are now more tangible in the

Public Employment Service, not least through the introduction of so-called complementary actors (staffing agencies and private or sector-specific services) involved in employment mediation and paid by the Public Employment Service to take over the responsibility for jobseekers (an arrangement wherein the state's role continues to be that of financing and overseeing the activities).

A second change is that the more disadvantaged groups receive more attention today. Although all jobseekers formally have the right to counselling, the activities are geared mainly to weaker groups. The 2013 budget bill clearly stated that the Public Employment Service's work should target mainly those furthest from the labour market (Prop. 2012/13:1, Appendix 14).

A third change is an accentuation of the task of matching. The Public Employment Service's arsenal of measures has largely shifted from training and practice to job search activities and mediating employment. The government is concentrating efforts on providing a greater number of employment officers and coaches, but less on labour market training. The labour market training that used to be a core programme has been radically reduced in favour of preparatory initiatives with a clearer focus on individual case management (now called 'the job and development programme' and 'the youth job programme'). These measures lack an outside time limit and target people who have been registered as unemployed for extended periods. The preparatory programmes also lack the ambition that the labour market training had, which is that the measures should lead directly to employment. Prioritized groups include youths with low education, older unemployed persons, non-Nordic immigrants and people with disabilities (Olofsson and Wadensjö 2009: 24–27). Most people who take part in labour market policy programmes today fall under the job and development programme, the youth job programme or the new start jobs. Other, more recent measures are introductory guides and introductory plans in order to increase immigrant participation.

## LABOUR MARKET POLICY GOVERNANCE

If we look now to the governance of labour market policy, up until the beginning of the 1990s, unions and employers were very influential. Public labour market policy had for many years been governed by 'corporatist'[6] arrangements between the state, unions and employers. Labour market policy was a key area of policy in which it was important to be able to adjust intervention programmes quickly according to upswings and downturns in the economy (Elvander 1969; Rothstein 1992). Unions and employers were therefore represented in decision-making bodies of the National Labour Market Board and on the county labour boards. These governance arrangements were to a large extent based on negotiation and compromise.[7] The Labour Market Board had a very independent role in relation to parliament and government. The government's appropriation directive was vaguely formulated and left much room for interpretation when it came to goals, tasks and funding. The critical point was to avoid binding oneself in advance to *one* solution or *one* goal.

Up until the 1970s, the corporatist arrangements were extremely important in the governance of labour market policy. They were weakened to some extent, however, by the enactment of three laws that strengthened workers' social security and influence: the Employment Protection Act (*Lagen om anställningsskydd*, LAS),[8] the Employment Act, which covers co-determination in the workplace (*Lagen om medbestämmande i arbetslivet*, MBL),[9] and the Board Representation Act for private sector employees (*Lagen om styrelserepresentation for privatanställda*, LSA).[10] In the 1980s, the corporatist arrangements were further weakened after several management policy investigations drew attention to the problems of this form of governance holding governing actors accountable. The arrangements were formally terminated in 1991 when the employers' confederation at the time (SAF, now *Svenskt Näringsliv* – Confederation of Swedish Enterprise) withdrew its representatives from government boards and committees, including the Labour Market Board. It was obvious that the old systems of governance were no longer considered up to the task. But what would replace them?

### Management by Objectives and Results Enters the Scene

Parallel with the phasing out of the corporatist arrangements in the early 1990s, a new administrative order was introduced in Swedish public administration, so-called 'management by objectives and results',[11] the general purpose of which was to make administration more manageable, actionable and effective. Through management by objectives and results, the intention was to address inefficiencies, the wasting of resources, and detailed regulation. The new governance model gave government authorities more decision-making freedom over their separate organizations. The formulation of overarching goals was also to be made clearer and demands on follow-up and reporting results more stringent (Premfors et al. 2009; Sundström 2003). The administrative change is part of a larger trend in which the state has been given a less dominant role in society. It has become more dependent on cooperating with other actors. New forms of governance in the form of networks, partnerships and similar arrangements have emerged – that is, a shift from what is described as *government* to *governance*. This implies a shift in governing logic from a redistributing, operative state to a regulating state that governs more by control, oversight and sophisticated systems of accountability (see, for example, Hood et al. 1999).

It would be some time before this governance model gained a foothold in labour market policy, however. After unions and employers withdrew in the early 1990s, and unemployment skyrocketed, labour market policy began instead to lose its compass and rudder. It began for a time to list towards social policy with no employment policy content. Neither was it clear how the policy should be organized. The decade was characterized by a number of short-term solutions, including, for example, a period when the municipalities were given more responsibility.[12]

The big breakthrough for management by objectives and results came at the beginning of the 2000s when a number of auditing bodies, including the National Audit Office (*Riksrevisionsverket*, RRV), Parliamentary Auditors (*Riksdagens revisorer*, RR), Agency for Public Management (*Statskontoret*), National Financial Management Authority (*Ekonomistyrningsverket*, ESV), and a number of internal ministerial investigators, drew attention to weaknesses in the Labour Market Administration's organization. Several management and efficiency analyses drew attention to shortcomings in the follow-up, operational planning and responsibilities between the local, regional and central levels of government (RRV 1997: 58; RRV 2000: 3; Agency for Public Management 2000:4; Ds 2000:38; ESV 1999:7).[13] These analyses also indicated that local politicians lacked the ability to effect labour market policy that looked beyond local priorities. An extensive recentralization was thereafter initiated, in which the role of the Labour Market Board as head authority was strengthened. Even the director-general received a stronger position in relation to the executive board. The change in regulatory structure also meant that county labour directors became more closely tied to Labour Market Board management. In 2001, the Labour Market Administration was considered to have resolved most of its internal organizational problems.[14] The catchword for 2002 was that it should be a 'line management' organization (AMV 2003: 5–8).

In conjunction with the introduction of the management by objectives and results model, the Labour Market Administration was given more autonomous power to decide how government funding was to be used in order to attain the overall goals. The local employment offices in turn were given more freedom to choose how they would use the funding, as long as they provided the feedback required.

The shift towards goals that could be verified and improved evaluation instruments in labour market policy was praised by government and the responsible authorities and auditors. They agreed in their recommendation that audit-based instruments (such as ranking, benchmarking and indicators) should be further developed. Having verifiable, measurable goals, where goal achievement cannot be manipulated, is considered desirable.

One explanation as to why objective and results-based management had such a strong impact can be gleaned from historical institutionalism. A fundamental principle of this theory is that political institutions' propensity to change is generally very limited. Public bureaucracies are sluggish operations, where change tends to occur very slowly.[15] The theory indicates, however, that there are occasions when political institutions become more open to new influences. The greatest opportunity for new ideas, new actors or new organizational bodies to gain political ground is during shorter, turbulent times (that is, critical junctures, windows of opportunity, or formative moments) (Collier and Collier 1991; Krasner 1989; Pierson 2000). Here, the difficult years, when initiatives largely departed from previous quality requirements, constituted an opportunity for a new beginning. The occasion also presented a textbook example of the success that can be achieved with revolutionary policy reforms. If we study the criticism from the auditors more closely, it not only dealt with changes introduced in connection with the municipalization, but also administrative procedures that prior to this were routinely seen as acceptable.

### New Key Players and a New Governance Model

There is no doubt that objectives and results management is very different from the earlier governance by authorities and, as we will see below, from labour market policy's corporatist governance in particular. The corporatist governance arrangement between the state, unions and employers was based on negotiation and a weighing of economic objectives against social ones. This could result in striving one day to meet employers' need for an efficient workforce, and the next providing support for those furthest from the job market, all depending on what current needs looked like. One executive at the Ministry of Enterprise, Energy and Communications had the following to say about this line of thinking: 'Yes, well, there's a bit of sacrificing the one to get the other, in the belief that the whole will still turn out better.' But these arrangements were not only about flexibility. They also related to negotiation techniques. Having many vague and negotiable goals also increased the chances of accommodating the priorities of different interest groups in the agreements – everyone could get something. That the negotiations took place within the executive board of the Labour Market Board also provided confidentiality; behind locked doors, one could reach compromises and establish support for proposals that might otherwise have been seen as unrealistic (Öberg 1994; Rothstein 1992).

Today's audit-based governance rests on another type of thinking entirely, about how goals should be formulated and what they should be used for. At the beginning of the 2000s, the Parliamentary Auditors pointed out the problem of there being as many as four or five different target levels and 15–20 goals in the area of labour market. They saw the complicated structure of objectives as one of the 'more serious governance problems of labour market policy' (RR 2002).

The current leading idea is instead that goals should be transparent, based on promises, and that external auditors should be able to assess the degree to which they have been achieved. Earlier vague and un-operationalizable goals have thereby been replaced by verifiable and (often also) quantifiable goals. The shift towards quantitative goals has meant that goal pluralism, earlier seen as a part of the success story, is now seen as a problem. But even this governance model has certain weaknesses. Not least, the political scope for those responsible for the policies has been narrowed. Here, there is a risk that the political governance may become rigid, and too highly governed by the ability to attain the goals that have been set in advance and that are closely monitored by the media and other actors in society – at the cost of other measures that are more difficult to demonstrate from an opinion standpoint or that appear more effective in the long term.

### The Audit Model Replaces the Corporatist Model

To sum up, one can describe the development by saying that the previous governance model based on the principle of *doing the right things* has been left in the wake of a governance model that rests on the principle of *doing things right*, in terms of controllability, follow-up and reporting.

The two governance models rest on entirely different notions about how goals should be formulated and what they should be used for. Certain components that were earlier considered fundamental to governance have even come to be seen as problems today. Here, it is obvious how differently governance is viewed today compared to 20–30 years ago. An administrative process of change has crept in, leading to new power relations, where both the key players and the rules of the game have changed.

Table 2.1 summarizes the corporatist model as based on the idea of being able to remain flexible to the needs that arise. Typical features of this model are that governance occurs by way of compromises, that the responsibility for policy is shared between public and private actors in society, that measures are adjusted to existing needs, that there is some room for confidential agreements between the main actors, that the division of power is determined through internal negotiation between the actors involved, and that goal pluralism is viewed as a part of the governance concept.

*Table 2.1   The corporatist model and the audit model*

| Corporatist model | Audit model |
| --- | --- |
| Goal pluralism as a governance concept | Goal conflicts as governance problem |
| Corporatist interests have influence | Auditing bodies have influence |
| Problem-based (adjust measures to existing need, to the economy) | Promise-based (adjust measures to set goals) |
| Confidentiality | Transparency |
| Internally controlled accountability | Externally controlled accountability |
| Flexibility | Predictability |

Today's governance model, the audit model, places the emphasis instead on predictability and transparency. Typical features are that the governance is based on formal rationality, that auditors and government officials have been given more power and responsibility, that quantifiable goals are prioritized over those that are not quantifiable, that actions are more promise-based, that transparency is sought in the decision-making process, and that the policy is controlled externally by auditors and other overseeing bodies.

## CONCLUDING DISCUSSION: SWEDEN TAKES A NEW APPROACH TO PUBLIC EMPLOYMENT SERVICES

Looking back at the development in labour market policy over the past 50 years, the largest organizational changes have taken place in the last 20 years. For someone who became unemployed 20 years ago, the road to seeking a new job was still quite clearly marked. The person would register with the Public Employment Service, book an appointment, maintain a certain level of job-seeking activity, and have regular contact with his or her employment officer. If jobseekers could not be matched to a job, there were a number of labour market policy instruments at their disposal, including labour market training, a work experience programme, or grants for starting their own business (see, for example, Thedvall 2004). Today, there are a multitude of actors and alternatives.

Important organizational changes include that corporatist governance has been replaced by audit governance, that the influence of unions and employers has been replaced by that of controlling bodies and auditors, that the Public Employment Service must now compete with online job sites, companies and organizations specializing in recruiting and job coaching, that the Public Employment Service's task of matching has been given more weight, and that society's weakest groups have become the main target for Public Employment Service activities. These are some of the most important organizational characteristics of the country's current employment services system that Swedish jobseekers now encounter. In the next three chapters, we step inside the Public Employment Service organization in an attempt to understand how the new job market is taking shape.

# NOTES

1. The research for this chapter was made possible by funding from the Swedish Research Council within the framework of *The politics and practices of capability: Lifelong learning for all in a knowledge-intense worklife?* – a project led by Christina Garsten, and by funding support from The Swedish Foundation for Humanities and Social Sciences for a project on *Social affairs: Governance for a normative economy*, also led by Christina Garsten.
2. There are, however, researchers who have traced the active aspect back to the 1830s (Ohlsson and Olofsson 1998:68).
3. Near the end of the decade, for example, the state-owned Samhällsföretagen (now Samhall), offering employment solutions such as sheltered employment, was formed.
4. Public employment offices existed far earlier, however. As early as 1902, the first public employment service offices were established under municipal management. These were nationalized during World War II.
5. Or, as one interviewee in a management position at the Labour Market Board laconically put it: 'On only one single occasion that I know of was there a county labour board director who did not choose to follow the director-general's decisions. And that labour board director was handily removed ...' (Personal interview, spring 2003).
6. *Corporatism* is defined here as a legitimate form of cooperation between stakeholder groups and government. There are many definitions and versions of corporatism (see, for example, Öberg 1994).
7. While public labour market policy was governed by way of this three-party cooperation, other parts of the labour market were regulated by a two-party arrangement, that is, by the

principal organizations of the labour market with no government involvement. In issues such as the setting of wages, organization of the workplace, work environment, worker safety, and occupational health, the employer organizations and union traditionally entered agreements at a central level in the form of collective agreements. This form of decision process still exists today, though the agreements are now made mainly at the industry level.

8. LAS requires that there be justifiable grounds for a permanent employee to be terminated. A lack of work or personal reasons can constitute such grounds. LAS was amended in the 1990s, and today employers are permitted to exclude two key individuals from seniority rules.

9. MBL strengthened the negotiation rights of unions. The act also applies to employers without collective agreements when it is a matter of collective redundancies or of a takeover by another owner. In this context, employers and employees are counterparties.

10. LSA allows representatives of the employees to participate in a company's decision process on the same terms as representatives elected at the company's general meetings, presumably with the company's best interests in mind. MBL and LSA give union representatives a dual role: they are responsible both for the entire company's operations and for the employees they represent. Employee representatives are seen as an asset owing to their insight about the company and longer perspective than other board members. The legislation regarding discrimination in the workplace was also strengthened in the 1990s.

11. The changeover has in fact been going on since the 1960s but under different names (Sundström 2003).

12. Municipalities were given the responsibility for unemployed youths up to the age of 20, and a majority in the local labour market boards; the county labour boards got more decision-making power, with some counties introducing trial programmes with a freer use of labour market funding; and the local employment offices were given responsibility for outcomes. Further efforts included local test collaborations between employment offices and municipalities. Organizationally, local anchoring was enhanced by instituting a number of new 'soft' regional instruments such as regional development agreements, local jobs pacts, development councils, and local and regional partnerships.

13. The Labour Market Administration ranked very low in the Financial Management Authority's 1998 economic-administrative valuation of government agencies (ESV 1999:7).

14. In 2000, however, they managed to rank among the highest category: *completely satisfactory* (ESV 2001:10).

15. The principle was originally formulated as a critique of rationalistic explanations for political action, but also questioned anarchistic models in which rational logic was seen as having been taken out of the equation. The theory of historical institutionalism maintains instead a certain constancy in political patterns over time.

# REFERENCES

Agency for Public Management (2000), *Att styra arbetsmarknadsinriktad utbild-ning*. Stockholm: Swedish Agency for Public Management 2000:4.

Allians för Sverige (2006), *Fler i arbete – mer att dela på*. Election Manifesto 2006.

AMV (2003), *AMVs verksamhetsberättelse 2002*. Stockholm: National Labour Market Administration.

Calmfors, Lars, Anders Forslund and Maria Hemström (2002), *Vad vet vi om den svenska arbetsmarknadspolitikens sysselsättningseffekter?* Report 2002:8, Uppsala: Institute for Evaluation of Labour Market and Education Policy (IFAU).

Collier, David and Ruth Berins Collier (1991), *Shaping the Political Arena: Critical junctures, the labor movement and regime dynamics in Latin America*. Princeton, NJ: Princeton University Press.

Dagens Nyheter (2009), 'Tio extra miljarder till arbetsmarknadspolitik', by Anders Borg and Sven Otto Littorin, 15 April 2009.

Ds 2000:38, *En effektivare arbetsmarknadspolitik*. Stockholm: Fritzes.

Elvander, Nils (1969), *Intresseorganisationerna i dagens Sverige*. Lund: CWK Gleerup.

Esping-Andersen, Gøsta (1999), *Social Foundations of Post-industrial Economies*. Oxford: Oxford University Press.

ESV 1999:7, *EA-värdering avseende 1998 av statliga myndigheter*. Stockholm: National Financial Management Authority.

ESV 2001:10, *EA-värdering avseende 2000 av statliga myndigheter*. Stockholm: National Financial Management Authority.

Hood, Christopher et al. (1999), *Regulation Inside Government*. Oxford: Oxford University Press.

Junestav, Malin (2004), *Arbetslinjer i svensk socialpolitisk debatt och lagstiftning 1930–2001*. Uppsala: Uppsala University.

Krasner, Stephen (1989), 'Sovereignty: An institutional perspective', in James Caparasso (ed.), *The Elusive State*. Thousand Oaks: Sage.

Lindvert, Jessica (2006), *Ihålig arbetsmarknadspolitik. Organisering och legitimitet igår och idag*. Umeå: Boréa bokförlag.

Öberg, PerOla (1994), *Särintresse och allmänintresse – korporatismens ansikten*. Stockholm: Almqvist and Wiksell International.

Ohlsson, Rolf and Jonas Olofsson (1998), *Arbetslöshetens dilemma – motsättningar och samförstånd i svensk arbetslöshetsdebatt under två hundra år*. Stockholm: SNS förlag.

Olofsson, Jonas and Eskil Wadensjö (2009), *Arbetsmarknadspolitik. Förändrade förutsättningar och nya aktörer*. Stockholm: SNS förlag.

Pierson, Paul (2000), 'Increasing returns, path dependence, and the study of politics', *American Political Science Review*, 94(2), 251–67.

Premfors, Rune, Peter Ehn, Eva Haldén and Göran Sundström (2009), *Demokrati and byråkrati*. Lund: Studentlitteratur.

Prop. 2012/13:1, *Budgetpropositionen för 2012*.

Rothstein, Bo (1992), *Den korporativa staten*. Stockholm: Norstedts.

RR (2002), *Styrningen av AMS och länsarbetsnämnderna*. RR 2002/03:2, Stockholm: Swedish Parliamentary Auditors.

RRV (1997), *Lokal samverkan i arbetsmarknadspolitiken: slutrapport*. Stockholm: Swedish National Audit Office.

RRV (2000), *Försöksverksamheten med friare medelsanvändning i arbetsmarknadspolitiken*. Stockholm: Swedish National Audit Office.

Salais, Robert and Robert Villeneuve (2004), *Europe and the Politics of Capabilities*. Cambridge: Cambridge University Press.

SFS 2007:1030, *Förordning med instruktion för Arbetsförmedlingen*. Swedish Code of Statutes.

Sundström, Göran (2003), *Stat på villovägar*. Stockholm: Stockholm University.

Thedvall, Renita (2004), 'Do it yourself: Making up the self-employed individual in the Swedish Public Employment Service', in Christina Garsten and Kerstin

Jacobsson (eds), *Learning to be Employable: New agendas on work, responsibility and learning in a globalizing world*, Basingstoke: Palgrave Macmillan, pp. 131–51.

Van der Berg, Axel, Bengt Furåker and Leif Johansson (1997), *Labour Market Regimes and Patterns of Flexibility*. Lund: Arkiv förlag.

# 3. The dual role of the Public Employment Service: to support and control

## Lars Walter

---

Unemployment – and society's responsibility for the unemployed – has been one of most intensely debated issues in recent years. The debate occurs mainly at a general level, with political and ideological arguments juxtaposed. More rarely discussed is the everyday practical work: the methods used by the Public Employment Service for administrating the flow of people from unemployment into new jobs – labour market policy converted into action. For the individual, unemployment not only means a lack of employment, salary, and a social work context, but also taking on a new role as jobseeker. This is a role that requires that the jobseeker acquire the skills, knowledge and routines expected of him or her. The Public Employment Service and its case officers thus have a central role in supporting and teaching unemployed individuals to look for work – to become jobseekers. It also has a controlling function, since it is the case officers of the Public Employment Service who determine who is employable and who qualifies for unemployment insurance.

This chapter looks at how the Public Employment Service's dual function of both supporting and controlling is evinced in the practical work of the case officers.[1] The focus is on the methods used to translate labour market policy into action through three phases of the jobseeker's contact with the Public Employment Service: registration, drawing up of an action plan, and the job and development programme. This study is based on interviews conducted in 2008–2009 with case officers, managers and representatives of other employee groups at a local Public Employment Service office in a city in western Sweden.[2] The office is a so-called city district office, to which both jobseekers and employers in the vicinity can turn. The office is staffed by approximately 40 employees, most of whom work as case officers, more precisely as employment officers, or placement officers. There are also other occupational groups represented at the office, including social workers and occupational psychologists. There is also an office director and an assistant director. The case officers are divided into three teams according to sector: technology and economics; construction, industry and transport; and services and the public sector. This breakdown is meant to enable individual case officers to gain advanced knowledge and build up networks in separate segments of the labour market. There are also a number of specialist functions at this office: one group that works exclusively with jobseekers in the job and development programme, and another that works specifically with issues regarding rehabilitation and interdisciplinary cooperation with authorities like the Social Insurance Agency, primary care, and social services.

The discussion of the case officers' work that follows is arranged in chronological order from a jobseeker's perspective. It focuses on three particularly close and critical situations and meeting-points between case officer and jobseeker during the various phases of unemployment. All jobseekers do not complete the entire process, however, as many find another employment (or do not show up for other reasons) before it is time to register in the job and development programme, or even before an action plan has been drawn up. According to the office director, during the period in question more than 40 per cent of the jobseekers were gone within 90 days of registering with the office.

I begin by describing what happens when unemployed individuals visit the office for the first time and register with the Public Employment Service, who they meet, what information they receive, and what is expected of them. I then present a description of how the jobseeker and case officer work together to create an individual action plan and what this involves. The drawing up of an action plan is regulated by law. It is done in an attempt to streamline the job-seeking process and has great significance for the jobseeking process. The chapter concludes with a description of how conditions change dramatically when a jobseeker has been unemployed for so long that he or she no longer qualifies for unemployment benefits and is registered instead in the job and development programme.

## REGISTRATION – FROM JOBLESS TO JOBSEEKER

To be eligible for unemployment insurance benefits, a person must visit the Public Employment Service on his or her first day of unemployment to register. Normally this is done at the local Public Employment Service office, where one meets a Public Employment Service case officer. In conjunction with registration, jobseekers are placed in an appropriate sector team and assigned an employment officer. As noted above, the staff at the employment office studied are divided into three sector teams: technology and economics; construction, industry and transport; and services and the public sector. The employment officer therefore has specific expertise in the area relevant to the jobseeker. The first part of the registration process usually takes 15–20 minutes. Included in the process is an assessment of the jobseeker's skills and the type of work he or she is looking for. The jobseeker's background is classified based on the Public Employment Service-wide system. The jobseeker thereby becomes searchable and accessible for matching and being directed to jobs. The employment officer also tries to assess whether the jobseeker may for some reason have a need for more extensive support from the Public Employment Service. The case officer also goes through what the jobseeker needs to do to gain access to unemployment insurance, and how to start looking for work. The jobseeker must make a return visit within three days to meet with his or her advisor. The Public Employment Service has a dual role already at this stage: both supporting and controlling. As one employment officer explains: 'If you don't show up, you are de-registered. And you don't want that. Because then, no unemployment insurance benefit is paid out'.

At the return visit, the jobseeker normally meets his or her placement officer for the first time, and the goal is that this person's experience and knowledge of the industry should match the jobseeker's experience. On this visit, the aim is primarily to validate transcripts, certificates and references, and so on, and to generally get the jobseeker's profile in order.

> The validation is done to ensure that the matching information we have is correct. It's actually a really good step that was introduced a couple of years ago. We go through everything so that the qualifications registered are in keeping with the jobs people are looking for, that they have the experience or training, and that the descriptions of their skills entered are correct. We go through the whole profile. (Case officer at the Public Employment Service)

After this, the jobseeker is called within two weeks to a general information meeting about the Public Employment Service's role and the different options available to support the jobseeker. About 20 people usually attend. More are invited, but the drop-out rate is quite high because a fair number of them have already found a job. The meeting takes just over an hour, and the information provided has to do with the Public Employment Service's control function, what it means to search for work, what the process looks like, what is required of the jobseeker, the rules that apply, the controls carried out, and what the penalties are for non-compliance. A description of the various services offered by the Public Employment Service is also given, including important things to think about when seeking a job, tips on useful websites, CV databases, upcoming recruiting activities, and other practical tips and advice. One employment officer describes the aim of the information meeting as follows:

> It's important, but it can be too dry. We want people who attend the meeting to feel that it was worthwhile. Yes, that's the feeling we want them to leave with. Not so that they think – *Well, now I've done what I had to!* But it should exceed their expectations. And they do, the meetings are well-liked.

A portion of the time at the information meetings is used to encourage the jobseekers to use the job placement system and the tools available to present themselves, their skills, experience and knowledge, as a part of their search for work.

In connection with registration, much importance is placed on informing the jobseekers. Here, the Public Employment Service's dual role quickly becomes clear. On one hand, it means teaching jobseekers the rules, requirements and routines that apply to qualify for compensation from unemployment insurance. Everyone registered as unemployed must actively seek work, must seek the jobs they are referred to, must be able to be reached and available for meetings, and in other ways be at the disposal of the labour market and the Public Employment Service. The registration represents a formalization of the unemployed person as looking for work. This is a prerequisite to be eligible for unemployment insurance and means that the jobseeker also accepts the Public Employment Service's controls and regulations. On the other hand, the Public Employment Service's role is to support the jobseekers. The placement officers teach them how to look for work, how to write and generate application documents, how to use the job bank, and what recruiting and online employment websites exist. The goal is 'help to self-help'; the jobseekers are themselves made responsible for looking for work on their own.

## AN ACTION PLAN – FROM AUTONOMY TO AGREEMENT

The next contact the jobseeker has with the Public Employment Service is to create an individual plan of action. The action plan is a tool to streamline the applicant's work search and specify the jobseeker's possibilities and responsibilities or, as one of the employment officers expressed it: 'The purpose of the action plan is for us to try to pinpoint what type of services and support the individual needs. It's appropriate to have some form of a plan' (case officer at the Public Employment Service).

According to law, an action plan is to be drawn up within three months of the individual jobseeker registering with the employment office, but the Public Employment Service's ambition is for this to be carried out faster than that. The goal is for 80 per cent of all action plans to be established within 30 days. An action plan is drawn up by a Public Employment Service case officer and the jobseeker, laying out a plan for what types of job are applicable, the relevant geographical region, which employers the jobseekers should contact, what support is needed in the search process (for example, help with writing a CV), possible training interventions (for example, labour market training programmes) and any limitations that exist. Such restrictions can involve everything from the jobseeker having some form of occupational handicap and thus the types of support that he or she can get, to the practical and social conditions that may exist. For example, does the jobseeker have adequate childcare or access to a car? The case officer should also determine whether these restrictions are legitimate and valid.

One requirement for the case officer and jobseeker to be able to formulate such goals together is that they share a fairly similar understanding of the jobseeker's requirements and conditions, and the types of employment that could be of particular interest. In connection with the drawing up of the action plan, a mapping out of the jobseeker's experience, knowledge and skills is therefore carried out. This occurs based on the Public Employment Service's standardized classification and categorization system, which is described in more detail below.[3]

Based on these standard classifications, the individual jobseeker's background is defined and evaluated. This in turn means that what is emphasized as important and relevant in a jobseeker's background forms the basis of the expectations that Public Employment Service representatives have for the jobseeker, and what measures and support are available for that individual. As a whole, the drawing up of an individual action plan can be described as a process in which the criteria and goals for the individual jobseeker's actions are formulated, actions that can be evaluated and controlled in the next step. The action plan is often described as a jointly produced contract that the jobseeker is expected to live up to in his or her continued search for employment. 'One could say that the action plan is like an agreement, and it's also used as a part of the process when we get to the control function. Everyone who has an action plan and receives unemployment insurance must follow it' (case officer at the Public Employment Service).

However, the action plan is an agreement drawn up between two parties with very different positions of power. In cases where the jobseeker does not accept the action plan, there may be sanctions, which in the worst case may threaten the livelihood of the person in question. The action plan is in its nature more an asymmetrical agreement where the jobseeker's autonomy is limited and subordinate to Public Employment Service regulation and control.[4] The ability to control is also underlined by the clear connection to penalties in the form of reduced or lost unemployment insurance benefits if the jobseeker does not live up to the action plan. There is, at the same time, reciprocity in that the action plan's content, at least in part, governs the Public Employment Service as well: 'We direct jobseekers to jobs based on the profile in the action plan. I don't think that would hold up legally, so what's in the action plan is important' (case officer at the Public Employment Service).

Once an action plan has been drawn up, the jobseeker is in contact with his or her case officer every six to eight weeks, most often by telephone. After three such contacts, they meet again. At this new meeting, the case officer and jobseeker go through the action plan and revise the goals previously formulated. Particular attention is given to following up points that may be perceived as problematic. This can involve things such as the jobseeker feeling that there are no relevant jobs to apply for or that he or she is having trouble getting an interview.

The drawing up of the action plan therefore changes the nature of the relationship between the jobseeker and the Public Employment Service. The action plan is perceived as an agreement between the jobseeker and the case officer. Its purpose is twofold: firstly, to facilitate, streamline and adapt the job search so that it suits and supports each individual jobseeker; and secondly, the action plan provides the possibility of check up on the jobseeker, meaning in turn that the individual's autonomy is limited. Here, the Public Employment Service's dual function is particularly apparent. Jobseekers are expected to continue to look for work on their own – but how and the extent to which they do so is regulated by the Public Employment Service.

## THE JOB AND DEVELOPMENT PROGRAMME – FROM AGREEMENT TO MICRO-MANAGEMENT

The next phase of unemployment begins when the jobseeker has used up most of the 300 insurance days and is at risk of losing his or her insurance benefits. After 300 days, one normally enters the government job and development programme. The step from unemployment insurance to the public job and development programme means, firstly, that the jobseeker is de-registered from the income insurance system and registered in a government-funded labour market measure. This comes with substantially lower levels of compensation, which often leads to the jobseeker also having to apply for municipal income support. The job and development programme has, at the same time, considerably more resources to offer. The jobseeker meets a case officer at least once a month and sometimes more frequently (compared to one telephone call every six to eight weeks for those receiving unemployment insurance). In this phase, jobseekers also have access to other professional expertise such as psychologists, social workers and career coaches. There is, in addition, a greater availability of support measures such as practical work experience, occupational training, grants for starting a business, vocational training, employment aid in the form of 'new start jobs', and special employment aid for jobseekers.

At this stage, the activities are set up as a programme or a course where one group of jobseekers conduct a series of activities together, which are expected to lead, in various ways, to a more active and focused job search. Examples of such activities are job coaching, analysis and improvement of CVs and application texts, as well as identifying and applying for work experience positions. Another essential part of the job and development programme is the further mapping of the individual jobseeker's qualifications with the aim of identifying additional experience, skills and qualities that may increase the possibility of finding employment. The point of departure here is a reassessment of the strategies and goals earlier used as the starting point.

A form designed for this purpose is filled out, about the individual's job search, what type of job he or she could imagine doing, how he or she feels about moving, and whether there are any obstacles. For example, there may be physical or mental work-related disabilities detected in this phase that were missed earlier. In the interviews, a number of different explanations were given as to why they had not been detected prior to this. To begin with, it is not uncommon that jobseekers are hesitant to acknowledge an occupational disability, in some cases because they worry that it may impede their ability to get a job, or because they do not see themselves as occupationally disabled. It may be a matter of the person not wanting to admit to having problems with addiction, or that it in some other way threatens his or her self-image. When a jobseeker enters the job and development programme, however, and has been out of the labour market for more than a year, he or she usually begins to understand that the road back into the labour market is not that obvious or simple. This can be accompanied by a greater inclination to accept that one has some kind of occupational handicap. There may also be economic incentives that make it more attractive for a jobseeker to be classified as occupationally disabled. For example, it may give the Public Employment Service case officers access to many more tools in the form of financial assistance measures and subsidized wages. In some cases, this can make it much easier for a jobseeker to enter the workforce.

The job and development programme also means that the jobseeker's search for employment becomes more regulated. Jobseekers look for work in the manner and to the extent dictated to them by their Public Employment Service case officers. Deviations can be and are penalized. Entering the job and development programme also means that the individual's different characteristics and capabilities are mapped out more explicitly. The case officer goes through the Public Employment Service's standard classification and categorization system with the jobseeker once again in order to broaden the search area. The importance of the jobseeker's own preferences and previous experience also receives less emphasis. Therefore, in application, the idea of a broadened search area means that the relationship between the jobseeker and case officer is fundamentally changed.

> One of the points that we talk a lot about is broadening the search area. Many interpret this as geographically – *Now I have to start looking for cleaning jobs up in Kiruna* [Sweden's far north] – but that's not what a broader search area really means. Instead, it involves the jobseeker being expected to be able to apply for the jobs that he or she can take, not just the jobs that he or she wants. At some point, jobseekers are expected to take any job that will provide them with a livelihood. The basic idea of unemployment insurance is for it to be a transition to supporting oneself, regardless of what that might look like. (Case officer at the Public Employment Service)

To be deregistered from unemployment insurance and registered instead in the job and development programme thus has significant consequences. The jobseeker receives a lower level of compensation. He or she also receives more support in the form of resources and tools that become available through the job and development programme. However, these are accessible based on different criteria than earlier. From previously having been defined as finding a suitable job, given the jobseeker's experience and preferences, 'matching' is redefined as finding any job at all, regardless of the individual's wishes and ambitions, and the qualifications he or she may have. The tie between the jobseeker and the case officer also becomes closer, as they now meet at least once a month. At this stage, the case officer has the task of supporting the jobseeker, but it occurs in an increasingly controlled form since the jobseeker must satisfy the conditions for the job and development programme.

## THE POWER OF CLASSIFICATIONS

One instrument that is particularly important in the work of case officers is the classification of jobseekers' skills and experience. How they choose to classify the jobseeker changes the longer into unemployment the jobseeker gets. The classification expands and becomes more specific, thereby providing less and less scope for individual preferences and interpretations. The determining factor here is how and with what ambition people are classified and categorized, as the descriptions constituted by the classifications become an expression of power and control. The work to couple the knowledge, skills and experience of jobseekers to a standardized taxonomy means defining which aspects are important (included) and which are less important (excluded). The taxonomy also means that a norm is established for how the various aspects are described and defined. A person who has the power to define what you are, what you are capable of, and what you should strive for, also has the power to monitor and control that you live up to these definitions. This way of looking at the exercising of power has been noted earlier by, among others, Michel Foucault, who stated that the ability to exercise control over a classification system gives those who govern the right of interpretation (Foucault 1966). A classification system that is in part legitimized based on its internal logic, and in part developed and controlled by the Public Employment Service, thereby gives the authority interpreting rights. More pointedly, one could say that the Public Employment Service is able to define what you *are* and demand that you act in accordance with this definition. The categorization system is at the same time not completely immutable. Descriptions must be worded such that they are meaningful, fair and legitimate for the jobseekers, prospective employers and other actors that come into contact with the Public Employment Service. A jobseeker can in addition always sabotage employment opportunities or not take a particular job, despite the risk of sanctions, and a prospective employer can choose not to employ a particular jobseeker.

The Public Employment Service's method of using its classification systems has other consequences as well. The systems help the Public Employment Service to establish a system of categories and consistent principles for classification, in which each category is unique and mutually exclusive. Bowker and Star (1999: 13) write that if a standardized classification system requires 'agreed-upon rules for the production of (textual or material) objects' that span more than one 'community of practice', it creates special opportunities to make things work at a distance and between different contexts. This is an important feature for case officers' and jobseekers' ability to describe and relate the jobseeker's prior knowledge and experience acquired to suitable jobs or job postings. Using the same categorization system to describe and classify jobseekers and potential jobs thereby makes it easier for the Public Employment Service to act as an intermediary, to match jobseekers to potential jobs. The classification system quite simply becomes a determinant for the Public Employment Service's ability to match jobseekers to jobs. Furthermore, the standardized classification system means that the Public Employment Service is able to use similar methods and activities to match different categories of jobseekers to various types of jobs and employment positions. The case officer's work of mapping, classifying and categorizing jobseekers similarly helps to change jobseekers' own descriptions of their previous experience and qualifications. This in turn helps to create distance to the surrounding environment and adds integrity to the case officer's task of matching workers and jobs. Matching thus becomes more of an internal and joint activity for the jobseeker and the case officer, separated to some degree from the environment, regulations and controls (Manning 1982). It becomes an activity where, on one hand, the jobseeker 'owns' his or her experience, and the case officer, on the other, 'owns' the language for describing this experience. Moreover, it means, somewhat paradoxically, that the work of classifying and categorizing the jobseekers enables the job search to occur more autonomously and more independently of the regulatory requirements than might have been intended by legislators and regulators.

## CONCLUDING DISCUSSION: FROM SUPPORT AND CONTROL TO SUPPORT BY WAY OF CONTROL

As mentioned in the introduction, unemployment often entails a person taking on a new role as a jobseeker, a role that in many ways requires one to acquire new skills, knowledge and routines expected of jobseekers. The Public Employment Service and its case officers play a central role in teaching people who are unemployed to become jobseekers. The Public Employment Service's assignment is to offer forms of support, to match, and in other ways help people to find employment. The work of the case officer also contains significant elements of evaluation and control of jobseekers and their behaviour.

It is also evident that a jobseeker's autonomy in relation to the case officer depends on how long the jobseeker has been out of work. In an initial phase, jobseekers have a relatively high degree of autonomy. If they register as looking for work, follow the rules and maintain contact with the Public Employment Service, they can themselves choose to describe and present themselves in the way that they want to, and to seek the jobs that they want.

In a second phase, once a joint plan of action has been established, the relationship changes such that the search for employment is increasingly based on a notion of jointly formulated goals and strategies. At this stage, the Public Employment Service has an obligation to monitor compliance and has more power to initiate sanctions. When, in a third phase, a jobseeker's unemployment insurance runs out and he or she is registered in the job and development programme, the individual's autonomy is even further eroded in that the jobseeker's actions in connection with the job search are increasingly regulated, made visible and standardized, and thereby also easier to monitor and control.

Here, the Public Employment Service has a dual function. It must both support and control. However, the longer a person has been unemployed, the more emphasis is put on the case officer's controlling function. This becomes apparent in the methods used in relation to the jobseekers. The work with the jobseeker is increasingly governed by standardized, well-defined and closely regulated handling procedures that limit the case officer's freedom to make individual considerations. The scope to act that nevertheless does exist is dependent on the regulatory system's chronology and the demand for increasing activities that can be followed up, evaluated, and specified in detail as they are carried out.

In their ambition to improve and to make the search for work more efficient, political institutions and authorities have chosen to regulate the jobseekers' behaviour and actions closely, through, among other things, individual action plans, as well as to link compliance with the rules for unemployment insurance benefit eligibility. The ability to micro-manage how jobseekers behave is to some extent dependent on how, with what precision, and to what extent the jobseeker's knowledge, experience and qualifications have been assessed and documented. It is this everyday practice of sorting people into different piles and affixing them with labels that determines the terms under which the jobless seek jobs.

# NOTES

1. The research that this chapter is based on was made possible with funding from CEFOS (Center for Public Sector Research) within the framework of a project on trends in social insurance and the interaction between law and governance (*Den nya socialförsäkringen: Samspelet mellan juridik och organisering*), led by Sara Stendahl.
2. Unemployment in Sweden in rose from 6.4% in January 2008 to 8.6% in December 2009, which tells about the urgency of the issue at the time of the study (*Arbetskraftsundersök-ningar*, AKU, www. scb.se).
3. The Employment Service uses the official Swedish standard for classification of occupa-tions, SSYK 96. SSYK 96 applies primarily to the classification of occupations according to the type of work done. The standard can also be used to organize information about job vacancies, jobseekers and occupations.
4. Establishing a mandatory and closely regulated individual action plan for unemployed persons is also an explicit policy aim.

# REFERENCES

Bowker, Geoffrey C. and Susan Leigh Star (1999), *Sorting Things Out: Classi-fication and its consequences*. Cambridge: MIT Press.

Foucault, Michel (1966), *The Order of Things*. London: Routledge.

Manning, Peter K. (1982), 'Producing drama: Symbolic communication and the police', *Symbolic Interaction*, 5, 223–41.

# 4. Public employment officers as brokers and therapists

## Julia Peralta

Public employment officers have a key position in the labour market. In Sweden the state was the sole player in the design and execution of the labour market policy during a large part of the 1900s. Since the 1990s, there are many actors executing labour market policies, including private employment agencies. In this chapter, the Public Employment Service is in focus. They find themselves at a number of intersecting points: between politicians and jobseekers; between employers and jobseekers; and between employers and politicians. The public employment officers operate in a force field of different demands and expectations. The category of public employment officers can in principle be broken down into two specializations. Their work is oriented either to placement tasks or to guidance and counselling tasks. This chapter provides insight into the significant differences between these specializations – into where priorities are made, what tools and resources the public employment officers have at their disposal, and how their relationships with jobseekers and employers take shape.[1] The placement officer (employment officer) and the counsellor reflect two ideological versions of contemporary society: the broker society and the therapy society.

## THE DIVIDE BETWEEN COUNSELLING AND PLACEMENT TASKS

Despite a formal divide between (employment) counsellors and placement officers having disappeared since the early 2000s, the informal division continues to be decisive for how the day-to-day work is organized. It governs which tools are available, how the work is conducted in relation to jobseekers, the characteristics associated with the employment officers' work and their relation to employers. Here, employment officers assume two main roles: *the role of the placement officer*, which has a clear connection to the broker society and market ideals; and *the role of the counsellor*, associated with the therapy society where problems earlier seen as structural and socioeconomic are today seen as individual and psychological.

By *the broker society* is meant a society permeated by services that are in one way or another associated with sales, and where various types of agents play an important part in how the market functions. The broker society thus has strong connections with the market society. In this model of society, brokers act as middlemen between buyers and sellers in a specific market and can engage in mediating, presenting, transferring and/or coordinating information, goods, assets or, in this case, labour and job opportunities.[2]

By *the therapy society* is meant a society where people have become more dependent on experts, who know best how we can attain success and happiness with neither the moralism of religion nor government (Furedi 2004; Holmes 1991; Nolan 1998). This is seen, for example, in the increased authority of therapists in social contexts. The therapist's status has increased, and the therapeutic perspective has gained more influence in many institutions and organizations in our society, for example among teachers, lawyers and social workers (Rose 1990).

The emergence of the broker society and the therapy society is related to an individualization of working life. Here, individualization refers to the process by which unemployment has slipped from being defined as an effect of social structures to being seen as a phenomenon rooted in individual circumstances.

This chapter is based on interviews and participant observation carried out in 2004 at two Public Employment Service offices. One of the offices is situated in a mid-sized Swedish city with a large public sector and knowledge-intensive industry, and the second in a smaller factory town where heavy industry makes up an important part of the economy.[3]

## THE BIG RESTRUCTURING OF THE 1980s

At the end of the 1980s, big changes occurred in the organization of local public employment offices. The Public Employment Service's activities underwent a restructuring, moving from a search-oriented way of working to a more job-oriented way of doing things. In the previous, search-oriented organization's time, the search process took its point of departure from the needs of the jobseekers. The Public Employment officers looked for employment opportunities for jobseekers among job vacancies listed with the Public Employment Service. Employers often had long waits before they were sent suitable workers. In conjunction with the reorganization, the ambition became to gain an overview of the employers' recruiting needs as quickly as possible (Ahrne et al. 1985; Ahrne 1989; Delander, Thoursie and Wadensjö 1991). Along with the job-focused method, activities came to be governed by which jobs were listed and the task became finding suitable applicants for the vacant positions (see also Chapter 2).

The restructuring also meant an extensive reform of staffing, whereby the categories of placement officers (*platsförmedlare*) and employment counsellors (*arbetsvägledare*) were introduced. The placement officers were given the responsibility of maintaining contact with the employers, and every placement officer was assigned a number of specific employers. The aim was to increase knowledge about local companies' recruitment needs. The placement officer was also expected to work to find suitable jobs for jobseekers. Both sides in the job placement process were to be given equal weight (Delander, Thoursie and Wadensjö 1991). In connection with the introduction of employment counsellors (or simply *counsellors* as they were and are still called today), three personnel categories merged: vocational counsellor (*arbetsvårdare*), occupational counsellor (*yrkesvägledare*), and case officers (*handläggare*) (Delander, Thoursie and Wadensjö 1991). The counsellors' activities were in turn oriented toward labour market training.

As will be shown in this chapter, the division between placement officers and counsellors lives on, although these particular titles have formally disappeared. The rather incisive wording 'in job placement, the starting point is the job openings; in counselling, however, it is the jobseekers' coined 20 years ago still applies today in practice (Delander, Thoursie and Wadensjö 1991: 132). Completely different starting points apply for placement officers and counsellors and, by extension, possibly also different value systems.

## JOB PLACEMENT IS A PROCESS OF MATCHING

The matching of jobseekers to employers is a central role for the placement officer. For a welfare state like Sweden, the connection between matching and unemployment is of crucial importance: it has to do with issues of economic stability and social security (Walter 2005: 18–19; see also Chapter 3).[4] The Public Employment Service is a public institution tasked with facilitating matching in the labour market, a marketplace where workers and opportunities for work meet.

The placement officers are responsible for registering jobseekers (which jobseekers do themselves via computer). After a jobseeker is registered, he or she is given an interview appointment and an appointment for a return visit. On this occasion, jobseekers are also given information materials and the placement officer offers relevant job search courses or online seminars. Placement officers are also responsible for the reception desk. This responsibility often falls on the placement officers who work with jobseekers in the first phase of unemployment, when jobseekers can search for employment on their own, at their own discretion, and without too much oversight.

Some placement officers work exclusively with matching jobseekers to jobs. This involves activities related to quickly teaching jobseekers to *manage on their own*, to use a computer (one of the first tasks given to a new jobseeker is the digitalization and uploading of his or her personal CV to the Public Employment Service website), and to look for job openings on the internet.

The matching work of placement officers is aimed at jobseekers who can be described as self-reliant. As one placement officer puts it:

> I mean, he's self-reliant, healthy, self-assured and has self-confidence. He's not someone who's missing that aspect. If he could just get a job, you would see him, really, as a fish that you catch and release. He won't need me at all, he won't need any of the employment office's services. It's just circumstances that have led to his unemployment. Mostly external factors. You can trust that he's looking for jobs.

Independence, drive and the ability to take initiative are central components in the categorization of jobseekers as self-reliant. The placement officers often also describe the self-reliant jobseeker as healthy, creating a link between self-reliance and being healthy. Being self-reliant is also an expression for the construct of the 'good' jobseeker. Self-reliant jobseekers are contrasted with 'problematic' jobseekers.

Being computer literate and being able to search the web are important components of self-reliance. Since the 1990s, computerization and, more specifically, the use of the internet have made matching in the labour market much easier (Bergström and Storrie 2003). One placement officer expresses it as follows:

> Things didn't used to be as computerized as they are now. There's always information to be had now. In practice, we've put more responsibility on jobseekers to gather that information. They need to be up-to-date and active. But it's apparent that, as case officers, we have a lot less time for personal contact with the jobseeker, mainly because it's more responsibility. In the future, it will be the jobseekers' responsibility.

As the above placement officer describes, computerization reinforces the normative starting point of this system, where jobseekers who are computer literate constitute the model for many of the Public Employment Service's activities. The technology requires jobseekers to be independent and to have computer knowledge, and in turn enables assigning high numbers of jobseekers to each employment officer. This norm is made visible in clear contrast to activities of jobseeking among people for whom personal computers are not as obvious a part of everyday life, as is the case for many workers in production and manufacturing whose work tasks date from the 1960s.

To effectively match jobseekers with job opportunities requires that placement officers have good assessment abilities. The task of assessing jobseekers is partly about knowing how to differentiate between the various needs of jobseekers for help or services. It is a matter of being able to quickly determine where in the organization the jobseeker can best receive help:

> I had one fellow here a couple of weeks ago who was hearing impaired. When he came in, I immediately noticed that he was hearing impaired. So I refer him to Hearing and Vision [a special team at the Public Employment Service]. He needs some other kind of help, like Work Rehab. It's the same as, if the person can look for work and they're on it, then I direct them to jobs and stay in touch with them. But if I notice that it's maybe not going that great, it's taking a long time and they don't get a job but need a bit more help, a little more time, or they may have some problems or need to talk about training or something, then I refer them to counselling where they can sit down and have this longer conversation with them.

The above quote illustrates how the work of placement officers largely has to do with assessing and categorizing jobseekers and thereafter referring them further (see also Chapter 5). The role of the placement officer as a creator of order is in turn reinforced by the personal qualities sought. A placement officer should have good assessment abilities, be able to work quickly, and, in brief conversations, be able to determine and refer jobseekers to the right employment officer category. The placement officer is also a broker between supply and demand in the labour market. One placement officer explains why he prefers the job of placement officer to being a counsellor, by comparing himself to a colleague:

> He takes the people that are past 100 days, who've been registered longer, who've been trying for a really long time. I can contribute to a certain degree. But I don't have the work hours to dedicate to this and also feel that I'm not a counsellor. I'm someone who likes these brief, brief contacts. I have

conversations with them too, but I also feel that I want to see that they have opportunities really fast like this. That's why I work with employers. I like working with employers. Then I know what they want. I go in and look on the computer, and I can see right away which jobseekers have what's needed.

Efficiency is another important characteristic in the work of a placement officer. It is a matter of handling, for the Public Employment Service, a large number of jobseekers (300–400 per employment officer at some employment offices). It is above all a matter of being able to handle the exposure involved with working on the front line in reception. Placement officers are exposed in the sense that they are expected to be able to answer all of the questions asked and to serve as the organization's public face.

A placement officer's work also includes assisting employers to recruit workers with specific knowledge and skills. Ordering labour like this illustrates the proximity to the open labour market that characterizes the work of the placement officers. One placement officer had this to say about her work:

I don't have to do the long-winded story thing. I'm not the type that has to investigate like that. I don't have the patience to sit and listen to people. What is it really they should train to become? That is, I prefer to have the kind of contact where I get recruiting assignments and then I can get in touch with a jobseeker who either has or doesn't have what I'm looking for. If they've got what I want, then: *Great, then I'll do this, and then I'll be in touch with you.* It's immediate. That's the way I like it.

This placement officer uses a language similar to what other brokers use. It is a question of selling a product (the labour sought) in a market, which should occur in an efficient manner. In the same way as brokers package and sell a product, placement officers match suitable jobseekers to employers and companies. The meeting between jobseekers and employment officers reflects the value that the labour market places on factors such as training, work experience and social competence. Here, the employer can be seen as a consumer and the employment officer as a mediator between supply and demand (see also Gustafsson et al. 2013). The work of placement officers resembles the activities carried out within the framework of private staffing agencies. This is yet another clear trend in the placement officer's work.[5] The more the placement officers refer 'suitable' workers to employers, the higher the confidence in the Public Employment Service among employers and in society in general. In this way, jobseekers are made into a commodity.

The focus on matching, however, becomes successively weaker the further into unemployment the jobseeker gets, and the labour market policy's activation measures gradually take over. Time represents a linear order, whereby jobseekers are first seen as self-reliant and, as time goes on, they are directed to other categorizations of more or less negative types. To not succeed in keeping a job or to fail to become employed is interpreted as a deviation (see also Chapter 3).

## TO COUNSEL IS TO NURTURE

The work of the counsellor targets mainly those with a large need for help and support, primarily long-term unemployed. Their work is largely structured around the so-called activity guarantee (now: job and development programme),[6] which comprises individually adapted full-time labour market policy activities that include courses on job-seeking, work experience and recruitment aid. The work of counsellors has less to do with matching, and more to do with activating. The counsellor's task is also to ensure that jobseekers receive the remuneration they are entitled to (unemployment insurance or activity grant). A second task for counsellors is to assess whether a labour market policy program is right for a specific jobseeker.

Counsellors also conduct assessments of work experience placements. They investigate whether an organizer is reputable and whether the trainee's experience can lead to knowledge and further development. In cases where labour market training is applicable, the counsellor and training groups in the counties in question assess whether or not there is a possibility of finding work after training. The counsellors also help jobseekers who are eligible for an individual recruitment incentive, a subsidized employment support form sometimes used for jobseekers who have been registered for longer periods.

The counsellor's work is aimed to a large degree at so-called weak jobseekers. The weak are here contrasted with those who are self-reliant. Other metaphors used include the marginalized or disadvantaged. Weakness refers here to the difficulty these jobseekers have asserting themselves in the labour market, coupled with a lack of desired personal qualities or the presence of qualities that are less desirable in today's labour market. The characteristics that counsellors define as problematic are shyness, awkwardness, passiveness, lack of knowledge of Swedish and how Swedish working life and the labour market function.

Counsellors have access to a number of instruments to exercise control over jobseekers, a form of control that also translates to a form of self-disciplining in the jobseekers (cf. Chapter 3). For the counsellor, however, it is also important to build a relationship with the jobseeker based on respect and friendship, a relationship that expresses empathy. Demonstrating that they understand and empathize with the jobseeker is a way for counsellors to build a relationship. As one counsellor says:

> I think you have to build a relationship with the jobseeker. It's crucial to have a relationship that builds on friendship and respect. My job is to provide a clear picture of myself as the authority, but an authority with a human face who can put myself in other situations, in other people's shoes, who can understand unemployed people, and who can truly feel their suffering, but who can nevertheless set demands, work in a professional manner. I've noticed that this is actually appreciated, absolutely.

The counsellors believe it is important to have confidence in the jobseeker's own capacity to act. At the same time, it is important to conduct frequent follow-ups of the jobseeker's efforts. The counsellors say this is a way of showing the job-seeking individual respect, of not excluding anyone, and of making sure everyone gets attention. One counsellor describes the task as follows:

> As a counsellor, my job is to get someone to see the light. That is, I start with a person who finds him- or herself in a dark room, and my job is to get that person out of there, that is, to lead or guide them, or however you want to put it. By acting as an advisor, the person should be able to slowly but surely find the light in his or her surroundings. And once there, this person should be able to open his or her eyes and see what he or she wants. I mean, they certainly know what they want, they know, but they don't see everything. I mean, as soon as they get to that lit place, they can themselves define what they want. They want nothing more than to get out of there, and I show less respect for the person when I start deciding what he or she wants. And it's really important that we set demands. I mean, my job is to lead you out of here, then you have to manage the rest of the way yourself.

The above quote expresses the jobseeker's situation as being 'in a dark room'. The counsellor describes himself as someone who sees the light, and who in turn can show it to others. (The job title itself in Swedish – *vägledare* – literally means someone who 'leads the way'.) That is, the counsellor can show the way to employment and thereby to a brighter existence. The term awakes thoughts about the emergence of a therapy society, which is seen as strongly linked to a process where the focus has shifted from social aspects to the individual's subjective experiences. Social problems are often understood as individual, with no connection to the social sphere: they are increasingly perceived in terms of psychological dispositions, such as, for example, personal unsuitability, feelings of guilt, anxiety, conflicts, qualities that are lacking, and psychoses (Beck 2002). As in the UK, the role of therapy in labour market policy initiatives that target the unemployed have become more and more important in Sweden, most clearly expressed in the use of, for example, solution-focused therapy in the work with the jobseekers (Peralta Prieto 2006).

By getting the jobseeker to understand and arrive at what he or she wants to do, the individual can be wakened from a state of inability to act. A fundamental element is the talk about the counsellor's task in terms that resemble the task of the priest as a caretaker of the soul. The counsellor can help the jobseeker to act and to fit in with the norm. As a whole, the counsellor's work differs from that of the placement officer in several respects. As one counsellor explains:

> I rather like this aspect of – a little analysing, discovering new ways forward, seeing the possibilities in things, and finding ways to remove the barriers. I therefore really like working as a counsellor. I'm not their mother and I don't solve their problems. But I try to get them to solve their problems. And show them the possibilities to maybe finding a way out.

Important characteristics in the work of a counsellor are patience, the ability to express oneself clearly, to show understanding, and being able to put oneself in the jobseeker's situation. It is partly a matter of a clear professional identity strongly tied to the image of long-term unemployed people as jobseekers in need of some form of employment, assistance and nurturing. But the above quote also expresses a partially divided professional identity, which in turn can be associated with a change in labour market policy. This change has been interpreted as a shift from labour market policy to social policy (Junestav 2004; Peralta Prieto 2006).

Similarly to placement officers, counsellors have frequent contact with employers, but their tasks are different. The counsellor's activities comprise mainly establishing contact with employers who could potentially take long-term unemployed people under the activity guarantee. These contacts are often informal and based on the jobseeker's needs – not the employer's, which applies for placement officers. Like the placement officers, the counsellors stress the importance of long-term and good employer contacts for being able to create employment or other subsidized positions for jobseekers considered to lack their own contact networks and other possibilities of finding work themselves. This reinforces the counsellor's role as a middleman between employer and jobseeker. This observation also supports the theory of the importance of social networks in working life for entrance into the labour market (Granovetter 1995).

Informal contacts between counsellors and employers are important in two respects. Firstly, the counsellor's social networks play an important part in referring jobseekers to employment or activation measures. The counsellor's social networks constitute a resource. The work to get more jobseekers into some form of employment can in turn be exchanged as symbolic capital by the counsellor within the Public Employment Service. Such a counsellor is seen to be effective and also receives confirmation that his or her work methods are correct. If the activities lead to some form of employment, it also reflects positively on how the Public Employment Service is seen in society as a whole. This is an important basis for the labour market policy's justification.

Secondly, the counsellor's contacts with employers can be seen as a way of developing new forms of social responsibility, in a broader sense than state responsibility. In this case, it is a matter of a responsibility that lies in the hands of public employment officers and employers as citizens. One counsellor comments: 'I would like in some cases for us to have the option of saying: *Hey – hire this person, it won't cost you anything.* That the employer would feel, along with us, this social responsibility. They could give the person in question a job'.

The role of counsellors is shifting from being primarily the long arm of the state in preventing long-term unemployment and social segregation, to becoming socially accountable professionals. This trend can be seen as a part of a process in which the problem of unemployment is increasingly individualized, as a problem largely in the hands of the jobseeker and the case officer.

## CONCLUDING DISCUSSION: SHIFTING RESPONSIBILITIES – FROM SOCIAL TO INDIVIDUAL PROBLEMS

There are differences between the work of placement officers and employment counsellors, in the priorities they make, the tools and resources they have at their disposal, and how their relationships with jobseekers and employers are formed.

These roles reflect two ideological manifestations in society: the broker society and therapy society. On one side of today's Public Employment Service are the placement officers (the brokers), whose work is aimed at quickly and effectively matching suitable jobseekers with job opportunities. This is a way of offering the market the right expertise, and the employers' needs are central. It is a matter of being receptive to shifts in the market and its needs, and reading demand, but also of being able to quickly assess the skills and expertise of the jobseeker.

On the other side of today's Public Employment Services are the counsellors (the therapists), whose work focuses more on conversation and confidence to get so-called problematic jobseekers to return to normalcy. This normalcy is expressed in terms of activity, which is an important element in the construction of the active citizen. It is also a question of disciplining, which is demonstrated in that certain personal characteristics are described as problematic and become the object of change measures.

These ideological manifestations are part of a historical process in which the responsibility for unemployment is becoming individualized. As opposed to earlier times, when the state was held responsible to a larger degree, today it is the individual's responsibilities and obligations that are stressed. Today, it is the individual's personal qualities that are seen as problematic. And it is these characteristics that are the focus of measures that are to be taken. This individualization means a de-politicization of the labour market. Descriptions and solutions for complex social problems are attributed to individuals rather than to structural matters pertaining to the functioning of welfare society. Individual citizens now to a large extent get to carry the responsibility for making the labour market work.

## NOTES

1. The research that this chapter is based on was made possible within the framework of a faculty-funded PhD position in economic history at Uppsala University.
2. For a further description of the emerging market society, see B. Dahlbom (2003).
3. This chapter builds on a doctoral thesis on the ills of unemployment and Swedish labour market policy and practice, *Den sjuka arbetslösheten. Svensk arbetsmarknadspolitik och dess praxis 1978–2004* (Peralta Prieto 2006). A full presentation of the study can be found in the thesis.
4. For a detailed description of matching as a process with respect to staffing agencies, see Walter (2005) and, in connection with recruiting, see Bolander (2002).
5. For an informative description and analysis of the work of temporary staffing firms, see Walter (2005), Garsten (2008) and Turtinen and Garsten (2000).
6. The activity guarantee was replaced by the job and development programme in July 2007.

# REFERENCES

Ahrne, Göran (1989), *Byråkratin och statens inre gränser*. Stockholm: Rabén and Sjögren.

Ahrne, Göran, Karl-Erik Johansson and Roine Johansson (1985), *Vad gör de där inne på arbetsförmedlingen?* Uppsala: Department of Sociology, Uppsala University.

Beck, Ulrich (2002), *Individualization: Institutionalized Individualism and its Social and Political Consequences*. London: Sage.

Bergström, Ola and Donald Storrie (2003), *Contingent Employment in Europe and the United States*. Cheltenham and Northampton, MA: Edward Elgar.

Bolander, Pernilla (2002), *Anställningsbilder och rekryteringsbeslut*. Stockholm: Economic Research Institute (EFI), Stockholm School of Economics.

Delander, Lennart, Ragnar Thoursie and Eskil Wadensjö (1991), *Arbetsförmedlingens historia*. Stockholm: Allmänna förlaget.

Furedi, Frank (2004), *Therapy Culture: Cultivating vulnerability in an uncertain age*. London: Routledge.

Garsten, Christina (2008), *Workplace Vagabonds: Career and community in changing worlds of work*. Basingstoke: Palgrave Macmillan.

Garsten, Christina and Jan Turtinen (2000), '"Angels" and "Chameleons": The construction of the flexible temporary employee in Sweden and the UK', in Bo Stråth (ed.), *After Full Employment: European discourses on work and flexibility*. Brussels: Peter Lang, pp. 161–96.

Granovetter, Mark (1995), *Getting a Job: A study of contacts and careers*. Chicago, IL: University of Chicago Press.

Gustafsson, Johanna, Julia Prieto Peralta and Berth Danermark (2013), 'The employer's perspective on supported employment for people with disabilities: Successful approaches of supported employment organizations', *Journal of Vocational Rehabilitation*, 38, 99–111.

Hertzberg, Fredrik (2003), *Gräsrotsbyråkrati och normativ svenskhet. Hur arbetsförmedlare förstår en etnisk segregerad arbetsmarknad*. Stockholm: National Institute for Working Life.

Holmes, Mark (1991), 'Bringing about change in teachers: Rationalistic technology and therapeutic human relations in the subversion of education', *Curriculum Inquiry*, 21(1), 65–90.

Junestav, Malin (2004), *Arbetslinjer i svensk socialpolitisk debatt och lagstiftning 1930–2001*. Uppsala: Uppsala University.

Nolan, James (1998), *The Therapeutic State: Justifying government at century's end*. New York, NY: New York University Press.

Peralta Prieto, Julia (2006), *Den sjuka arbetslösheten. Svensk arbetsmarknadspolitik och dess praxis 1978–2004*. Uppsala: Acta Universitatis Upsaliensis.

Rose, Nikolas (1990), *Governing the Soul: The shaping of the private self*. London: Routledge.

Walter, Lars (2005), *Som hand i handske. En studie av matchning i ett personaluthyrningsföretag*. Gothenburg: BAS.

# 5. A labour market of opportunities? Specialists assess work ability and disability

**Ida Seing**

---

Both labour market policy and the labour market today are characterized by demands and expectations on people to market themselves, have the right attitude and personality, in order to get a job. Human abilities, knowledge and skills are put forward as central tools for competing in the modern labour market and being resistant to unemployment and social exclusion (Fogde 2009; Garsten and Jacobsson 2004). This is a development that reflects a new view of the individual, who is expected to take responsibility for unemployment and employment. The trend has been formulated in terms of an ideological shift, where social responsibility has shifted from society to the individual – from the right to employment to an obligation to be employable (Garsten and Jacobsson 2004). In the labour market policy in Sweden, the Public Employment Service's orientation towards self-service, courses in entrepreneurial business, learning to write CVs and practice job interviews are examples of how such ideas are expressed in a local context (Benson 2008; Fogde 2009; Thedvall 2004).

In recent years, the number of groups outside the regular labour market has grown. Research and public reports show, for example, that the number of people referred to sheltered employment and receiving wage subsidies has increased markedly in the last decades (Holmqvist 2009; Jacobsson and Seing 2013). According to Public Employment Service statistics (AKU) for 2014, 27.4 per cent of all registered jobseekers between the ages of 16 and 64 have a registered disability. As a comparison, in 1992, 10 per cent of all registered jobseekers were classified as disabled. What is especially notable is that the number of people with so-called sociomedical disabilities and mental disabilities has continued to increase over the past two decades. This poses many questions, encouraging more research and political initiatives.

Societal norms and values influence how bureaucratic organizations categorize work ability and work disability. Here, the concepts should not be understood merely as administrative categories, but also as social categories influenced by norms and assumptions about desirable charac- teristics for an individual in order to get a job and 'to fit' in today's labour market (Fogde 2009; Garsten and Jacobsson 2004; Peralta Prieto 2006). In the area of labour market policy, qualities such as flexibility and adaptability are regarded as self-evident characteristics one must have to be viable in the modern labour market. Being averse to change or having difficulty adapting can in this context be seen as problematic and limit the individual's work ability and employability.

This chapter focuses on the Public Employment Service's activities for jobseekers with a reduced ability to work, that is, limited work capacity.[1] The starting point is that it is in the interface between citizens and street-level bureaucrats that practical policy is shaped (Lipsky 1980). The chapter illustrates how bureaucratic processes lead to jobseekers being classified as disabled. How does the work of assessing and categorizing individuals actually occur? What assumptions does this work rest on? The chapter draws attention to how activities are structured, what the investigation process looks like, which actors are involved, and how the concepts of work ability and disability are operationalized. The ambition is to gain a richer understanding of how the Public Employment Service works at the local level, how it organizes and designs its activities for jobseekers who are considered to have limited ability to work.

Implementation of national labour market policy guidelines in Sweden is carried out by the Public Employment Service and its local Public Employment Service offices, and street-level bureaucrats. Michael Lip- sky's theoretical framework regarding the importance of street-level bureaucrats and the room to manoeuvre they have can be used to understand and explain the local outcomes of the policy (Lipsky 1980). Local Public Employment Service offices and their street-level bureau- crats represent the lower hierarchy of the organization, who have daily contact with citizens. Street-level bureaucrats must execute their work tasks based on tight budget constraints, within the limits of laws and regulations. Studying the Public Employment Service from the street- level bureaucrat's horizon enables us to increase our understanding and knowledge of the preconditions for the organization and implementation of welfare policy in practice.

The current study is based on semi-structured interviews with admin- istrative employees at central and local levels of the Public Employment Service and the Rehabilitation to Work Department (hereafter called *Work Rehab*). The empirical data has been complemented with document studies of case officer support from the Public Employment Service and public government reports.

According to the official government ordinance on labour market policy activities (SFS 2000:628), the task of the Public Employment Service is to operate so-called occupational rehabilitation. This is a term used for the counselling, assessment and rehabilitation efforts the authority provides for people with disabilities. Labour market support for jobseekers with disabilities consists of measures such as wage subsidies, publicly sheltered employment, and adaptation of the workplace. The purpose of the measures is to compensate for reduced work ability and to improve the jobseekers' prospects of finding work in the regular labour market.[2]

The Public Employment Service and the street-level bureaucrats at local level decide which jobseekers are eligible for the special support initiatives for people with disabilities. This work includes an investigation process where the concept of the work ability constitutes an important assessment category for differentiating between jobseekers who are healthy and able to work versus those who are not (cf. Lindqvist 2008). In this process of investigation and assessment of work ability, the Work Rehab unit at the Public Employment Service has a specialist consultative function for local employment officers. Work Rehab has access to professional groups such as occupational psychologists, occupational therapists and social workers, referred to as 'specialists'. Jobseekers who have a diagnosed disability or seen as potentially having a disability are referred to the Work Rehab department for counselling and to undergo further investigation of their work ability.

## MEDICALIZATION AND INDIVIDUALIZATION OF LABOUR MARKET POLICY

In order to understand and explain how welfare policy is shaped and organized, we must also consider the prominent role that professional knowledge has come to play (see, for example, Dandeker 1990; Prior 1993). Research shows, for example, that human conditions to an increasing extent tend to be diagnosed and labelled as illness according to medical models. This trend, which in the literature is called *medicalization*, is explained by the fact that professional knowledge and professional occupational groups have become more important and more influential in welfare policy institutions both at the central institutional level and in the interface between street-level bureaucrats and citizens at the local level. Alcoholism, eating disorders, obesity and anorexia are examples of how social phenomena are medicalized (Conrad 1992; Peralta Prieto 2006).

Medicalization processes have also received attention in the area of labour market policy. Concepts such as occupational handicap and work disability have, for example, been identified as medicalized phenomena. This is explained by an increasing number of jobseekers, since the 1990s, having come to be perceived and treated as problematic, for example, as having an 'occupational handicap'. In this way, solutions to unemployment are found in characteristics attributed to the individual, which are considered to be the reason for a particular jobseeker not getting a job (Holmqvist 2009; Peralta Prieto 2006).

Earlier research indicates that the application of medical frames of reference, for classifying unemployed people, for example, is associated with an increased individualization of social responsibility, where individuals are expected to be responsible for their employment and unemployment. Being unemployed thereby becomes a problem connected to the individual's own personal shortcomings and actions, as well as health-related factors. The labour market policy problem therefore lies primarily with the individual, who is the subject of measures and adaptation (Peralta Prieto 2006; see also Chapter 4).

As Jessica Lindvert described in more detail in Chapter 2, from the latter half of the 1900s onward, Sweden has pursued an active labour market policy with the aim of combining economic development and social security. A basic assumption of this policy model is that the willingness of workers to adapt to economic changes increases if society is able to offer an extensive social safety net and acceptable alternatives to unemployment. Instead of passive measures in the form of financial compensation (in the form of cash support), unemployed people are offered – at both high and low unemployment levels – active measures such as Public Employment Services, labour market training programmes, opportunities for retraining and mobility support. The purpose of the active labour market policy is to reduce unemployment and for society to do as much as it can to prevent people from ending up outside the labour market for long periods of time (Lindvert 2006).

The implementation of the so-called job placement reform (PLOG) at the end of the 1970s, however, was the beginning of a new direction for labour market policy and the Public Employment Service in Sweden. The economic boom of the 1980s meant that labour market policy was targeted at adapting the supply of labour to the labour market's needs. Thus, the Public Employment Service's activities came to be demand-based and the interests of jobseekers were downgraded in priority. Job placement meant that the main work task of employment officers was to find the right staff for the job vacancies listed. The prioritizing of job openings over unemployed people has been described as a radical change in direction for Public Employment Service activities (Ahrne et al. 1985). This has also influenced the emphasis on identifying jobseekers' abilities and possibilities.

## FROM SEEKING LABOUR MARKET MEASURES TO SEEKING JOBS

In step with the Public Employment Service's increased market adaptation, we also see an increased emphasis on the individual's responsibilities and obligations to society, where social rights are increasingly tied to work. The focus on activating and rehabilitating reflects an institutional change and a political ideological shift in the area of labour market policy and social policy (Junestav 2004). We are seeing the growth of a new work strategy, where labour market policy measures are in decline in favour of employment in the regular labour market. One of the managers at Work Rehab describes it as follows: 'We find ourselves faced with new thinking today no matter which party we vote for. There's an ambition to have more people working in Sweden today. More people getting jobs in the usual way and not as many activities.'

In national labour market policy guidelines, the matching assignment specifically has been intensified. According to this labour market policy assignment, the Public Employment Service's main activities should be to match jobseekers to job vacancies in the regular labour market. In recent years, funding allocated to activities and support initiatives has decreased. The support initiatives that the Public Employment Service has at its disposal today are, according to the respondents, for the most part aimed at jobseekers whose eligibility for unemployment insurance has expired, that is, whose unemployment insurance days have run out. One employment officer believes that the focus today is on the jobseeker being active. Instead of seeking measures, one should be seeking jobs.

When I started in 1994, there were numerous different programmes. There was public relief work, a work experience scheme (*arbetslivsutvecking,* ALU), we talked about workplace introduction for immigrants, improved general employment support. Now most of these support measures have disappeared ... We've tightened up the demands on people who are unemployed in the form of having reduced unemployment insurance benefits; we've reduced the number of unemployment benefit days. And labour market policy programmes no longer count towards benefit days. It's only real work that provides eligibility for new benefit days. So, here, there's more of a focus on the jobseeker being active. And to really actively seek work and not measures. (Employment officer)

The understanding of unemployment has changed. Instead of a labour market policy focusing on the labour market's system, it is now the individual's human abilities, knowledge and skills that are put forward as central tools for counteracting unemployment (Benson 2008; Peralta Prieto 2006).

## FROM REHABILITATION TO EMPLOYMENT

In order to prevent social exclusion in the labour market, the welfare state has invested extensive resources in efforts to prevent and rehabilitate illness and disability. In 2000, the Riksdag (Swedish parliament) took a decision regarding a national action plan for disability policy (Prop. 1999/2000:79). In the area of labour market policy, which the Public Employment Service is responsible for, the goal is for people with disabilities to have the same opportunities as others to participate in working life (Prop. 2007/08:1, Expenditure Area 13). In one of the government's so-called intermediate targets, the level of employment for the segment of the population with disabilities shall in the long term be equal to that of the population as a whole. The target group's employment level shall also increase more rapidly than the rest of the labour force.

The emphasis on people's ability to work has also given rise to new forms of cooperation. Actors at the policy level have warmed to the idea of multi-stakeholder cooperation between labour market and welfare administrations. The street-level bureaucrats at the Public Employment Service are at the same time critical of cooperation. Reasons given for this, is that cooperation in itself has always been a 'popular concept to talk about' but difficult to realize because rules, guidelines and professions differ between the authorities. One interviewee describes the situation as a 'game of musical chairs', where groups of unemployed people and sick-listed unemployed people fall between the cracks and are forced to make the rounds between the authorities:

So we've got a fun game here, that I call musical chairs. The Social Insurance Agency sits in one and wants great numbers, great numbers for Curt Malmborg [former director-general] to show. And at the Public Employment Service, sits Bo Bylund [former director-general], who wants great numbers to show government. And then there's the municipality, who wants great numbers for the municipal executive. This is something that has to be addressed. This game of musical chairs drives me crazy. Where no one wants this person who is basically really struggling. (Occupational therapist)

Earlier research shows that cooperation, in the form of partnerships, for example, places demands on public organizations that are hard to meet. Strong organizational identities within the public sector have emerged and authorities are mainly focused on their own affairs. Collaboration may hence be a popular term to use, but difficult to realize because regulations, goals and guidelines between organizations are different (Brunsson and Sahlin-Andersson 2000). In the area of social and labour market policy, there is therefore a risk that cooperation itself becomes merely an empty slogan (Lindvert 2006). Despite ambitious goals at the policy level, that is, that people with reduced work ability should participate more in working life, the target group's position in the labour market has not improved.

## SPECIALISTS AT WORK

According to constitutional law, the Swedish Riksdag and the Swedish Government set the guidelines for labour market policy as formulated in the ordinance (SFS 2007:1030) that instructs the Public Employment Service. The assignment is further clarified in the annual budget proposal and government appropriations. The Public Employment Service's over-arching goals are to work towards and improve the function of the labour market. This shall occur through: 1) effectively bringing together those who are looking for work with those who are seeking staff, 2) prioritizing those who are far from the labour market, and 3) contributing to a steady increase in employment in the long term (SFS 2007:1030). The Public Employment Service organizes its labour market policy assignment into nine service areas, which are: 1) job-seeking, 2) improving your job-seeking, 3) counselling for employment, 4) training for employment, 5) starting your own business, 6) clarifying your work capabilities, 7) adapting your work situation, 8) recruiting new employees, and 9) pre-recruitment training.

Occupational rehabilitation is a term used for activities at the Public Employment Service undertaken for people with disabilities with reduced ability to work and conducted within the framework of the above-mentioned services: *Counselling for employment, clarifying your conditions to work* and *adapting your work situation* at the Work Rehab department. Thus, when the case ends up on the specialist's desk, the investigative work into the jobseeker's work ability begins.

From a formal standpoint, the Work Rehab unit only has a consulting function, but it can still be described as relatively freestanding and independent, run by professions with significant influence and responsibility. Work Rehab has approximately 600 employees comprising mainly occupational psychologists, occupational therapists and social workers. The department also comprises a small number of audiologists, counsellors for the deaf, teachers for the deaf and hearing impaired, hearing technicians, physiotherapists, nurses and low vision teachers. These street-level bureaucrats have advanced investigative skills in occupational rehabilitation, and knowledge about assessing the ability to work. The scope of the specialists to act is founded on professional and experience-based knowledge, which creates legitimacy and credibility in the execution of their professions.

Jobseekers who have been assessed as having an impaired ability to work in the form of physical, mental and social disadvantages that prevent them from getting a job in the labour market are referred to the Work Rehab department. According to the people interviewed, those who come to the department may have earlier diagnosed and documented problems such as addiction, criminality, acquired brain injuries, intellectual problems, physical disabilities, or some combination of these. The target group is stated to be people in need of more qualified knowledge and support to analyse why their job search is not yielding results. The service area of *clarifying your work capabilities* is emphasized as the specialists' main task. The purpose of the assignment is to find out, by way of the assessment process, whether or not the jobseeker has a disability that entitles him or her to special labour market policy measures. The Public Employment Service's investigation is often a precondition for disabled persons with reduced ability to work to be allocated extra labour market support initiatives such as wage subsidies, publicly sheltered work, or a job at Samhall (a state-owned Swedish company assigned to provide meaningful work that furthers the personal development of people with disabilities).

## The Investigations

Within the limits of the *clarifying your conditions to work* service area, and with the support of the investigative methods used there (occupational psychological assessment, social assessment and activity-based assessment), the jobseeker's possible physical, mental and social limitations are detected and identified. Investigations include interview sessions, testing and work ability assessments intended to lead to an overall assessment in the form of a written report of the jobseeker's work ability.

The criteria used in the assessment of work ability include, in broad terms, a focus on skills, personality, capabilities, interests, lifestyle, social situation and health status. These criteria are all associated with a vocabulary that belongs to professions like occupational psychologists, occupational therapists and social workers. In medical terms, for example, occupational psychologists call conditions like depression, fatigue syndrome and dyslexia and neurological disorders such as autism, Asperger syndrome and ADHD, disabilities. In the assessment of possible medical diagnoses, occupational psychologists also underline that the Public Employment Service does not give a diagnosis but is only able to provide a description of the problem.

In the work-related social assessment, the social workers may also methodologically concentrate on the social situation and identify things such as criminality and addiction as sociomedical disabilities. The focus of the assessment rests on so-called social factors that affect a jobseeker's prospects of getting a job. According to the social workers interviewed, jobseekers may often demonstrate a history of various forms of addiction (gambling, drugs and alcohol), or a criminal past that limits their chances of getting or keeping a job.

Within the framework of the activity-based assessment, the occupational therapists are responsible for compiling underlying material for decisions regarding things like technical aids. According to the occupational therapists interviewed, investigations are used in cases where the jobseeker has musculoskeletal impairments. According to an occupational therapist at a larger Public Employment Service office, the purpose of the investigation is to gain an understanding of the jobseeker's individual experience of pain. More precisely: 'What demands can be placed on this person based on his or her perceived pain?'

The activity-based assessment usually occurs at the regular workplace or an adapted workplace. In these settings, the occupational therapist observes the jobseeker in action. These observations can, for example, involve the fine and gross motor skills, dexterity and attention of the person in question, as well as how he or she cooperates and communicates with other co-workers.

According to a senior manager at the Public Employment Service, at the Work Rehab department, the occupational therapists are clearly the professional group with the most refined knowledge on assessing work ability. Occupational therapists are also described as a professional group that will become more and more common in welfare authorities in the future:

Occupational therapists are the professional category assigned to do – to look at the ability to work. Because if you think of the occupational therapist's work in rehabilitation in medical care, it's often a matter of people who've been injured somehow that are trying to return to jobs they already have. Or that they have to adapt their homes because they've acquired a disability. So they're very practised in observing this. How the person functions and what they need to think about. So I think it's a category that's going to grow in this sphere of work ability. (Manager at central level of the Public Employment Service)

According to an occupational therapist with extensive experience in working life, coordination of occupational therapy activities began mainly in the late 1980s and early 1990s. Prior to that, activities were managed more locally, using methods and instruments that they had developed themselves. In her words:

And then when occupational therapists came on the scene, they started to think: *We've got to be able to evaluate what they do and be able to make assessments; we've got to have some kind of form; we need to give the assessment a structure.* And so they began to create a lot of different homemade solutions, different ones everywhere. And when I started in the early 1990s, maybe at the end of the 1980s – we started to coordinate things. *Those of us who work with the same issues – shouldn't we create the same solutions so that it's all the same?* And then we started to use Valpar[3] and tools like that. *Yes, this is what we need, we can use this.* There are other methods, too. We created process charts and lots of things for rehabilitation, for how we should work. (Occupational therapist)

Thus, there has been and remains an ambition to make the investigation work more standardized and uniform.

**The Importance of Measuring Instruments and Testing**

All of the specialist groups use standardized and accepted methods to carry out their investigation processes regarding the ability to work. Conversations and interviews have long been important but are complemented also by various forms of occupational psychology testing and occupational therapy assessment instruments in an attempt to provide a holistic assessment of the individual's work ability in relation to the work environment and work duties. The test instruments that occupational psychologists at the Public Employment Service say they use are personality tests, preference inventories and aptitude tests. The personality test is often used when the occupational psychologist feels the jobseeker in question may be deviant in some respect. This can be in his or her level of motivation, drive or ability to take initiative. Moreover, the personality test can also identify aspects such as impulse control and self-discipline, and provide indicators of a personality disorder, as one experienced occupational psychologist articulated it.

In the interview data, the occupational psychologists point out that there are a wide range of test instruments for assessing the jobseeker's work ability. One occupational psychologist with extensive experience at the Work Rehab department notes that there can be a big difference from one occupational psychologist to the next in how they decide to organize the investigation:

> If, as a psychologist, you're very textbook-oriented, then you'll probably use many different instruments because you don't dare trust your own instrument, which is you, yourself. If you're more artistically inclined, then you use more of yourself and fewer instruments. So there's a lot of variation. If you know what's going on in these talk sessions, say, for 10 different psychologists, things can be very different. And you'd probably be very surprised and think: *Wow, if Karl had talked to that person, then the outcome would've been completely different than if he'd talked with someone else.* So there are very few norms for what these conversations really look like. And there can't be either. There are no manuals for how you establish contact and reach people, and get them to understand. There just aren't.

Like the occupational psychologists, the occupational therapists also state that there are many test instruments that can be applied in the assessment of the jobseeker's ability to work. One interviewee points out that there are, at the same time, many factors that affect a person's prospects of getting a job. Therefore, the instruments cannot provide a unified picture, but instead serve an important guiding function:

> Sure you can have a lot of instruments. But there are so many other factors behind people getting a job. And it can be what we talked about in the coffee room – that it just happens to work at that particular place, for example. But no-one could've known that it would happen just like that, right there and then. Because you just can't predict that. But sometimes you just get lucky: *Yes, well, it was as easy as that – that the person wound up right there and then, and it turned out.* So it's really difficult to find a concrete solution for the individual based on an instrument. On the other hand, the instrument provides a good guide to what the person can do and what the person should avoid doing, and so on. (Occupational therapist)

In the work-related social assessment, a so-called quality assurance checklist is used, with broad question areas concerning 'social factors that affect how the person behaves in society and as a jobseeker' (quality assurance work-related social assessment, ASU). The social worker looks at the jobseeker's current situation, networks, health, work/training, leisure activities and individual resources that affect his or her chances of getting or keeping a job in the labour market. In a labour market context, the jobseeker can thereby be assessed as having a sociomedical disability that is both based on expert knowledge and lives up to society's ideal regarding quality assurance.

## DISABILITY CODING

In order to be able to allocate and offer labour market policy measures reserved specifically for people with disabilities, the Public Employment Service has a classification scheme made up of different disability codes that the employment officers use to sort jobseekers. In order for a disability code to be applied, the jobseeker must demonstrate some form of physical, mental and/or social problem that restricts the ability of the individual in question to get a job. The coding is entered in the Public Employment Service's information system (AIS), a data bank that forms the basis for assigning extra support measures for people with disabilities. A jobseeker must always give his or her consent to being coded by the Public Employment Service as disabled. There are a total of 14 disability codes in which different kinds of physical, mental and social problems can be classified as disabilities. They are:

11    Cardiovascular and/or pulmonary disease
21    Congenital deafness
22    Hearing impairment
31    Severe vision impairment
32    Low vision
41    Mobility-related disability requiring mobility devices such as a walker or wheelchair
42    Other mobility-related disability
51    Other somatic disability
61    Mental disability
71    General disability
81    Sociomedical disability
91    Asthma/allergy/hypersensitivity
92    Specific learning difficulties
93    Acquired brain injury

The specialists interviewed state that the disability coding is used primarily for administrative reasons to facilitate case management and follow-up. The interviewees say that disability coding also enables the Public Employment Service to show outwardly to the public (the government and stakeholder organizations) that resources allocated to people with disabilities are being used efficiently. The following quote represents common thoughts among the specialists about the importance of and need for the disability coding in the Public Employment Service activities:

> The reason why we assign disability codes in the Public Employment Service system is mainly because we have to ensure the more exclusive assistance measures go to the right people. That's why we do these assessments and assign the disability codes. Everything from money and wage subsidy grants to SIUS support [introduction and follow-up support], as I mentioned, so that a person is able to get it. It's done to facilitate more help than [what you would get through, my insertion] the regular resources in the labour market. (Manager at Work Rehab)

This shows that the Public Employment Service has to have a bureaucratic system with rules, criteria and standardized work methods in order to be able to distinguish healthy jobseekers from those who are unwell. Therefore, for individuals, being assigned a disability code should not be seen as a definitive assessment but rather as a necessity to legitimately qualify them for extra efforts from the state (Holmqvist 2005). Thus, for the Public Employment Service, the classification is an administrative measure that the individual in question must submit to in order to gain access to measures such as wage subsidies, adaptation of the workplace, or sheltered employment. In welfare organizations, activities are based on mass handling and each individual case must be processed within a specified time period. Simplifying, classifying and sorting human characteristics can therefore be seen as a necessity for bureaucratic organizations (Johansson 1992). In the area of labour market policy, classification of people with disabilities should above all be seen as an administrative and technical phenomenon that enables bureaucratic organizations to implement policy guidelines and distribute welfare to citizens effectively.

The process chart (Figure 5.1) gives a schematic representation of how construction of the person to a bureaucratic case occurs within the framework of occupational rehabilitation in the Public Employment Service and Work Rehab department. The depicted case flow should be seen primarily as an ideal rather than an exact representation of the practice.

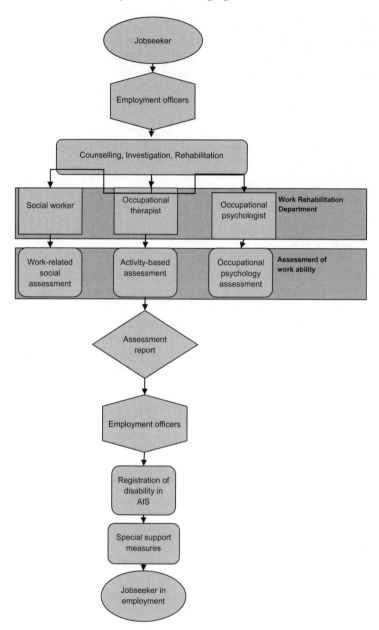

*Figure 5.1    Occupational rehabilitation – case flow*

# THE ROLE OF KNOWLEDGE IN THE PUBLIC EMPLOYMENT SERVICE'S LOCAL PRACTICE

As we have seen, the investigation activities at Work Rehab are based on profession-based frames of reference and assessment criteria that provide a seemingly objectified and standardized assessment of jobseekers' work ability. Having expert-oriented street-level bureaucratic activities in which established professional groups operate, also reduces the uncertainty brought on by the assessment of work ability. Thus, credibility is created within the organization and outwardly to the general public. Here, we can see the importance of knowledge and expertise for credibility and perceived fairness, where the professions, measuring tools and assessments are an expression of accuracy and objectivity (cf. Holmquist 2006).

In the implementation of labour market policy guidelines, ongoing medicalization processes are significant. Professional groups such as occupational psychologists, occupational therapists and social workers are given prominent roles in assessing jobseekers' work ability. The fact that there are specialists, investigations, assessment instruments, tests, assessments reports and disability codes indicates that the role and influence of professional knowledge has become increasingly important in the Public Employment Service at the local level and in the interface between street-level bureaucrats and citizens. In medical terms, the specialists cite depression, fatigue syndrome and dyslexia as conditions that can pose problems for people's employability. Autism, Asperger syndrome and ADHD are also disabilities noted as impairments to the ability to work.

Investigation and assessment processes at the Work Rehab department are based on the striving towards measurability, uniformity and control – terms which can be linked to professions but which can also be linked to the emergence of an 'audit society' (Power 1997). Assessment of work ability can therefore be seen in light of an audit society in which new norms for governance and control have been established (Beck 1992; Giddens 1998; Power 1997; Strathern 2000). In line with this, previous research shows that Swedish labour market policy has undergone a shift, from having focused on 'doing the right things' to a focus on 'doing things right' in the form of controllability, follow-up and reporting (Lindvert 2006).

The trend of using scientific knowledge and making the various components of the assessment work visible are ideas that are also expressed in a government commission appointed in 2008 on the topic of work ability. In the commission's directive, it is stated that there is a need to assess the ability to work based on science and evidence, which should increase uniformity and create the conditions for neutral and value-independent assessments (Dir. 2008:11). That is, this is not something that can be left to experience-based assessments or subjective criteria.

## CONCLUDING DISCUSSION: MEASURING WORK ABILITY IN A CHANGING LABOUR MARKET

While the Public Employment Service distinguishes itself in its expert street-level bureaucratic activities, the process of investigating and assessing the ability to work is complex in that the needs of the labour market, the work environment and the nature of the work tasks must be taken into account. One highly experienced occupational psychologist maintains that the Public Employment Service and the assessment specialists are influenced by changes in the labour market. Work ability and employability are not static concepts but are linked to existing demands in the labour market as well as the work environment and the nature of the work tasks:

> We've naturally been influenced a great deal. There's no denying it. Today, we sit and assess someone as disabled, that we might not have done 20 years ago. The threshold of difficulty needed for people to not do well in the labour market is low. That is, if we talk about the people who are a little 'odd', if you know what I mean? They don't really have a chance in today's labour market. And then in what respect they are odd. There are lots of different ways ... Today, they've been put on disability pension long, long ago. That is, there's no place for them. (Occupational psychologist)

The specialists interviewed stress how the labour market has become less inclusive in terms of there being less space for people who for various reasons are perceived as different and don't fit in. Having the ability to learn, to be flexible, and to take initiative and responsibility are ideal characteristics for being employable and for fitting in to today's modern work life. People who deviate from these ideals have a harder time asserting themselves in an increasingly knowledge-intensive and competitive work life. In the following extract, an occupational psychologist reflects on the Public Employment Service's role in a societal development that puts more and more emphasis on individuals' employability:

> But I also think that it's very dangerous if we, as an authority, decide that people aren't employable in some way. Because then we facilitate this trend,

which is quite negative. Because someone can be assessed as difficult to employ for so many different reasons. They may have a little Asperger's or something, that makes them less mainstream. But at the same time, if we push everyone who isn't mainstream out, what have we got left? Well, we maybe get a smaller and smaller group of yes-sayers, who think like everyone else. That's not very dynamic and, more importantly, it would be terrifying if that happens. I think everyone should have a chance to participate. And every child should have a chance to have parents who work in one way or another. That they belong in society. That they're part of society. (Occupational psychologist)

At the same time, another occupational psychologist interviewed points out that, within the Public Employment Service, there are differing views and values regarding disability assessment, in the form of two camps, where one takes a more critical stance and the other sees the classification as the only way for certain groups to enter the workforce:

Then parliament and government have demanded that we brand these people with a disability code so that they can access the money specially earmarked for disadvantaged groups. And so we've naturally had different views and values regarding this – everything from those who contribute only very unwillingly to disability assessments and feel that – *No, let diversity bloom. Let people be the way they are. Why do we have to sit here and stigmatize people?* – to the other camp, which I belong to, who as often as is humanly possible have made the assessment of disability. Because, in my opinion, it's the only chance this person has to actually access the money and get the help. You could say that the value debate about employability has always been there. (Occupational psychologist)

The disability assessment is also described as an 'opportunity code'. One social worker commented, for example, that problems with addiction, a criminal past and/or problems with pain can constitute barriers for jobseekers for getting and keeping a job in the regular labour market. The disability assessment is therefore one way for the specialists and job-seekers to gain access to more exclusive forms of support initiatives. For example, a wage subsidy makes the person in question more attractive in the labour market and raises his or her employability:

I see it more as an 'opportunity code', so to speak. We give a person who may have a criminal past an opportunity to come back into the workforce. Like, that person can re-enter the workforce. Similarly, someone who's had problems with addiction, who is not expected to function at a level where an employer could accept the odd relapse. No-one accepts that they're away from time to time – haphazardly – without warning – sporadically. It's very difficult because you can never plan production. These people who are struggling so much that they don't even get that far, a single mother with several kids and a kid with ADHD, and another with some other problem. You can imagine where the focus lies for someone like that, so to speak. If we can create an opportunity there, and take advantage of some of this person's time, when she can function in a job, it's worth a lot to society. (Social worker)

Against the background of the labour market placing higher demands on the workforce as a whole, long-term unemployment often ends in an assessment of disability at the Public Employment Service. When the Public Employment Service's main assignment has become matching, and where large parts of active labour market policy measures have been reduced, disability assessment is a way for the Public Employment Service and the jobseekers to access extra support. In the area of labour market policy, there is at the same time an assessment discourse with close ties to the labour market.

In conclusion, it can be said that the disability assessment is based on a complex and situation-bound process tied to norms and to the economic situation in the labour market. Disabilities are therefore primarily not a result of the discovery of illnesses, limitations and other difficulties, but of changes made to the assessment criteria to handle changes in the labour market and the demands of work life. To have work ability, to be employable and to have a disability are placed in relation to norms and to the current state of the labour market, as well as the work environment and the nature of the work tasks. The process for investigation and assessment of a jobseeker's work ability is thereby not an isolated process but coloured in part by changes, demands and expectations in the Public Employment Service's environment. At the same time, the specialists reflect and emphasize that they are party to a trend that they themselves consider to be quite negative – the labelling and excluding of people from the regular labour market. In step with the ongoing flexibilization of work life and increased competition between workers, measures such as wage subsidies and publicly sheltered employment are becoming the only prospect for many people to find work and activity today.

## NOTES

1. The research that this chapter is based on was made possible with the aid of funding from the Swedish Research Council within the framework of *The politics and practices of capability: Lifelong learning for all in a knowledge-intense worklife?* – a project led by Christina Garsten.
2. Support initiatives exclusively reserved for jobseekers with disabilities are: 1) support for a personal assistant, 2) work aids, 3) special grants for starting a business, 4) special introduction and follow-up support (SIUS), 5) wage subsidies, 6) development employment, 7) security employment, 8) Samhall, 9) publicly sheltered employment.

3. VALPAR Component Work Samples (VCWS) is an instrument used by occupational therapists to assess people's ability to perform work tasks. Simulated work tasks are used to test an individual's work capacity. The method was developed in the US in the beginning of the 1970s (Carlsson 2007).

# REFERENCES

Ahrne, Göran, Karl-Erik Johansson and Roine Johansson (1985), *Vad gör de där inne på arbetsförmedlingen?* Uppsala: Department of Sociology, Uppsala University.
Beck, Ulrich (1992), *Risk Society: Towards a new modernity.* London: Sage.
Benson, Ilinca (2008), *Organisering av övergångar på arbetsmarknaden: en studie av omställningsprogram.* Stockholm: Stockholm School of Economics.
Brunsson, Nils and Kerstin Sahlin-Andersson (2000), 'Constructing organizations: The example of public sector reform', *Organization Studies*, 21(4), 721–46.
Carlsson, Annica (2007), Metoder för arbetsförmågebedömning – en inventering. Project for Occupational Health Course for Physiotherapists/Ergonomists. Stockholm: National Institute for Working Life/Karolinska Institutet.
Conrad, Peter (1992), 'Medicalization and social control', *Annual Review of Sociology*, 18, 209–32.
Dandeker, Christopher (1990), *Surveillance, Power and Modernity: Bureaucracy and discipline from 1700 to the present day.* Cambridge: Polity Press.
Dir. 2008:11, *Översyn av begreppen sjukdom och arbetsförmåga samt en enhetlig bedömning av arbetsförmåga.* Swedish Ministry of Health and Social Affairs.
Fogde, Marinette (2009), *The Work of Job Seeking: Studies on career advice for white-collar workers.* Örebro: Örebro University.
Garsten, Christina and Kerstin Jacobsson (eds) (2004), *Learning to be Employable: New agendas on work, responsibility and learning in a globalizing world.* Basingstoke: Palgrave Macmillan.
Giddens, Anthony (1998), *The Third Way: The renewal of social democracy.* Cambridge: Polity Press.
Holmqvist, Mikael (2005), *Samhall: att bli normal i en onormal organisation.* Stockholm: SNS förlag.
Holmqvist, Mikael (2006), 'Medikalisering av arbetslöshet', in M. Holmqvist and C. Maravelias (eds), *Hälsans styrning av arbetet.* Lund: Studentlitteratur, pp. 27–60.
Holmqvist, Mikael (2009), *Disabling State of an Active Society (Welfare and Society).* Farnham: Ashgate Publishing.
Jacobsson, Kerstin and Ida Seing (2013), 'En möjliggörande arbetsmarknadspolitik? Arbetsförmedlingens utredning och klassificering av klienters arbetsförmåga, anställbarhet och funktionshinder', *Arbetsmarknad & Arbetsliv*, 1, 9–24.
Johansson, Roine (1992), *Vid byråkratins gränser: Om handlingsfrihetens organisatoriska begränsningar i klientrelaterat arbete.* Uppsala: Arkiv förlag.

Junestav, Malin (2004), *Arbetslinjer i svensk socialpolitisk debatt och lagstiftning 1930–2001*. Uppsala: Uppsala University.

Lindqvist, Rafael (2008), 'Funktionshinder, arbetsförmåga och socialpolitik', in L. Vahlne Westerhäll (ed.), *Arbets(o)förmåga – ur ett mångdisciplinärt perspektiv*. Stockholm: Santérus, pp. 169–94.

Lindvert, Jessica (2006), *Ihålig arbetsmarknadspolitik. Organisering och legitimitet igår och idag*. Umeå: Boréa bokförlag.

Lipsky, Michael (1980), *Street-level Bureaucracy: Dilemmas of the individual in public services*. New York: Sage.

Peralta Prieto, Julia (2006), *Den sjuka arbetslösheten: Svensk arbetsmarknadspolitik och dess praxis 1978–2004*. Uppsala: Uppsala University.

Power, Michael (1997), *The Audit Society: Rituals of verification*. Oxford: Oxford University Press.

Prior, Lindsay (1993), *The Social Organization of Mental Illness*. London: Sage.

Prop. 1999/2000:79, *Från patient till medborgare – Nationell handlingsplan för handikappolitiken*.

Prop. 2007/08:1, *Budgetpropositionen för 2008*.

Public Employment Service (2010), *Statistik över arbetssökande med funktionshinder på Arbetsförmedlingen*. Swedish Public Employment Service/Statistics Division, 2 February 2010.

SFS 2000:628, *Förordning om den arbetsmarknadspolitiska verksamheten*. Swedish Code of Statutes.

SFS 2007:1030, *Förordning med instruktion för Arbetsförmedlingen*. Swedish Code of Statutes.

Strathern, Marilyn (eds) (2000), *Audit Cultures: Anthropological studies in accountability, ethics and the academy*. London: Routledge.

Thedvall, Renita (2004), 'Do it Yourself: Making up the self-employed individual in the Swedish Public Employment Service', in C. Garsten and K. Jacobsson (eds), *Learning to be Employable: New agendas on work, responsibility and learning in a globalizing world*. Basingstoke: Palgrave Macmillan, pp. 131–51.

# 6. Temporary staffing: balancing cooperation and competition

## Gunilla Olofsdotter

They all compete. Most recently it was we who initiated a negotiation of the agreements. The pricing and conditions. We had one round that resulted in everything going down in price, but AAA,[1] who also pay their temporaries the most, had the lowest price plus that the quality of the group they delivered was really good. They've received almost all of the assignments. Before that, it was BBB that did the same thing to CCC, except their price was a bit higher but with much better quality. Then it was just BBB for a while. So it's gone a bit in waves. All of the staffing firms are there and ready: *Can't we get some people in there; we should do this and this*. It's a buying spree, you notice it in that way. You get a little spoiled.

These are the words of Martin, a manager at a call centre in Sweden that for a number of years hired in a lot of temporary agency workers. In the interview, Martin told me about the internal recruiting strategies of the company, and the competition for assignments that exists between different staffing agencies. He described how the company uses, at the same time, three staffing firms that must compete against each other for assignments. It is not just a matter of being able to offer the lowest price, however, but also of being able to deliver temporaries of sufficiently good quality. And to establish a good working relationship. The cited excerpt constitutes a starting point for the coming discussion about the role of staffing firms in today's labour market.

The study presented here was carried out in 2008 in two companies that have hired in staff for a number of years. The purpose was to study temporary staffing strategies in these client companies and their effects, both internally in the client companies and for the staffing firms.[2] The findings show how temporary staffing has become an obvious part of ongoing company operations and how the staffing firms have adapted to this change. The emerging market for temporary staffing has far-reaching consequences for the temporary staff's working conditions and the internal organization of client company operations. The extensive use of temporary staffing demonstrates how value differences are constructed between temporary and regular employees in the client companies. As a consequence of temporary staffing, new demands are also put on leadership and organization in the client companies, where expertise in purchasing services from staffing firms is an important part. In addition to this, the sizable level of temporary staffing means that there is competition between the staffing firms for these assignments and that the client companies have learned to handle and utilize this competitive situation. Excerpts from the interviews with managers from staffing firms and from the two client companies are used to illustrate this development.

In the companies that hire in temporary staff, various strategies are used for recruiting and temporary staffing. In some companies, temporary staffing is a temporary solution to acute staffing problems, while in others the hiring in of a large number of consultants is more or less permanent and new recruitment of regular employed personnel is minimal. The companies that make use of staffing services, the client companies, included in this study belong to the latter category, that is, companies with an extensive use of temporary staffing and limited new recruiting. The growing staffing industry together with these client companies' relatively standardized work tasks have made possible business operations in which almost half of the workforce is made up of temporary staff. This is accompanied by a change in recruiting processes, where parts of the responsibility are placed on competing staffing firms, at the same time as the client companies must handle negotiations of these services and manage a workforce with varying terms and conditions.

In recent years, temporary staffing has become an increasingly common element in the Swedish labour market.[3] There are, however, different views about the advantages and disadvantages of temporary staffing. Simply put, one could say that the 'pro' side feels that temporary staffing gives the client companies and the workers increased flexibility, and contributes to knowledge transfer between organizations and increased experience among the personnel. The 'con' side is of the opinion that employees are being exploited, that traditional forms of employment are being threatened, and that all of this leads to conflicts in the workplace (see Boje and Grönlund 2003; Garsten 2008; Karlsson 2007).

Despite these diverging views, opinions about temporary staffing have changed from earlier being seen as more or less socially unacceptable to becoming more and more acceptable. Temporary staffing is often understood as an exception to and, in certain cases, a threat to established labour market norms, such as the norm regarding permanent employment (Bergström et al. 2007).

For the individual client company, temporary staffing is often associated with both possibilities and problems. By hiring in temporary staff, companies are able to replace personnel who are absent and also find personnel that they may later hire. Temporary staff can also help the companies to overcome temporary peaks of demand for the company's goods and services, or to respond to increased competition in an increasingly globalized market. The staffing firms are quite simply assumed to be able to balance client companies' changing needs for staff (see, for example, Bergström et al. 2007; Håkansson and Isidorsson 2007; Håkansson, Isidorsson and Kantelius 2012). Staffing firms have become an important player in the labour market in that they offer services that can balance out the client companies' production cycles and peak demands for labour.

The use of temporary staffing entails, however, a paradox for an organization. Hiring in temporary staff can increase flexibility and economic efficiencies, but can at the same time make the organization difficult to manage as the workforce becomes increasingly heterogeneous (Koene et al. 2014). The use of temporary staffing can, in addition, lead to risks for the organization with respect to maintaining a skilled workforce in the long term (Bergström 2001). If more and more of the work is performed by a temporary workforce, a large part of the skill developed in the company can disappear when consultants' assignments come to an end. For the regular personnel, temporary staffing can, in addition, mean uncertainty about one's own job security. They can begin to wonder whether they themselves are at risk of being terminated and hired back later as consultants (Connelly and Gallagher 2004; Olofsdotter 2008). Despite this, the use of temporary staff can be seen as a solution to the client companies' problems. It is quite simply an obvious and recurring part of operations that does not require a particularly high degree of interest or attention (Bergström et al. 2007).

The use of temporary personnel also means that management's work tasks and areas of responsibility are divided between managers of staffing firms and client companies (Bergström 2003; Walter 2005). The responsibilities of managers in the staffing firms include supplying human resources, covering absences due to sickness, and paying wages. Managers in the client companies, on the other hand, are responsible for the quality and evaluation of the work actually performed by the consultant (Purcell and Purcell 1998; Ward et al. 2001). The result is that the client company's middle managers are in practice responsible for both the temporary and regular personnel. They are thereby expected to manage separate personnel groups with different employment forms, wages, benefits and job security (Ward et al. 2001).

In relation to the norm of traditional permanent employment, temporary staffing raises important questions about the organization of working life, and can even have repercussions for social relations within the client companies. In day-to-day operations, temporary and regular staff are expected to work together and cooperate. A job situation such as this, where regular employees and consultants work side by side is, however, not entirely unproblematic. Kalleberg (2001) points out, for example, that we have an incomplete picture of the consequences of this for the regular staff. He believes that organizations' strategies for minimizing costs through the use of temporary workers, at the same time as companies attempt to increase the motivation and commitment of regular staff, are not always all that successful. Such strategies can give rise to tensions and conflicts between temporary and regular personnel. Bergström et al. (2007) believe that, in the worst case, the use of temporary staff can contribute to a permanent imbalance in the labour market, regardless of whether temporary staff are offered better or worse conditions than the regular staff. The existence of temporary staffing contributes to and, in certain cases, invalidates the 'norms and values that have characterized the Swedish labour market' (ibid.: 208), such as the strong position of permanent employment and employees' fear of changing workplaces.

The entrance of temporary staffing onto the Swedish labour market can therefore be said to contribute to making certain tensions and imbalances in the labour market visible. The temporary agency worker's mobile work life, with short-term social relations and high demands on adaptability, are set against the norm of traditional permanent employment and the desire for long-term tenure at a single workplace. It can therefore be of interest to ask whether something that is understood as an exception to and in certain cases as a threat to established norms in the labour market has become more accepted. Bergström et al. state that we should see temporary staffing as a process whereby 'that which is seen as socially unacceptable is being institutionalized and becoming a part of the Swedish labour market' (2007: 18). In other words, it is a matter of an institutionalization process where what was earlier uncommon and abnormal is normalized and incorporated into business operations.

By studying how ideas about the organizing of temporary staffing are interpreted, legitimized and turned into practice in client companies, we can shed light on the institutionalization of temporary staffing. When actors embrace new ideas, and translate and transform them into concrete actions, new patterns of behaviour are created and established. These patterns can be seen as institutionalized when they are repeated to an extent where the patterns are taken for granted by the actors without this being expressed explicitly (Czarniawska and Joerges 1996; Czarniawska and Sevón 2005). The translation model shows what the actors *do* with different ideas and models to make them attractive and suitable for a particular target group (Tomson 2008). This means that the translation model can be used to show the different staffing strategies used in the client companies, and how these are adapted and changed to meet the needs and requirements of a company's activities. In the following discussion, I show how temporary staffing has been institutionalized and become an obvious part of the business operations in two client companies. The competition that exists between the staffing firms is also underlined, as the process through which they adapt their activities to the wishes of the client companies in the emerging market for temporary staffing.

## THE METHOD

In order to understand how ideas about temporary staffing affect and are integrated in to the activities of the client companies, it is important to study the roles and perceptions of the constituent actors. An analysis of their narratives about how the day-to-day work has changed is therefore necessary. My study aims to show how the actors interpret and assign meaning to the change, and how the organization and content of the work has changed over time.

The discussion is based on case studies of two client companies that hire in temporary personnel from staffing firms on a continual basis. The first company is a call centre where the staff provide customer support for telecommunications services (IT Support AB). The second client is a company in the manufacturing industry that produces telecommunications equipment (Telecom AB). Both companies hire in temporary staff from a number of staffing agencies simultaneously. Interviews have been conducted with supervisors and regular personnel in the client companies as well as managers and consultants employed by different staffing firms. At the time of the interviews, the consultants worked at one or the other of the client companies.

I have chosen to allow a small number of voices to illustrate the staffing strategies and the relationships between each of the client companies and the staffing firms. The selected quotations are taken from interviews with key people in management positions in the respective companies.[4] Martin is a manager at IT Support AB and has worked at the company for six years in a number of different management positions.

Tommy works as a production manager at Telecom AB. He has worked at the company for 20 years and has extensive experience of temporary staffing, everything from the company's first cautious attempts to today's extensive use of temporary personnel. Lena works as a consultant manager[5] at one of the staffing agencies used by the client companies. She has worked at the company for seven years. Signe has been employed for three years as a consultant manager at a staffing agency that has been supplying temporary staff for Telecom AB for many years. During the time of the study, their contracts with Telecom AB were terminated. For confidentiality reasons, the names used here are pseudonyms.

## IT SUPPORT AB

At the time of the interviews, IT Support AB had been hiring in staff from staffing firms for just over three years. When the company began to use temporary staff, the goal was that a maximum of 20 per cent of the personnel working in the team should be made up of temporary staff. This was a norm that was not always followed. At times, close to half of the company's workforce has been temporary.

The company's business is customer support, mainly for matters regarding telephony, broadband and TV services. This means that the support services are open for much of the day and night, every day of the week. In order to maintain these business hours, the personnel are divided into different groups with different work schedules. A distinction between first line and second line support is also made, where second line support staff handle the more complicated questions forwarded to them by the first line support staff. The division into different groups also means that there are differences between the groups when it comes to, among other conditions, working hours and wages. The division also distinguishes between temporarily and regularly employed personnel in IT Support AB. The way Martin expresses this is that the staff are divided into A, B and C groups. Group A is made up of both regular and temporary staff who work in teams or so-called expert groups. They have a fixed schedule and work during the day as well as evenings and weekends, though to a lesser extent. Group B is made up of a relatively permanent team of temporary personnel who are hired in to work only evenings and weekends. They have scheduled work shifts that amount to 75 per cent of full-time. Group C comprises only temporary personnel who work on an hourly basis, mainly evenings and weekends. This group is often made up of students working part-time alongside their studies.

No regular employees work in the B or C teams. When I asked Martin why the company uses temporary staff instead of hiring its own part-time employees, his response was that:

> We used to have casual part-time employees of our own, but we don't anymore; they've had to phase themselves out. The reason that we stopped that was because it was extremely demanding from an administrative standpoint. To sit there and call and book shifts all the time; it was a lot of work. (Martin)

He then went on to add that:

> But sure, we could've had full- and part-timers. But then we'd have had to keep track of the people working part-time, what shifts they were coming in to work. It takes a huge amount of overhead to do that, planners that is; it costs money. And if we have to reduce staffing then we've got to give them notice. I don't think it's doable so we're always going to have some temps. (Martin)

Here, Martin is describing a shift of the administrative responsibility for staffing from his own company to staffing firms. The staffing firms act as brokers and match the right person to the right assignment (cf. Bergström 2005). It's a matter of making the business more efficient and dividing the responsibility between customer and staffing companies.

Because much of the responsibility for personnel sits in another company, IT Support AB has to be able to rely on the staffing firm to take responsibility and send temps with the proper expertise, and at a reasonable cost. This means that the consultant managers play an important role in the cooperation. As boundary-spanning actors, they have to be able to balance the demands of the client company, the staffing firm and the individual consultant (Augustsson, Olofsdotter and Wolvén 2010). Martin underlines the point about how the staffing firms' varying service levels are dependent on how the consultant managers do their job.

In order to ensure a sufficiently high level of service, IT Support AB keeps a constant competition going between three different staffing firms. Pricing, terms and contracts are renegotiated on a regular basis. The company that has the lowest price at the same time as being able to offer 'top quality of the group they deliver' gets the assignments. When a need to increase staff arises, the client company contacts the staffing firms and informs them of its needs. The staffing firms in turn try to maintain a readiness to quickly staff assignments that come in:

> For the most part, the agencies are interviewing people all the time, so they are ready with suitable candidates. In the beginning, we had our own review process, too. The candidates came to us and we conducted a 10-minute confirmation process if it seemed like a good person. But we don't do that anymore. Now it's the staffing firms themselves that just send them to us. This is quite simply because they've come to know us so well that they know what we're after now. In the beginning, that wasn't the case. It's a maturing process; we've gotten to know each other. (Martin)

This shows how working with the staffing firms has become an obvious part of IT Support AB's operations. On business-like terms, the staffing agencies supply competent staff. They compete with each other to deliver the best solutions at a reasonable price. The use of temporary staffing has become an obvious and unreflected part of the company's daily activities.

The division of the workers into A, B and C teams also shows a hierarchical order between temporary and regular staff. Martin does not see the unequal working conditions as a problem, but rather states that temporary staffing is a precondition for the regular employees to be able to have 'a good job'. He continues:

> If we hadn't used temporary staffing as much as we have, it would have meant that everyone would've been forced to work a lot more evenings and weekends. Our staffing is adapted to the volume of incoming customer calls and, without the temporaries, it would've meant a lot more evening work. In that way, I think they appreciate it. (Martin)

The above quote demonstrates a conscious strategy to divide the personnel into groups with better and worse working hours. The regular employees have the advantage of not needing to work inconvenient hours and weekends (cf. Olofsdotter 2012a). There are, however, certain risks with a division such as this between temporary and regular staff. Kalleberg (2001) states, for example, that strategies like this can give rise to tensions and conflicts between the personnel groups.

The reasons behind organizations' choice to hire in temporary staff can also affect how the agency workers integrate. Connelly and Gallagher (2004) suggest that, if they are hired in to increase flexibility, they will likely integrate better and be compensated at a level similar to regular employees, compared to when they are hired in to minimize costs. This shows how the use of staffing firms creates clear differences in value between personnel groups and affects the work itself and the social relations in the companies. The introduction of market elements into the organization highlights how segregating tendencies between personnel groups are consciously integrated into business activities.

Apart from for a few highly qualified positions, at IT Support AB no staff are recruited directly. Instead, the company conducts a round of recruiting once or twice a year, where it offers some of the temporary staff a permanent position:

> The only times we've hired new people any other way in the past two years have been for management positions. We bring in all of the support agents via the consulting companies; they try it out for six months or a year, and then we hire them. Often we take in several at a time. We decide that we're going to hold a recruiting session in September and another in February. Then we see which ones are the best candidates. (Martin)

Martin's description of the staffing strategies shows how IT Support has systematically divided the staff into teams A, B and C. As a result of the different terms and conditions, and chances of being offered a job, the temporary staff are motivated to demonstrate that they are knowledgeable and worth hiring. This more or less official career path can be described as a promotion ladder where workers start as casual temporary workers paid by the hour, and then work evenings and weekends. After that, they are hopefully offered a position on a team as a scheduled temporary worker. When the company holds one of its recruiting sessions, a worker may then be one of those chosen to be offered a permanent position. This gives rise to a new type of competition between personnel groups and trying out of candidates, which is a direct consequence of the use of staffing firms and the influence of the market on the organization of work. The result is normalization of a structural inequality between temporary and regular personnel in the organization (see Olofsdotter 2012a). This inequality and preferential treatment consequently leads to a risk that the social relations between personnel groups will be affected negatively and that the consultants may have difficulty influencing their work situation (cf. Olofsdotter 2008).

## TELECOM AB

For the greater part of the 2000s, Telecom AB has used temporary personnel. An approximate estimate is that half of those who worked on the collective side were temporary employees at the time of the study. The company is involved in industrial production of telecommunications equipment. Even here we see a clear division into groups, into the A, B and C teams. In the A team, there are only Telecom's own regular employees. Team B is made up of people who have worked as temporary agency workers for a longer period of time, often many years. It is not uncommon that they were earlier employed by Telecom AB, but were let go in earlier personnel cutbacks. Here, differences in wages and working hours are not directly linked to belonging to one group or the other.

Tommy, who works as a production manager, describes the historical process from the first tries to the current extensive use of hiring in temporary staffing:

> For us, it began with several big staff cuts around 2000. I was involved in each one, giving people their notice; that wasn't much fun. The first time went quite well, the second time was really hard, the third was hell. That time there were people who'd been working here for 12–14 years. And then you get scared on the management side of things; all these dismissals naturally cost a lot of money. In the beginning then, they said there would be a bit of temporary staffing. Since then, it's accelerated. (Tommy)

Tommy's description shows how something that was at first seen as a temporary solution to acute problems has increased to become an obvious part of the business activities. In discussions about flexibility in the labour market, the use of temporary personnel is often presented as a viable way to meet the need for flexibility in the workforce. The size of the workforce can change along with changes in demand. Client companies also avoid hiring people on a permanent basis and being responsible for the whole redundancy procedure when demand slows (cf. Garsten 2008; Håkansson, Isidorsson and Kantelius 2012). Since the beginning of the 2000s, Telecom AB has organized its operations in such a manner. It recruits no new staff at all on the collective side. Instead, it uses temporary staffing for periods of increased demand or to replace absent workers. However, Tommy is somewhat hesitant about this method of approach and would like to see the company hire some of the temps:

> I think it's founded in a real fear of the slow times. But at the same time, I know what it costs per month for a temp. If you've had a temp for several years, I think that you could at least compensate for those who have retired. It would be nice to be able to hire a few more. There's no better reference than someone having been here as a temp for three years and done their job well with a high level of quality and all. (Tommy)

He is also critical of the extent of the temporary staffing:

> I would like to see us have a limit. We used to talk about an 80:20 split; that no longer exists. For the long term, it's better to have permanent employees; many consultants are extremely good at what they do but the regular staff are better if you're going to work long term. (Tommy)

Tommy's description shows there is a danger of long-term consequences with the extensive use of temporary staffing. The increased organizational complexity, in terms of a differentiated workforce, is difficult to manage and appears to be sidelined in favour of more short-term considerations. The attitude towards temporary staffing among the company's own employees also seems to have changed. Tommy explains: 'They're accustomed to it now. At one time, when I was in charge of two production lines, I had 72 per cent temporaries; I think that's way too much. So they've gotten used to it being like this ... Now it's a more natural part of things.'

Tommy describes here what he perceives as a normalization of the use of temporary staffing among the personnel. How the regular employees and the temps themselves see this is another question. Because temporary staffing has been extensive and gone on for many years, it is likely that the personnel have become accustomed to it, but whether or not the social relations between the groups function satisfactorily is more uncertain. The consultants must, as Barley and Kunda (2004) suggest, quite simply find their own way in a context where they can never become full members of the client firm. The temps who are able to cope with the differences in work conditions may therefore have what it takes to work as a temporary agency worker (Olofsdotter 2008).

As the use of temporary staffing has become an obvious part of the company's ongoing activities, Telecom AB's human resources department has also been affected.

> The HR department is now a fifth of its size, where we've cut back more and more. Administrative tasks have been given to us supervisors ... Rehabilitation therapy sessions were the last to go. We had a woman here who helped who was really good with that. It was easy when it was just a broken bone, but when it's up here [points to his head] it's worse. She retired two weeks ago and wasn't replaced. So now we have to do it ourselves together with occupational health. It's going to be a nightmare when it comes to illnesses like that. The mental aspects. Those things are being put on us more and more. (Tommy)

This means that when temporary staffing increases and the company's own employees decrease in number, the internal personnel-social functions in the company also decrease. The consequence of this is that regular staff are referred to their closest supervisor with their problems, in this case, the production manager. The temporary staff are expected to turn to the staffing firm's managers or people in their own human resources department. For the temporary workers, this is hardly a change. But for the regular employees the ability to get support when they are unwell or for work-related problems is probably limited. They must turn to the production manager who apportions the work and ensures that the set goals are met. Consequently, the staff may be afraid to bring their problems and conflicts to the attention of this person, who also monitors their performance. It is a matter of streamlining operations, where management's areas of responsibility are changing and are divided between the client company and staffing agencies. Certain areas of responsibility may thus end up in a grey zone.

Telecom AB has a freeze on hiring and has for some time now only hired in temporary personnel. The use of temporary staffing is extensive and has, over the years, become an obvious part of operations, even if there is some desire to hire more permanent employees. The staffing strategies that are implemented in Telecom AB operations involve a structural division of the personnel into three groups with different terms and conditions. The regular staff make up one group, and qualified temporary staff, who in some cases have been employees of the company, another. A third group is made up of more temporarily hired-in staff. This means a stratification of the workforce based on their value for the client company. A further consequence of temporary staffing is that the personnel-social function at the company has been reduced to a minimum. For the regular permanent staff, the responsibility for this has been placed on the production managers. This shift in responsibility for human resource matters demonstrates the distinction being made between personnel groups and how they are valued. Temporary staffing can therefore be said to generate a distinction between personnel groups and accentuate their relative valuation (see also Olofsdotter 2012b).

## STAFFING FIRMS AS COOPERATIVE PARTNERS

The Swedish temporary staffing industry is dominated by a small number of big staffing firms with both national and international operations. These companies represent approximately 75 per cent of the entire Swedish market for temporary staffing. In addition to this, there are about 400 smaller staffing firms in Sweden (Walter 2005). Since the deregulation of the temporary staffing sector in the 1990s, the industry has grown in size and been integrated into the Swedish labour market (Bergström et al. 2007). The staffing agencies that cooperate with the two client companies in this study are all big staffing firms with extensive operations across much of Sweden. The fact that these client companies work with several staffing firms at the same time has consequences for the staffing firms' activities. Because the contracts between the companies are negotiated for longer periods, it means that the staffing firms are able to plan their operations in a more long-term manner. They must, however, also be vigilant about the competitive situation that exists between staffing firms. In order to meet the needs of the client companies, their own strategies and business concepts have changed over time. Lena, who has worked for seven years as a consultant manager at one of these staffing firms, describes the company's change process as follows: 'When I started, the business concept was that we supplied a full range of staffing solutions. Today we're a strategic HR partner. Some of the customers I work with today, I've worked with since 2003. It's been both temporary staffing, recruiting and transitions.' She goes on to say that:

> As a company, we have changed strategies, from previously having said that 40 per cent of our consultants get jobs with the client. We see ourselves more as a long-term employer now. Before, it was more that we said – *Yes, they'll get permanent jobs with the assignments they have.* Then we said ourselves that it was a springboard. (Lena)

Lena's description demonstrates the company's change of direction. From having marketed itself as a more temporary solution, it now sees itself as a long-term employer for temporary agency workers, and a natural cooperating partner for the customer firms. The change from only supplying staffing solutions to wanting to be seen as a competent HR partner has also meant that the staffing firm has changed its views on the expertise needed to work as a consultant manager. This change is clearly shown when new consultant managers are hired:

> For a while there, it was common to have really young consultant managers. Things have changed a bit in the company. It's a demanding role, where you have to have the hard conversations – illnesses, cancer and stroke. So the last people we hired were 45 and over 50 years old – from earlier being a popular job for young women. Since we opted to call ourselves a strategic HR partner, we've taken on a bigger role. So we also have to be able to have those harder conversations. The same applies when we work with transitions, for example, of a person who has lost his or her job after 20 years. When you meet with someone, it has to be credible. (Lena)

It is clear here that they are trying to organize operations in such a manner that the consultant managers have sufficient expertise to be able to meet the needs and demands that the temporary personnel can place on them. They quite simply try to live up to the goal of being a full-value partner who can also offer their own consultants good social expertise. Another consequence of the increase in the temporary staffing market is that the requirements in the client companies for expertise in purchasing the services have grown.

Because the cooperation between the companies has gone on for a longer period of time, the staffing firms have become familiar with the needs of the client firms. Managers from Telecom AB and IT Support AB themselves rarely meet interview candidates; instead, the staffing agencies take care of the entire matching process:

> Because I've worked with Telecom AB for so long, I know what skills they're looking for. Then we either already have personnel who we know of, or we're interviewing new people all the time to maintain a candidate bank of fresh new names of people who want to come in and work. (Signe)

This shows how management's areas of responsibility have shifted between managers in the different companies (Bergström 2003; Walter 2005). The relations between client- and staffing firms have gone from being temporary solutions to staffing problems, to being increasingly institutionalized.

The contracted-out personnel are also covered by collective agreements that grant them considerable employment and economic security. When they have no assignments, a wage guarantee ensures them 75–90 per cent of their wages (Håkansson and Isidorsson 2007; Storrie 2003). This comprehensive labour legislation can be one of the reasons behind the change in attitudes towards temporary staffing:

> Before, it may have seemed like more of a threat when consultants came in; the regular staff and the unions thought the real jobs were disappearing. I think this has settled a little. Some companies we work for understand this when they get the same people back after several years – Karl has a secure job too ... You don't have the union against you like it used to be. It's the opposite, rather, it's them we're starting to work with – to get all the information about shift work and wages, for example. All of the practical aspects. I think it's more a complement. (Lena)

These descriptions of the internal changes in the staffing firm indicate the emergence of an industry striving for increased continuity and long-term cooperation with its customers. Lena's explanations imply an increased understanding and acceptance of their operations among the client firms' regular employees and even among the labour associations. Whether this is actually the case is something that these groups themselves must answer. Nevertheless, her statements, and those of the two client firm managers, demonstrate a normalization of temporary staffing. From having been an industry perceived as more or less temporary, and in some cases unacceptable, the sector has become an obvious part of operations.

# COOPERATION IN THE FACE OF COMPETITION

There is stiff competition between the staffing firms to reach far-reaching contracts with both Telecom AB and IT Support AB. When I visited Telecom in the autumn of 2008, they had just renegotiated the contracts. The renegotiations had resulted in the contracts with one of the agencies not being extended. I tried to find out the reasons for this decision, but it proved difficult. The consultant managers I spoke to implied that it could be a pricing issue, or also have to do with Telecom AB's having implemented a system of replacing one of the agencies at every re-negotiation. When a contract between a client company and the staffing firm is terminated, there are considerable consequences for the affected consultants, as well as for their responsible consultant managers:

> First, it's more work. There are a lot of temporaries that call and are concerned. *What's happening? What are we going to do?* I've received a lot of telephone calls, I've been out at the plants to answer questions, that's in addition to my regular work. Then, based on this, we work on our existing clients more, and we work on new clients. (Signe)

She also describes how, to start with, she was shocked by the news:

> First you think: *Oh God, what're we going to do? We've got over 100 temps out there. Where are they going to go? How are we going to place 100 temps?* That is, after all, quite a few. Then, at some point, when you've run through all of those thoughts, then you start thinking about yourself. *What about my job?* Then a bit of time passes and you have time to think about it. The fact is, really, that Telecom AB is really a terribly demanding customer. (Signe)

For the consultant manager, it is a matter of trying to find new assignments for these temporary workers quickly to avoid the financial burden that comes with the wage guarantee when the temps are without assignments (Olofsdotter 2008). The staffing firms have to be efficient in their matching of jobseekers to jobs in order that they are not forced to pay temps with no assignments (Bergström 2005). One solution in this particular case was that some of the temporary workers themselves contacted the remaining staffing agencies regarding the possibility of moving over to one of them. Consequently, the competition between the staffing firms means that the temps are left to take responsibility, themselves, for continued employment or for moving to a competing staffing firm. This shows how the market for staffing has a direct impact on the individual temp's situation.

At Telecom AB, they have strategically organized the use of temporary staffing to optimize the exchange. The company's long experience with temporary staffing has become an integrated part of its business operations. It is also aware of the possibilities that the use of temporary staffing provides, and has quite simply become a demanding customer:

> Over the years, these really polished companies, like Telecom AB, for example, that are practised buyers, have become a little cocky maybe, though that might not be the right word … But that's our business concept – that it be really flexible, that you're able to cancel from one day to the next. We've maybe gotten away from when it used to be a bit more person-based. As a buyer, they've gotten a little tougher … They count man-hours in a different way. They maybe exploit our business concept of flexibility much more aggressively than they used to. The more practised buyers that is, not the ones just starting out. (Lena)

She distinguishes here between the client firms with long experience and those with more limited experience of hiring in personnel. The two client firms described above can both be categorized as 'practised buyers'. They make use of well-developed strategies to be able to vary the size of their workforce along with changing demand for their goods and services. In order to be able to meet these needs for flexible numbers (Atkinson 1984), the staffing firm has to organize its activities in such a manner that it is quickly able to match temps with the appropriate expertise to the assignments coming in.

## CONCLUDING DISCUSSION

The study demonstrates a normalizing of temporary staffing in both of the client firms studied and in how the staffing firms have adapted to this development. The extent of temporary staffing used has far-reaching consequences for the personnel, both temporary and regular, as well as for the internal organizing of the client firm's activities. Despite the fact that both companies hire in temporary staff on a continual and extensive basis, they use different staffing and recruiting strategies. At IT Support AB, temporary and regular personnel work on different terms. The wages are considerably higher for regular personnel, and the personnel are divided into different groups with large differences in work schedules. After a period of time, temporary personnel may advance to be part of a team and, after about a year, some may be offered regular employment with IT Support AB, with a substantial pay rise. The company does not recruit personnel directly, with the exception of the odd highly qualified specialist.

At Telecom AB, no new personnel are hired at all on the collective side; instead, the use of temporary personnel is extensive. The personnel are divided into three groups: regular employees; qualified temporary personnel, who were often previously employed at the company; and casual temporary staffing, which varies according to demand. The long-term risks associated with using only temporary staff do not appear to garner much attention from management.

In both companies, the use of temporary staffing has developed into a natural part of operations. Although the companies' staffing strategies differ in certain respects, the similarities are nevertheless more significant. Both companies purchase a large amount of temporary staffing and have, in a well-thought-out manner, divided temporary and regular staff into a hierarchical order with different terms and conditions. These strategies mean that a structural inequality has been implemented in the organizing of company activities, where temporary and regular employees are valued differently.

Development of the market for temporary staffing has brought with it new needs for knowledge and skills in the client companies regarding the purchase of services from staffing agencies. The competition involved with being one of three staffing agencies that these client firms enter agreements with has consequences for the staffing firms. When re-negotiations occur, the firms must present competitive bids. Both the client companies and the staffing firms have learned to manage this competition between the staffing firms. The cooperation between client firms and staffing agencies is often lengthy, and transboundary relations between consultant managers and the responsible managers at the client companies have been established. The various functions of management have been divided between the companies. The relationship and cooperation with the staffing agencies have evolved. From being a temporary partner, the staffing firm increasingly resembles a permanent HR partner with a greater responsibility for solving the client firm's staffing on its own.

The results presented in this chapter are based on interviews with people in leadership positions. An analysis of the temporary and regular staff's experiences with respect to temporary staffing may yield a somewhat different picture. Regardless of possible differences between managers' and employees' attitudes towards temporary staffing, the results suggest a change in terms of increased acceptance and normalization. The market for temporary staffing has become a natural part of the Swedish labour market.

## NOTES

1.  AAA, BBB and CCC symbolize the three temporary staffing firms that this client company works with.
2.  The research that this chapter is based on was made possible with the aid of funding from the Research Council for Working Life and Social Sciences (FAS) within the framework of a project on the consequences of temporary staffing for working conditions, attitudes and social interaction in client companies (*Personalinhyrningens konsekvenser för arbetsvillkor, attityder och sociala interaktioner inom företag som hyr in personal*), led by Lars-Erik Wolvén.
3.  At present, there are approximately 440 authorized staffing firms in Sweden. An estimated 1.5 per cent of the workforce are temp workers whose primary employment is with a staffing firm http://www.bemanningsforetagen.se/.
4.  The interviews were conducted as a part of a project on the consequences of temporary staffing on working conditions, attitudes and social interaction in client companies (*Personalinhyrningens konsekvenser för arbetsvillkor, attityder och sociala interaktioner inom företag som hyr in personal*), in the autumn of 2008. The study was funded by the Research Council for Working Life and Social Sciences (FAS).
5.  'Consultant managers' are the managers at the staffing firms that place temporary agency workers in different assignments and have direct contact with the contracted-out temps.

## REFERENCES

Atkinson, John (1984), 'Manpower strategies for flexible organisations', *Personnel Management*, 16(8), 28–31.

Augustsson, Gunnar, Gunilla Olofsdotter and Lars-Erik Wolvén (2010), 'Swedish managers in TWA act as boundary spanners', *Leadership and Organization Development Journal*, 31, 4–17.

Barley, Stephen and Gideon Kunda (2004), *Gurus, Hired Guns, and Warm Bodies: Itinerant experts in a knowledge economy*. Princeton: Princeton University Press.

Bergström, Ola (2001), 'Externalization of employees: Thinking about going somewhere else', *International Journal of Human Resource Management*, 12, 373–88.

Bergström, Ola (2003), 'Beyond Atypicability', in Ola Bergström and Donald Storrie (eds), *Contingent Employment in Europe and the United States*. Cheltenham and Northampton, MA: Edward Elgar, pp. 14–51.

Bergström, Ola (2005), 'Temporary work agencies and labour market policy', in Thomas Bredgaard and Flemming Larsen (eds), *Employment Policy from Different Angles*. Copenhagen: DJØF Publishing, pp. 365–90.

Bergström, Ola, Kristina Håkansson, Tommy Isidorsson and Lars Walter (eds) (2007), *Den nya arbetsmarknaden – Bemanningsbranschens etablering i Sverige*. Lund: Academia Adacta AB.

Boje, Thomas and Anne Grönlund (2003), 'Flexibility and employment insecurity', in Thomas Boje and Bengt Furåker (eds), *Post-industrial Labour Markets: Profiles of North America and Scandinavia*. London: Routledge, pp. 186–212.

Connelly, Catherine E. and Daniel G. Gallagher (2004), 'Emerging trends in contingent work research', *Journal of Management*, 30, 959–83.

Czarniawska, Barbara and Bernward Joerges (1996), 'Travel of ideas', in Barbara Czarniawska and Guije Sevón (eds), *Translating Organizational Change*. Berlin: Walter de Gruyter.

Czarniawska, Barbara and Guije Sevón (2005), *Global Ideas: How ideas, objects and practices travel in the global economy*. Copenhagen: Liber and Copenhagen Business School Press.

Garsten, Christina (2008), *Workplace Vagabonds: Career and community in changing worlds of work*. Basingstoke: Palgrave Macmillan.

Håkansson, Kristina and Tommy Isidorsson (2007), 'Flexibility, Stability and Agency Work: A Comparison of the Use of Agency Work in Sweden and the UK', in Bengt Furåker, Kristina Håkansson, and Jan Ch Karlsson (eds), *Flexibility and Stability in Working Life*. Basingstoke: Palgrave Macmillan, pp. 123–47.

Håkansson, Kristina, Tommy Isidorsson and Hannes Kantelius (2012), 'Temporary Agency Work as Means of Achieving Flexicurity?' *Nordic Journal of Working Life Studies*, 2, 153–69.

Kalleberg, Arne (2001), 'Organizing flexibility: The flexible firm in a new century', *British Journal of Industrial Relations*, 39(4), 479–504.

Karlsson, Jan Ch. (2007), 'For whom is flexibility good and bad? An overview', in Bengt Furåker, Kristina Håkansson, and Jan Ch Karlsson (eds), *Flexibility and Stability in Working Life*. Basingstoke: Palgrave Macmillan.

Koene, Bas, Christina Garsten and Nathalie Galais (eds) (2014), *Management and Organization of Temporary Agency Work*. London: Routledge.

Olofsdotter, Gunilla (2008), *Flexibilitetens främlingar: om anställda i bemanningsföretag*. Sundsvall: Doctoral Thesis, 47. Dept. of Social Sciences, Mid Sweden University.

Olofsdotter, Gunilla (2012a), '"The Staircase Mode": Labor control of temporary agency workers in a Swedish call center', *Nordic Journal of Working Life Studies*, 2(1), 41–59.

Olofsdotter, Gunilla (2012b), 'Workplace flexibility and control in temporary agency work', *Vulnerable Groups and Inclusion*, 3, 1–17.

Purcell, Kate and John Purcell (1998), 'Insourcing, outsourcing, and the growth of contingent labour as evidence of flexible employment strategies', *European Journal of Work and Organizational Psychology*, 7, 39–59.

Storrie, Donald (2003), 'The regulation and growth of contingent employment in Sweden', in Ola Bergström and Donald Storrie (eds), *Contingent Employment in Europe and United States*. Cheltenham and Northampton, MA: Edward Elgar, pp. 79–106.

Tomson, Klara (2008), *Amnesty in Translation: Ideas, interests and organizational change*. Stockholm: Stockholm University.

Walter, Lars (2005), *Som hand i handske. En studie av matchning i ett personaluthyrningsföretag*. Gothenburg: BAS.

Ward, Kevin, Damian Grimshaw, Jill Rubery and Huw Beynon (2001), 'Dilemmas in the management of temporary work agency staff', *Human Resource Management*, 11, 3–21.

# 7. Transition programmes: a disciplining practice

## Ilinca Benson

In order to succeed in working life, it is not enough to simply do a good job or to develop in one's profession. It is becoming increasingly important to be good at *changing* jobs. We speak today less and less about employment *security* and more and more about employ*ability*. While employment security places an emphasis on the security in the employment relationship between an employee and employer, employability stresses the importance of being attractive and in demand in the market (Garsten and Jacobsson 2004). In other words, people need to learn to be competent market actors.

Transition programmes have become a central instrument in the Swedish labour market to increase people's employability. These programmes involve activities aimed at providing guidance and counselling for how to look for a job and, in the best case scenario, bridge the time from redundancy to new employment for those made redundant and those at risk of losing their jobs. The programmes strive to offer a set-up that is realistically as work-like as possible, where people who have lost their jobs receive support on how best to proceed to find a new one.

In this chapter, I argue that there is a discrepancy between talk and action in the transition programmes.[1] The programmes are presented as being individually based on each person: people are regarded as independent actors who have a choice. Great importance is put on introspection and self-development. In practice, however, the programme period stands out as a transformation process driven by adaptation to the environment – in which the individual's choices are highly limited. The programmes constitute a new form of individual disciplining where the participant is disciplined to think about him- or herself.

# TRANSITION PROGRAMMES – TWO CASE STUDIES

Transition programmes are offered within the framework of agreements on transition. A considerable proportion of all employees in Sweden today are currently covered by these agreements.[2] Transition agreements have existed in the Swedish labour market for several decades. As early as in the 1970s, the first trendsetting agreement between unions and employers was entered. The parties closing the agreement were The Confederation of Swedish Enterprise (Svenskt Näringsliv) and The Council for Negotiation and Co-operation (PTK). It applied to administrative employees in the private sector.[3]

The spread of transition agreements has led to rapid growth in the market for transition programmes. Regardless of whether they are organized by public or private providers, what most of the programmes share is that personal advice and guidance is an integral part of the programme, and that the search for employment is seen as a skill that can – and needs – to be taught.

This chapter is based on two case studies on the implementation of transition programmes at two large Swedish companies, one state-owned company and one publicly listed company. The study was carried out in conjunction with these companies being forced, during the economic downturn of the early 2000s, to make substantial cuts to staffing. Both of the companies studied have a history of being secure, long-term employers, and had also previously worked systematically and on a broad scale with transition programmes.[4] In connection with the labour cuts, both companies offered the redundant people an extended termination period (the state-owned company offered a period of up to 18 months, and the publicly listed company doubled its termination period, meaning a minimum of 5 months and a maximum of 12). A condition for extension of the termination period was, however, that the dismissed person participates in practical counselling on how to look for work. This meant that, for the transition support period, these participants were still formally employed.

The companies chose to organize their transition activities in somewhat different ways. The state-owned company built up an internal transition unit with personnel from its own organization. The publicly listed company instead brought in external partners to carry out the programmes. Both companies in the study were affiliated with the Employment Security Council (TRR), which became one of the external partners in the publicly listed company. In the state-owned company, TRR was used as a complement to the internal unit.

The chapter takes up four transition programmes – the state-owned company's internal programme and three external programmes that the private company offered (the first of the three programmes was built up in a cooperation between the company and a large commercial actor, the second was carried out by a small commercial consulting firm specializing mainly in senior management and specialists, and the third programme was a TRR programme). Most of the empirical data comes from interviews with the providers of and participants in the programme, along with written documentation. The chapter addresses initiatives for administrative employees, mainly at the middle management and project leader level.

## The Purchaser, Participant and Provider

A transition programme is a service between three actors: the purchaser, the participant and the provider. Firstly, there is the employer or purchaser who orders the programme in consultation with the union. Secondly, there is the person who has been made redundant – the participant. And, thirdly, there is the provider. The provider may be a joint security council (like TRR), a transition department within a company, or an external commercial consulting firm. The three different types of actors may have different goals concerning the programmes, and these do not always go hand in hand.

*The employer's* goals can be divided into three parts: to provide support to the people made redundant; to minimize the negative effects of the cutback process on the company's own operations; and to be seen as a responsible employer in the eyes of the employees, the people let go, and not least of the surrounding society.

*The participants* in turn may also have different goals for the programmes. Many take part mainly because it gives them access to the financial supplements the company offers. Another reason is that they see the programmes as a support in itself for dealing with redundancy and finding new work. However, others take it less seriously and see participation in the programme as an opportunity to do something other than work or look for a job. Two of the participants interviewed express it in this way:

> It was the chance of a lifetime, I think. If the employer is going to pay full wages for me not to work, and it's there, then I'm going to take advantage of it and see what I can get out of it for my own personal sake. I thought it was an opportunity. If someone is crazy enough to pay me for it, then why not?

To be honest, I was thinking: *What am I going to do then? Look for a new job?* No, I see an opportunity here, even if that wasn't the purpose, to take a sabbatical year. I've a lot of ideas. I'm not sitting at home twiddling my thumbs, but I was thinking that I would do something that I've wanted to do for a long time. So I've been busy renovating our house.

For *the providers*, it is a matter of completing their assignment, in part in relation to the purchaser, and in part in relation to the participants. In a perfect world, these two forces would coincide, but in practice, they often do not. The employers tend to prioritize that the redundant person gets a new job as soon as possible. But the programme providers not only have the ambition of actually finding the participants a new job, but focus more on teaching the participants how to become proficient at job search. The participants in turn have other priorities. Most try to find a new job corresponding to or better than the one that they had, rather than finding a job as quickly as possible. Others explain, as in the quote above, that they want to use the programme time for other things entirely, rather than looking for a job.

## The Dual Role of the Providers

During the programme period, the participants are still employed. They are in an employment relation where the employer has delegated the responsibility of supervision to the transition programme personnel. The programme providers therefore have a dual role in relation to the participants, acting as both supervisors and advisors at the same time. The relationship between providers and participants in a transition programme is, on the one hand, based on *hierarchy* and *economic forms of control*, where the programme's personnel have the task of monitoring whether the participants are doing their 'job', which in this case is to search for a new job. If the participants are not complying with these terms in a satisfactory way, they run the risk of having their wages withdrawn.

On the other hand, the providers studied see their relationship to the participants primarily as a service relationship, a specialist/client relation in which the personnel guide the participants in searching for a job. Such a relationship builds on *equality* and *normative forms of control* (see Goffman 2007 [1961]). The underlying conception in this kind of relation is that the client (in this case, the participant) does as the specialist (the programme's personnel) says, because he or she has confidence in the specialist's expertise and has been convinced that the specialist knows what is best for him or her.

**The Phases of the Programmes**

Despite the fact that there were four different providers included in the study, the similarities between the programmes studied are striking. They usually start a short time after the employee has been made redundant, and the dismissed person leaves his or her regular workplace because the programmes take place in special premises. The personnel of the programmes place great importance on how entry to the programme occurs and, in the introduction, endeavour to 'create the right expectations'. The providers explain what participants can get help with, what the personnel's role and function is, and the participant's own responsibility.

The participants are assigned a personal coach, advisor or consultant, who is the most important person for the participant in the programme. Despite the different titles, these people have a similar role. In addition to this function, there are a series of secondary functions, such as project coordinators, lecturers, so-called sellers of skills, interview coaches and educators of different types. The programmes also offer an arsenal of aids and activities. Examples of aids include self-assessment tests relating to areas such as personality traits, stress management, career options and motivation. Common activities include seminars, group exercises, and short courses on topics such as life and career planning, personal development, the work world and the labour market, skills analysis and skills inventory.

The most central part, however, are the interview sessions with the personal coach. Together with this person, the participant conducts an analysis of his or her situation and the so-called inventory of his or her background and skills. Questions such as 'What do I do now?' and 'What can I do and what do I want?' serve as a guide.

The message conveyed by the providers is that every participant's programme is designed according to his or her individual circumstances and conditions. However, all of the programmes are based on a similar model. They begin with an analysis, first of the participant him- or herself and then of the labour market, and thereafter transition to action – the concrete search for a job. One provider calls these phases 'analysis – opportunities – action plan – marketing'. Another calls them 'personal inventory – environmental analysis – jobseeker strategies'.

Although the providers maintain that the participants do not need to go through the phases in a certain order, or that the phases must take a certain portion of the programme time, the activities are governed by these phases. The set of functions and tools for each part of the process makes the programme a complex, complete service. As a whole, the model contributes to the job search process being depicted as something that requires special skills. Transition becomes a practice with specific requirements and conditions, the success of which is contingent on access to professional expert support.

## The Routines of Working Life Are Preserved

The programmes offer office premises where the participants can go to 'work' – that is, to look for a new job and participate in the various activities. At the 'workplaces', they also meet their personal coach and their 'colleagues', that is, other participants. The participants are encouraged to spend time at the office on a regular basis. As one provider describes it: 'We think it's important [for the participants] to have a structure during the day and a place to go. People also need another focus, other than when they're at home doing the laundry maybe, or doing something else.'

The participants are called in for scheduled activities that more or less demand their presence, such as regular meetings with the coach and different forms of group sessions, as well as voluntary activities like courses and seminars. A coach explains: 'The dream scenario would naturally be for everyone to be here from 9:00 to 3:00, every day. That it would feel that motivating to be here. Some people are. Some people come, but there are a number of people who choose to work from other places.'

When informing them about the programme, the employers make clear to the dismissed employees that a condition for taking part in a programme is that they must dedicate *all of their working hours* to 'increasing their employability and getting a new job'. Normally this work should be done during the daytime. They have the same obligation to work as before, but in the programme 'you actively work on your own future', and the assignment is to 'come out into the labour market'.

Stress is put on the participant's own responsibility. The participant should be active and follow an approved action plan. If a participant does not do this, he or she can be barred from the programme and his or her wages terminated. It is thus seen as important for participants to continue to behave as if they had a regular job. The boundaries between working hours and leisure time, as well as between the workplace and home, remain intact.[5] The interviews show that there are various ways of meeting these demands. One participant explains:

> I get up at the normal time. I try to see it as a job. I've trouble just lying at home in bed. I feel a certain responsibility. So it's hard to truly comprehend

this, which is maybe a good thing too, about getting full wages and permission to do a few things that are fun and exciting, that I've been wanting to do.

The programmes are made up of components that are typical for gainful employment: wages, office premises, supervisors, certain work procedures, routines and control bodies. One can see this set-up from two different points of view. On the one hand, one could say that it is a matter of protecting the workers in the sense that they need to be taken care of; they are seen as incapable of organizing their search for a new livelihood on their own. On the other hand, the structure gives the employers and the unions the ability to exercise control over the workers. From this perspective, it is a matter of the workers not being regarded as dependable; the employers and the unions do not trust that the workers will apply themselves and actively seek employment if they are not bound by the employment relationship and the monthly wages.

## Positive Change and Self-Development

One idea that permeates the transition programmes is that change is positive and necessary. This is expressed in different ways. One provider expresses it as follows:

> They avoid all of this [the problems that arise in regular staff cuts when the redundant staff remain in the workplace during the termination period] when they're released from the workplace, and get to come here, and work on themselves. The focus is only on yourself. It's a dream existence really. Even if we should use that word carefully maybe, because being unemployed is no-one's dream. But it's really something to be able to spend so much time on yourself.

None of the providers interviewed trivialize the fact that the participants have been made redundant. However, how they interpret the situation can vary. From having been a positive solution to a negative situation, the transition programme can be seen as something positive in itself. Despite the fact that what triggered the situation (termination) might be negative, and perhaps traumatic, the personnel claim that the programme holds possibilities for turning the situation into something good – a change of life as a whole. This potential to change decouples the situation from its link to the company's economic difficulties and the need to reduce its workforce. Instead, another framing of the situation occurs, where the situation is related to individuals' needs to change their job situation, or even their life situation. These needs are actively constructed in the programmes. One argument presented is that the transition programme, at least for some participants, is itself a better alternative to remaining in the old job. One of the coaches explains: 'I often get the question: *But Ulf, don't you find it hard to work with people who've lost their jobs?* And my response is: *It's precisely the opposite!* I see so many examples of people who say: *Wow, this should have happened a long time ago.*'

But there is also an instrumental dimension to all of this. In order to find a new job, the participant *must* have a positive attitude and be willing to change.

## Dependence and Independence

Right from the start, the providers strive to establish a relationship with the participants that builds on voluntariness. They come back to the point that it is important for people themselves to choose to participate in the transition programme. A manager for one of the transition programmes stresses that it is a matter of a mutual choice, both those leading the programme and the dismissed employees must make the assessment that the programme is 'right' for the person in question:

> This means that both of us can say yes to it, and both of us can say no. It surprises many clients, or potential clients, that we can both say no, too. But our view is that an active choice creates the best conditions for good cooperation and good results.

This initial procedure articulates the providers' explicit attitude towards the participants: they see them as responsible, independent individuals. One of the coaches puts it like this: 'We make the assumption that all the persons here, even if they've been let go and aren't feeling that great, are capable, mature adults, who essentially have everything they need to manage their own life.'

The ideal is expressed in various ways. The activities of the programmes, above all the personal interviews, are described as having to do with 'tapping into the participant's own wants'. Finding a new job is presented as 'the participant's project and responsibility' because it is 'his or her life'. The personnel will 'never take that responsibility away from the partici- pant'. One project coordinator reflects on the division of responsibility:

> It's the clients who come in here, who possess the knowledge really, both of a certain area and about themselves as persons. The consultant is the one who can ask the questions and ensure that the pieces needed come to light. But then it's the client who has to do the work. That's important, it's the responsibility part of it.

The message is that it is important to take responsibility for your own life. One provider described it in the following way:

> When you see, in some people, that there are possibilities here – then you try to inspire people. Above all, inspire them to do things on their own. That's the best that can happen, that they find a job and can look at themselves in the mirror and say: *I did this. It wasn't some goddamn coach who did this.* It makes them stronger individuals.

However, the study shows that the programme providers rarely feel that the participants, at least in the beginning, behave independently or responsibly. Here, taking responsibility is seen as a desirable ideal, rather than a condition that is presupposed in the programmes. In this way, the shortcomings of the participants motivate the existence of the pro-grammes; the programmes help the participants to become responsible and to take action. The following description by a coach of a typical coaching session illustrates this:

> We want them to find the answers themselves. It's not for us to say what they should do, but we should help so that they figure out on their own that *This is what I should do.* This is important because when it comes from inside, when they're your own ideas and your own thoughts, then it's more appealing than if I say: *Do this, do that, do this.* Many like it that way. But there's a completely different engagement when they figure something out themselves. That's what happens in the coaching session. I can see that a person, as a participant, may need to do certain things. They maybe need to up the tempo or make some other change. But I don't tell them that, instead I ask: *What do you think the consequences will be if you don't do this?* So that the person him- or herself gains the insight that he or she needs to improve something.

The coach quoted above has an opinion about what the participant should do, something that the participant is not aware of. She describes how her role is to ask questions and, in doing so, to increase the participant's self-awareness. In practice, however, this approach does not simply mean that the participant's own self-image should be affirmed. The coach uses her questions to convey a *certain* view of how the participant should behave and see him- or herself. The purpose of the questions is to lead the participant in a predetermined direction, even if it is described as a matter of the participant him- or herself figuring out what he or she wants.

The fact that every participant must take responsibility for his or her situation and future is, in sum, a central idea in the programmes. In the end, it is up to the participants themselves to find a new job. According to the programme personnel, this is for the participants' own good. At the same time, the division of responsibility makes it difficult for participants to express dissatisfaction with the programmes if they do not get a job. Because the role of the providers is to offer advice, not to deliver jobs, they cannot be held responsible if the participants have not found work by the end of the programme.

## On Being Coachable and Uncoachable

Despite the fact that the providers want the redundant employees to take part in the programmes of their own free will, the practice proves different. Most of the participants have de facto not wanted to leave their jobs, and taking part in a transition programme is to be regarded more as a necessary evil than a voluntary choice. One provider articulates this by saying that many view it as 'choosing between cholera and the plague'. Another provider says that there is 'a lot of resistance' and that participants have sometimes felt forced to take part in the programme:

> There's a lot of resistance. You have to make an individual assessment based on the state they're in when they come. Some need a longer process, because they're not really up to it. They didn't really want to go into it [the transition programme], but felt that they had to because, bluntly put, they're redundant.

Yet another provider divides the participants into coachable and uncoachable. She tells how she often has to take care of participants who are 'difficult to handle', because she is good at it and, with her, they 'become coachable'. She describes this as 'putting pressure on their sore spots' but that, at the same time, she has great respect for the participants. When participants enter the programme, they are often angry and disappointed. In her opinion, 'they must be allowed to feel like that', but they must also 'accept the situation' and 'move on'. For the ones who don't, the work becomes very difficult and then 'their anger is projected onto the coach':

> I had one participant with the wrong attitude completely. He was really snarky. Everything was wrong and everything I said was wrong. It didn't matter to me, but I said to him: *Well, the fact is that you have a problem. Your attitude is getting in your way. And it's apparent. Experienced recruiters, who meet many people, they see right through that. There's no point in being like that and thinking that you can hide it in an interview.* After that he became really nice, and coachable, and pleasant to work with, and fun in the group. And it's very liberating for the person to let that go.

Here, an initial tension between the provider and participant is reformulated as something characterising the participant. The participant is described as uncoachable, as if he does not know what is best for him and does not acknowledge the coach's expertise either. When the participant later behaves in accordance with the programme's way of looking at things – that is, he adopts the prescribed identity – he is described as having become coachable. This development is presented as favourable, 'liberating', above all for the participant himself. An alternative interpretation is that the participant has not been converted at all, but rather has yielded to the process. He has adapted his behaviour to the programme's system, rendering him a more agreeable participant to have to do with, 'nice' and 'pleasant to work with'.

Providers often describe how, in the beginning, the participants find themselves in a crisis-like state that may be expressed as anger, bitterness and an unwillingness to cooperate, or an inability to work – that is, to search for a job. It can take a while before a participant is 'ready' to begin to look for a new job. In the end, after having gone through the programme's exercises, the participant is transformed and wants to cooperate and look for a new job. This is described as that the participants 'grow as people' or 'become stronger as individuals'.

### CVs Should Look in a Certain Way

A large part of the programme is dedicated to teaching the participants to behave in what is regarded as the correct manner in the labour market. This involves seminars on how the labour market works, lectures given by headhunters and employers etc., courses in how to map out and use your networks, and interview techniques. The resumé – the CV – appears to be an important symbol for the process of presenting and marketing oneself in the labour market. It marks the start of the job search process. It is virtually unthinkable to look for a job without a CV. Production of the CV also appears to be an activity that is anything but trivial. CV courses and CV panels are arranged within the programme framework. These activities offer advice, recommendations and templates for how to compose a CV. Writing a CV is described as a particular skill that must be taught and learned, and needs to be updated. One provider comments: 'I'd say that when it just comes to putting together a CV, 10 years ago no-one knew what it was. With programmes like these, you get good at coping with a situation like becoming unemployed. Therefore, I don't think they're as afraid of becoming unemployed next time.'

The participants are taught to carefully consider their formulations, to describe themselves in terms that are understandable and saleable, and to adapt to the demand in the market. A person should not present him- or herself as too good, but not as unattractive either. The provider's role becomes both to boost the participants and to downplay the CVs. What should be highlighted about the different participants is not a predetermined given. The programme provides an opportunity to 'repackage yourself' and bring different qualities to the fore. This might be skills that people have previously performed in their leisure time, or characteristics that have, until now, not been articulated as work-related. A programme representative describes the process:

> You begin by looking at: *Where does my expertise lie?* and *What skills do I possess?* We talk about the analysis phase, analysing: *What is it I can do?* and *What kind of skills do I bring?* These can also be skills that someone has engaged in in their leisure time, but not at work, but that could actually lead to employment.

It can also be a matter of leaving out certain details that the participant earlier included in the CV, for example, titles that are not regarded as generally applicable. In that all of the CVs are formulated in a similar way, employers are able to compare different candidates to each other. The CV thus helps to standardize the jobseeker. On one hand, emphasis is put on how important it is that one's CV stands out – that it is somehow unique and catches the attention of employers. On the other hand, the CV makes the jobseeker appear more similar to other candidates. This represents a common dilemma for something to be sold in a market: a good should be both comparable to other goods and, at the same time, be special in some way, and therefore appealing.

One aspect regarding formulation of the CV is that the participants are not formally unemployed. One provider suggests that this improves the participant's situation in the labour market: 'When they're in the transition programme, they're still employed. So, on their CV, they write that they're still employed at the company. They're not unemployed. This means that the employer knows that these are people who still have a job.'

However, the participants no longer work with what they were hired to do. The content of the work, and its purpose, is radically changed. Instead of engaging in their previous work tasks, their task is to search for a job, 'increase their employability' and 'work on themselves'. That is, they do the same things as people who are de facto unemployed. The objective is for them not to need to become unemployed in a contractual sense. They should be able to present a CV with no gaps that need explaining. The programmes therefore reflect that uninterrupted careers are still the reigning ideal. The line drawn between people categorized as employed and those categorized as unemployed in the labour market is also hereby strengthened.

**The Personal Network Matter**

The providers emphasize the importance of using personal contacts in the job search process. They encourage participants to build their own network of relationships. A coach explains:

> Many people get jobs via their own contacts. And there I usually recommend that they really spread their CV around. It's a generous gesture to send your CV to friends and others in the network and offer your services. And who doesn't read a CV that comes from a friend? I try to inspire this type of activity.

Participants in turn tell how they have been advised to take advantage of every opportunity to tell people they are looking for work, people they meet in the laundry room, or other parents they meet at their children's daycare. Just as one needs to invest some of one's private self in marketing oneself as labour, one must also invest one's private relations to be successful in the labour market.

# CONCLUDING DISCUSSION: MAKING A VIRTUE OF NECESSITY

The purpose of transition programmes is to increase the employability of redundant people and of those whose jobs are threatened – that is, their viability in the market. The programmes presuppose a large measure of adaptation. It is in part a matter of adapting to the programme methods, and in part of adapting to the labour market. It is not only jobseekers who must be employable. Rather, improving one's employability is described as something that all of today's workers should embrace, all of the time. In this respect, the aim of the programme is to bring about lasting change in the participants.

In theory, the starting point for the programmes is the individual. The programmes are presented as individualized. They emphasize that people are independent actors and are able to choose. They encourage individual participants to see the situation as an opportunity for self-development. The first priority is for the participant to put what he or she wants and is able to do into words.

The programmes' message is that an ability to change and a positive attitude are necessary. The goal is to create responsible, independent people. In the ideal situation, the individual chooses the career that best articulates and develops him or her. A person's career is presented as a means and expression for that person's development as 'him- or herself'. People are assumed to choose a job that reflects who they are.

In practice, however, many run into barriers that limit their options. The transition programmes can therefore be regarded as a disciplining process – where the disciplining has to do with adapting, under the pretence that one is engaging in self-development. In the end, for prosaic reasons such as the responsibility to make a living, most of the participants must accept the offer they get.

One conclusion is that many people must make a virtue of necessity. It is often more a matter of wanting what one must, rather than choosing what one wants.

## NOTES

1. The research that forms the basis of this chapter was made possible with the aid of funding from the Economic Research Institute (EFI) at Stockholm School of Economics.
2. The contracts also commonly involve financial supplementation of unemployment insurance.
3. The Public Employment Service was not considered suited to the needs of the administrative employees. First, special severance packages were introduced as a supplement to unemployment insurance. Thereafter support in the process of seeking a new job was also introduced, which was to be explicitly based on the needs of the individual. A special foundation, the Employment Security Council (*Trygghetsrådet*, TRR), was formed to administrate and organize the support.
4. It has long been relatively common for large Swedish workplaces to offer custom solutions and more extensive support than what the law and central collective agreements demand in redundancy situations. These expanded forms of transition support constitute a part in negotiations with the union organizations. They make it possible to reach agreements in individual cases where the Employment Protection Act (LAS) is overridden in favour of a negotiated order. (Stjernberg and Tillberg 1998; Sabel 2002; Bäckström 2006; Bergström 2007).
5. This can be contrasted to current ideas about how these types of boundaries are in the process of disappearing and even to the notion that we are living in a '24-hour society', where activities go on around the clock and it is merely a matter of 'plugging in' when it suits you.

## REFERENCES

Bäckström, Henrik (2006), *Omställningssystemets agenter och försäkringar på den svenska arbetsmarknaden. Bemanningsföretag, försäkringsbolag, myndigheter och trygghetsråd i helig allians?* Report 2006:4. Stockholm: National Institute for Working Life.
Bergström, Ola (2007), 'Translating socially responsible workforce reduction – A longitudinal study of workforce reduction in a Swedish company', *Scandinavian Journal of Management*, 23, 384–405.

Garsten, Christina and Kerstin Jacobsson (eds) (2004), *Learning to be Employable: New agendas on work, responsibility and learning in a globalizing world*. Basingstoke: Palgrave Macmillan.

Goffman, Erving (2007) [1961], *Totala institutioner*. Stockholm: Norstedts.

Sabel, Ola (2002), *Posten Futurum – Utvärdering av verksamheten i Postens omställningsprogram*. GRI Report 2002:8, Gothenburg Research Institute.

Stjernberg, Torbjörn and Ulrika Tillberg (1998), 'When structure and meaning break down – Taking responsibility in downsizing', *European Journal of Work and Organizational Psychology*, 7(3), 355–74.

# PART II

# People in the new labour market

# 8. Market-oriented relationships in working life: on the perception of being employable

## Erik Berntson

At both the national and international levels, employability is emphasized as a key to attaining success in working life and to an ever-increasing extent it is also a requirement for the individual to be able to cope with the variations that increasingly occur in working life. The concept of employability has been highlighted in EU labour market directives as an important factor for achieving full employment in Europe (European Commission 1997) and has been implemented as one of the central goals of the EU's joint training initiatives in the Bologna process (European Commission 1999). Employability has, however, also been brought forward as a concept in various national labour market and education policy strategies, for example in Denmark's so-called flexicurity model (see, for example, Kongshøj-Madsen 2002), in labour market directives in Britain and the Netherlands (see, for example, Weinert et al. 2001), as well as in target documents of Swedish universities (see, for example, Stockholm University 2007). The increased occurrence of the concept is also seen in the research literature, in both occupational psychology (for example De Cuyper and De Witte 2008; Van der Heijde and Van der Heijden 2005) and management (for example Bloch and Bates 1995; Hind and Moss 2005).

Why has the concept of employability come to play such a significant role in the labour market policy debate and in the occupational psychology research? There are several reasons for this, but the one that I will address in this chapter has to do with the relationship between employer and employee, which, in occupational psychology, is referred to as the psychological contract.[1] This relationship has changed and shifted towards a more market-oriented relationship, where the responsibility for one's career rests to a higher degree on the individual. A consequence of this shift is also that it has become critical for individuals to continually update their skills in order to guarantee their attractiveness in the labour market. In other words, it has become more important for the individual to be employable.

The main argument in this chapter, however, is that it is essentially not the actual employability that is most important, that is, an individual's ability to change jobs. Rather, I argue that the perception itself of being employable has become increasingly essential in working life today. Being employable has always been important in the sense that everyone has at some time or another had to establish themselves in the labour market and get their first job, but the central point of being employable today is not establishing oneself but retaining employment. Today's working life is not characterized by having a single job at a single employer for one's entire life. Rather, it has become a reality for many to change workplaces, voluntarily or involuntarily, with regular frequency. Employability can therefore be a matter of retaining one's current job or advancing in an organization, to be equipped and ready in the case of reorganization, but it can also be a matter of retaining work in a broader sense, that is, being able to switch jobs if necessary.

In that the focus has moved from establishing oneself to retaining employment, two aspects have become increasingly important. Firstly, the *perception* of being able to change jobs has become more central in working life. Whether a person changes jobs or not, the feeling that one has this possibility yields the sense of control and security needed when security is not necessarily found within an organization. Secondly, there are higher demands on individuals to *continually* stay up to date and to increase their knowledge and skills in order to be able to change jobs even after establishing themselves.

The chapter begins with a discussion about the so-called psychological contract, which plays an important role in the emergence of the concept of employability. A description is then given of the concept of *perceived employability*, followed by a description of what it is that shapes an individual's perception of employability and the importance this has from a health and well-being perspective.

## CHANGED RELATIONSHIPS AND A SHIFT IN EXPECTATIONS IN WORKING LIFE

The research on the psychological contract can, from an occupational psychology perspective, serve as a relevant inroad to understanding why it has become more important to believe that you can get a new job if you need to.

The psychological contract is an abstract contract that exists between an individual and an organization. Many occupational psychologists have written about the psychological contract, which is why it has been defined in somewhat different ways, but Denise Rousseau describes the contract as follows: 'the term *psychological contract* refers to an individual's beliefs regarding the terms and conditions of a reciprocal exchange agreement between that focal person and another party' (Rousseau 1989: 123). Although there are different ideas about what the psychological contract is, it is clear that the *individual beliefs* regarding the terms and conditions, and *reciprocal exchange* are key concepts. In other words, the psychological contract has to do with how I as an employee perceive the terms and conditions regarding my employment – both what is required of me and what I can expect of my employer.

Like a legal employment contract, the psychological contract has to do with the relation between employer and employee. In contrast to the legal contract, however, the psychological contract focuses on the implicit rather than explicit conditions. Where an employment contract establishes the terms and conditions of a job with respect to work content, wages, benefits and the like, the psychological contract has to do with the expectations an employee has, both of what he or she will receive from the employer and what is expected of an individual in employment. When we start a job, we bring with us expectations about a number of things relating to the new workplace, including: What are the possibilities for working from home? What possibilities do I have to influence the structure of my work? What will the managers be like, what feedback will I get? The list is naturally long, but the point is that these types of expectations are never or rarely stipulated in an employment contract. Rather, they constitute more or less implicit expectations that we bring with us to a job. There are, at the same time, expectations of what is required of me, both by myself as an employee and by the employer. This can be a matter of whether or not I have the right knowledge and skills to carry out the job, how much overtime I will be required to work, or whether I will be expected to perform tasks that fall outside my position. On the part of the employer, there are expectations about how capable I am, how I will fit into the organization, etc. Conditions such as these can be more or less known and explicit; I may have found out about them in the recruiting interview (implicitly or explicitly), by way of the company's values, website, other employees or through my own experience, but the point is that they are not written down in a contract and it is this that forms the psychological contract.

Even though the psychological contract is highly individual, that is, it is a contract that exists and is 'owned' by a particular individual, there is also reason to speak about it from a social-psychological perspective. From such a perspective, the psychological contract is not entirely individual, but can be shared by groups of individuals. For example, one can imagine that people who work in the same industry and have the same profession have relatively synchronized expectations about the terms and conditions that apply within that sector. Secondary school teachers likely have certain beliefs about what should be included in their work in terms of their development, relations to management, etc. These expectations can also be expected to differ from the expectations that, for example, nurses have about their work. But expectations can also be grouped at the organizational level, that is, that secondary school teachers have different expectations depending on which school they work at. This distinction is important because socially shared expectations can also change over time and context, a discussion that has been important in the occupational psychology literature (see, for example, Conway and Briner 2005). The result of this is that, when the context changes over time – that is, the labour market and its written and unwritten rules – individuals' expectations also change, and we can thereby speak about a change in the psychological contract.

## CHANGING THE PSYCHOLOGICAL CONTRACT – FROM 'OLD' TO 'NEW'

Occupational psychologists often talk about a shift in the psychological contract. This expression refers to the shift that is a theme throughout this book, namely, the shift towards an individualized working life. The discussion of this shift furthermore captures the flexibility found in today's working life. In such contexts, we often speak about a 'new' and an 'old' psychological contract (for a more detailed discussion of this, see, for example, Anderson and Schalk 1998; Arnold 1997; Conway and Briner 2005; Kluytmans and Ott 1999). I emphasize these concepts with quotation marks because they can be somewhat misleading. There is in actuality nothing that says that there are not relationships today that resemble the 'old' ones or vice versa, but they mark a change and a tendency in working life that is important, which is why I retain them.

The 'old' psychological contract was at its core characterized by security, loyalty and sustainability. This means that, once hired, as workers we expected a long-term relationship with our employer. It was not unusual to work in the same organization for all of one's working life, and to expect also that the company would be responsible for some degree of job security even in poor economic times. Even when things were not going all that well for the company, one did not expect it to start letting employees go – and particularly not in times when things were going well for the company. Several researchers have similarly pointed out that, within the framework of this older contract, it was also more common for the organization to expect long-term loyalty – job-hopping was not appreciated and could make getting future employment more difficult (Anderson and Schalk 1998; Kluytmans and Ott 1999). In a way, one could say that the relationship between employer and employee was predictable and relatively stable. Careers were made primarily through seniority, that is, by working for a long time within an organization – loyalty enabled one to have a career within a company, and careers such as this were to a large extent driven by the organization (Arnold 1997).

But the content of the psychological contract has changed over the years. The change has been gradual and is continuing, which is why it is not possible to talk about a particular year as the breaking point between these different perspectives. The most critical element of the change is that we have gone from a situation characterized by sustainability, loyalty and security, to a situation of a more transactional nature. This transactional character means that the employment relationship and the expectations placed on it have become more market-oriented. There is a focus in the relationship that is oriented more towards a market exchange between the parties. The worker has a set of skills, which can be regarded as a product that can be marketed and must be constantly developed. The exchange between employer and employee occurs around this skill set – the worker delivers his or her skills and receives in exchange the opportunity to continue to develop and improve them.

In other words, the key constructs of the 'new' psychological contract are *exchange*, *flexibility* and *development*. Researchers have described workers' expectations as being comprised of professional development, self-realization and challenges. The central issue when we take a job is how it helps us to attain our personal goals and take us further to the next job. Our career path does not necessarily remain within an organization but rather winds its way through different companies and positions and possibly across different occupational fields. In this way, careers have changed from having to do with seniority to having to do with an individual's own development and dreams of attaining his or her own goals. The path is no longer controlled by the organization but it is the individual him- or herself who takes initiative for the development of his or her own career. Douglas T. Hall (1996) speaks, for example, about the protean career, alluding to the Greek god Proteus who could change his shape whenever he wanted or needed to. The expression suggests that the concept of career today means that, as a worker, one must be able to change shapes in order to drive one's career towards self-realization.

The employer has at the same time other expectations of the employee. Loyalty is expected, though perhaps not so much towards the organization and from a long-term perspective, but rather to the immediate work task and the organization's current situation. Companies today are prepared to pay higher wages and they do not expect everyone to stay within the organization. They do expect, however, that while workers are in their employment, they will dedicate everything to the task and the company; they are in the organization to create 'added value'. We can thus talk about a shift in the relationship between employer and employee. Conway and Briner (2005) refer to a shift away from a relational contract, that is, a contract that is long-term and vaguer in nature, with a focus on security and loyalty, to a transactional contract whose emphasis is on the exchange of skills and monetary rewards, where the focus is on short-term, explicit relations. The reason for this shift has been explained by several researchers by the shift in working life towards individualization and an increasing flexibility that leaves people, firstly, exposed to more and more frequent changes and, secondly, to handle these changes on their own (see, for example, Anderson and Schalk 1998; Kluytmans and Ott 1999).

To summarize, the psychological contract has come to be given a more prominent place in the occupational psychology research for several reasons. Two key reasons are the importance it has for employees' actions and for the change in working life in a broader sense. Research has shown that expectations such as those in the psychological contract play a role in people's attitudes and behaviours in the workplace. A breach of the contract or when one party does not fulfil his or her obligations has been shown to be linked to performance and commitment, as well as well-being and a willingness to remain in an organization (Conway and Briner 2005). But what makes the discussion about the psychological contract really interesting is that it captures two central and important trends in working life, namely, individualization and flexibilization. It describes a situation in which the worker must be able to be flexible and adapt in order to attain success, but also where it is the workers themselves who drive their careers. The employer no longer offers a given career path; this is instead something that the worker, admittedly together with the employer, pursues. It is in this meeting between working life's tendencies of flexibilization and individualization that the concept of employability gains its legitimacy. The essence of the 'new' psychological contract is precisely continuous professional development, adaptation and, not least, being employable in order to be able to profit from this development by changing jobs when needed.

# EMPLOYABILITY AS A SUBJECTIVE PHENOMENON

As the relationship between worker and employer has become character-ized by short-term exchanges with skills development at the core, it has also become more important for employees to have control over their working life by being able to change jobs. In a flexible environment where the organization does not take responsibility for the individual's employment in times of economic adversity, and perhaps not even in times of economic prosperity, there are greater demands on the individual to be able to change jobs when necessary. Security is no longer gained by having employment but by being employable (Kanter 1993 [1977]). It is therefore not only important to *be able* to change jobs, it is also important to *believe* that one can.

Using my starting point, where the focus lies on people's subjective perceptions, employability has been defined as 'an individual's percep-tion of his or her possibilities of getting a new, equal, or better employment' (Berntson 2008: 15). This definition emphasizes four aspects of the concept of employability that appear especially important to discuss in order to understand its content.

Firstly, from an occupational psychology perspective, the definition is based on an individual's own perception, placing the individual at the centre, rather than a focus on how the concept is used at a group level or in policy documents, which is otherwise very common (for example, Lefresne 1999). Secondly, 'a new job' suggests that the definition is limited to individuals who are employed. Employability is relevant and can be discussed from several perspectives. The literature has often focused on employability from the perspective of those who are un-employed, have disabilities, or are new graduates (Bricout and Bentley 2000; Finn 2000; Knight and Yorke 2004). For obvious reasons, it has previously not been as important to show an interest in the employability of people who already have work. But, as working life has changed, employability has taken on a broader and somewhat different meaning, that is, that it does not in the first place have to do with establishing oneself in the labour market but retaining employment over time.

Thirdly, the definition's qualification 'equal, or better' means that the focus lies more on security than on career. We can speak about employabil-ity from a career perspective, that is, which factors play a role in an individual being able to climb in a predetermined hierarchy. There are, above all in the management literature, a series of books that draw attention to tricks and techniques to get that next, slightly better job (see, for example, Hind and Moss 2005). But this is not what is central in today's discussion about employability. Rather, today it is a matter of feeling secure in one's ability to retain employment – it is important to be employable in order to be able to keep a job or position in the labour market.

The fourth aspect is that the definition of employability is aimed at the perception of being able to get a new job. Throughout the literature, one speaks of what is referred to as *objective employability* that is, an individual's *actual* possibilities of getting a new job (see, for example, Fugate, Kinicki and Ashforth 2004). Against the background described above, however, the perception of employability becomes more interesting. Perceptions in general are interesting because they affect individuals' actions as well as affective and cognitive reactions (Magnusson 1981; McLean Parks, Kidder and Gallagher 1998; Meyer and Allen 1997). When it comes to employability, perception is important because it is the very perception of employability that creates the sense of control – regardless of whether this perception is based in reality or not. And it is this very sense of control or security of being able to get a job that has become important.

Theoretically, we must differentiate here between an individual's actual possibilities of getting a new job and the individual's perception of these possibilities. An objective event or situation is characterized by its ability to be described based on a number of physical, biological and socio-cultural parameters, and if one of these parameters changes a new event or situation is formed. A perception, on the other hand, is linked to an individual's interpretation of a situation or event and can thereby vary from one individual to the next, and may also deviate from what can be defined as the objective event or situation (Magnusson 1981). In relation to employability, this means that an individual can have an objective level of employability but perceive it differently. And different individuals with seemingly similar situations can perceive their possibilities of getting a job differently. And while distinguishing between objective and subjective employability is fundamental from a theoretical standpoint, one can naturally question the extent to which it is possible to differentiate between them in practice. Several researchers, among them Albert Bandura (1986), suggest that perceptions, situations and behaviours shape one another in interaction. How an individual perceives his or her ability to get a job is related to the individual's actual possibilities of getting a job, and it is moreover possible that objective employability is affected by the subjective. How closely objective and subjective employability are coupled is an empirical question, but the point here is that, regardless of how employable an individual is, the perception of being employable plays a role in a person's actions and perceptions.

To sum up, the perception of employability has become more central through the shift in the psychological contract that I touched upon earlier in the chapter. It is particularly the four aspects of the concept of employability addressed (the focus on the individual, employability of people who already have jobs, security in working life, and the subjective perspective) that have become important in this context. This does not mean that employability has not become more central, for example, from an unemployed individual's perspective, or when taking an objective perspective. Rather, a dimension has been added that makes it more relevant to feel employable. In other words, it is not necessarily important to be able to change jobs, but the key is to believe that one can change jobs – it is the feeling or perception of employability that is important. The reason for this is that it is the perception of employability that creates a sense of control in the individual and can influence the individual's behaviour.

## HOW IS THE PERCEPTION OF EMPLOYABILITY FORMED?

What is it then that makes an individual feel employable? There are a number of different psychological theories that indicate that the formation of perceptions is the result of the interaction of factors that individuals carry with them (for example, age and earlier experiences) and the situation in which the individual finds him- or herself (see Magnusson 1981). Such interactionist theories (where perceptions are formed in the interaction between individuals and contexts) enable us to understand what it is that forms an individual's perception of his or her ability to get a job. Based on this perspective, it is useful to identify in part individual factors and in part situational factors that affect an individual's perception of his or her employability.

### Individual Factors

Knowledge and skills are the category most often put forward in the literature as important for an individual to feel employable (see, for example, Hillage and Pollard 1998; McQuaid and Lindsay 2005; Van der Heijde and Van der Heijden 2006). The category of knowledge and skills includes a series of different competencies that have been judged to be important for perceiving oneself as employable. Some of these come from experience and skills development in working life, while others are gained through formal education and training.

A number of studies have shown that different types of competencies and skills are positively linked to the perception of employability (see, for example, Berntson, Sverke and Marklund 2006; Van der Heijde and Van der Heijden 2006). Profession-specific expertise has been shown to be especially important for an individual's employability (McQuaid and Lindsay 2005). This expertise comes in part from experience in one's field, the tacit knowledge accumulated over time in the profession, but it is also attained through successive skills development. There is reason to believe that skills development is of particular importance for employability, since the changes in working life, for example, technical advances, mean that the individual must continually stay up to date in order to be attractive in the labour market.

Reference has also been made to so-called transferable knowledge and skills as important for employability (McQuaid and Lindsay 2005). Transferable knowledge is knowledge that an individual can take with him or her from one job to another. It is a type of knowledge that is general or generic, and that we can apply in many types of situations. These situations can vary widely at times, and very high demands are therefore set on finding this transferable knowledge that enables the individual to take jobs that are not very closely related to what they are doing now. Examples of such transferable knowledge include basic skills in language and presentation, communication, problem-solving and entrepreneurship.

It is naturally the case that there is variation between professions with respect to how important these knowledge and skills are for making an individual feel employable. Some professions have formal requirements for attaining certification or licensing before one begins to work (for example, medicine), while in other professions no special educational background requirements for recruitment may be more common. Several studies have, however, shown that formal training as well as profession-specific experience are associated with the perception of employability (see, for example, Berntson, Sverke and Marklund 2006). There are, in addition, naturally a number of other individual factors noted in the literature as important to making us feel employable. Some of the factors presented include social capital, that is, how strong and broad an individual's personal networks are (Fugate, Kinicki and Ashforth 2004). According to several researchers (McQuaid and Lindsay 2005), having the right attitude is also of importance. Attitudes that are mentioned include a willingness to change, a willingness to adapt oneself, and a willingness to learn new things.

**Situational Factors**

Even if individual factors are central to employability, we cannot overlook the fact that the situation also plays a decisive role. If there are no jobs, there are no requirements and conditions for individuals to believe that they can get a new job either. In other words, the jobs that are available play an important role in how individuals perceive their employability. This has been shown in, among others, a Swedish population study of over 11 000 participants (Berntson, Sverke and Marklund 2006), where both the economy and local labour markets were shown to be linked to how individuals perceived their employability. The study was conducted during an economic slump (1993) and an economic boom (1999), and the findings showed that during the slowdown only 17 per cent of the people surveyed believed that they had good possibilities of getting a new job, a figure that in booming economic times was 43 per cent. The findings also showed that where a person lived in the country was linked to the degree of perceived employability. In large urban areas, people believed, in both slow and booming economic times, that they had better possibilities of finding a new job. The explanation for this may lie in the fact that people living in large metropolitan areas have access to a more varied and dynamic labour market, which in part enables them to change jobs, and in part generally leads them to believe in their ability to change jobs. The empirical evidence indicates that the structure of the labour market, which can vary over time or depending on geography, plays a role in how individuals see their possibilities of getting a new job. These findings are also supported by the international research, which presents similar arguments (McQuaid and Lindsay 2005).

As a whole, there are a number of factors that affect a person's perception of his or her prospects of getting a new job if needed, and it is likely that these factors change somewhat over time. Knowledge and skills appear, however, if we consider the international research in the area, to be extremely important factors for individuals to judge their chances of getting employment as good. This applies both to basic knowledge and transferable and profession-specific knowledge. These knowledge and skills need to be kept up to date and added to continually throughout one's working life, which is why lifelong learning is seemingly central in working life.

## THE IMPORTANCE OF THE PERCEPTION OF EMPLOYABILITY FOR HEALTH AND WELL-BEING

Earlier in the chapter, I touched upon the point that changed relationships in the labour market mean that people today must to a greater extent continually update their knowledge and maintain their attractiveness in the labour market, partly to be able to be in control of their situation.

When an organization changes, a period of uncertainty and insecurity ensues, which is to some extent harmful for the individual (see, for example, the research on job insecurity, Sverke, Hellgren and Näswall 2002). One way of coping with this is to know that you can get a new job. Then the consequences of what happens in the organization need not be as grave – if the situation becomes untenable for the individual, there is always the possibility of switching to another, more favourable work situation.

From a health perspective, we can therefore say that employability is an important factor for one's ability to maintain good health in working life today. Empirically, there are studies that have shown a relationship between the perception of employability and health and well-being. In one population study, 1918 people (employed individuals in Sweden, aged 25–50 years) responded to a questionnaire on the topics of employability and health and well-being (Berntson and Marklund 2007). The study found a positive correlation between perceived employability and general health and mental well-being. Health was measured by a question that asked participants to estimate their general state of health and mental well-being. Their responses reflected, among other things, the individual's feeling of being calm, relaxed, at ease, energetic and active. The findings showed that even when taking into account a number of known factors that influence health (including age, level of education, work environment and earlier health status), the link between employability and health remained. One year later, individuals with higher employability reported better general health and better mental well-being than people with lower employability.

That the perception of being employable has a positive effect on individuals' health and well-being can be explained on the basis of Lazarus and Folkman's (1984) appraisal theory. They claim that any individual on any given occasion assesses the situation, what potential threats it presents and, if it poses a threat, his or her possibilities of managing that threat. Lazarus and Folkman call this primary appraisal and secondary appraisal. Allow me to illustrate with an example. When a company undergoes organizational change, a person can perceive the situation as irrelevant – perhaps the change does not affect the person's department. But the change can also be perceived as either positive or potentially stressful. These three outcomes are examples of a person's primary appraisal of the situation. If the situation, in this case an organizational change, is perceived as potentially stressful, the individual makes a secondary appraisal, that is, of his or her possibilities of coping with that change. If such possibilities exist, the change may be perceived as a challenge; but if no possibilities exist to manage the stressful situation, there is instead a risk that it will be perceived as a threat to the individual. Lazarus and Folkman emphasize the importance of control for the secondary appraisal to lead to a positive outcome. When individuals do not perceive themselves as having control, there is a significant risk that a stressful situation will be perceived as a threat, with negative health outcomes as a result. The perception of being employable is a way to gain control over one's working life, which can lead to someone not being negatively impacted by stressful situations, from a health and well-being perspective.

In addition, there is a risk that the reverse situation, that is, where an individual does not believe that he or she will be able to find new employment, may be harmful for that person. In one study, Gunnar Aronsson and Sara Göransson found that individuals who felt 'locked in' reported worse health than people who did not feel locked in. By 'locked in', they mean that the person either finds him- or herself in an undesired profession, or in their preferred profession but at an undesired workplace. In other words, there is a risk that being locked into the organization like this may contribute to the individual not having the ability to influence his or her situation, with negative health outcomes (Aronsson and Göransson 1999).

As a whole, one can say that, given that working life is characterized by flexibility and general turbulence, the perception of being employable contributes to individuals having a certain control, or perception of control, over their work lives and careers. At the same time, it also sets higher demands on the individual, who can no longer be complacent about performing his or her current work well, but must also, to a greater and greater extent, change and update his or her knowledge and skills in order to have the possibility of getting a new job if the need should arise. There is thus a risk that lifelong learning becomes a quest to be employable, not necessarily to get a new job, but to be ready and able to if necessary.

## CONCLUDING DISCUSSION: ON THE IMPORTANCE OF PERCEIVING ONESELF AS EMPLOYABLE

There are many important aspects in the research on employability, whereof only a few have been addressed in this chapter. The two central issues in the chapter are, firstly, the increased importance of the perception of being employable and, secondly, that individuals need to continually update their employability, regardless of whether this is internally in the organization or externally in relation to other employers.

Developments in working life have meant that the relationship between worker and employer has become more market-oriented, with a particular focus on lifelong learning and employability. Instead of describing working life with keywords like *loyalty, seniority* and *sustainability*, it is described based on the concepts of *self-realization, development* and *short-termism*. Within the framework of the 'new' psychological contract, there is also an increased focus on flexibility and adaptation. Instead of an organization offering long-term employment and security, the security lies with the individual in that this person can be independent and find a new job whenever needed – in other words, it is more important to feel employable to be able to face the turbulence and flexibility that arise in working life.

I would like to stress the importance of this perception because it is a determinant for a series of aspects for individuals in working life. While actually being able to get a job is only important if an individual is forced to find a new workplace, the perception is important all the time. This applies even in the case of individuals who never change workplaces in their entire lifetime of work. Though a person may work in one organization for his or her entire working life, changes may arise in the organization such that a previous job disappears even though employment itself remains. Knowing that the prospects of performing one's job may be put in jeopardy by way of organizational change can give rise to a great deal of uncertainty and concern, and it matters very little that the individual is secure from a legal perspective, that is, via the Employment Protection Act (LAS). In a situation such as this, the perception of employability is essential to feeling one has control over one's working life.

At the same time, the emphasis on perceiving oneself as employable also raises a number of paradoxes. Because it is the perception that is important, whether a person would actually be able to get a new job is less important. As long as he or she feels that it is possible, it can contribute to this perception of control and, vice versa, when this perception is lacking, there may be strong feelings of concern that may be harmful to one's health. That it is a matter of a perception thereby means that individuals who would actually have difficulty finding a job may still feel a sense of control, through a strong perception of employability, and, similarly, there may be individuals who perceive themselves as having a very low employability even though it is not at all impossible that they could find a new job.

Regardless of whether or not an individual is employable, the development in the labour market and the changed relationships in working life now place higher demands on individuals to continually learn and reinvent themselves in order to be attractive to employers. There are greater demands for individuals to actually engage in continual updating of their knowledge and to learn new things, which applies irrespective of whether an individual intends to change jobs or not. An individual's sense of security and control over his or her working life therefore lies in the perception of being employable.

## NOTES

1. The research that this chapter is based on was made possible with the aid of funding from the Swedish Council for Working Life and Social Research (FAS), and the project 'Employability perceptions – relationship with gender, age and health. Is the labour market divided into segments?' led by Staffan Marklund.

## REFERENCES

Anderson, Neil and Rene Schalk (1998), 'The psychological contract in retrospect and prospect', *Journal of Organizational Behavior*, 19, 637–47.

Arnold, John (1997), *Managing Careers into the 21st Century*. London: Paul Chapman.

Aronsson, Gunnar and Sara Göransson (1999), 'Permanent employment but not in a preferred occupation: Psychological and medical aspects, research implications', *Journal of Occupational Health Psychology*, 4(2), 152–63.

Bandura, Albert (1986), *Social Foundations of Thought and Action: A social cognitive theory*. Upper Saddle River, NJ: Prentice-Hall.

Berntson, Erik (2008), *Employability Perceptions: Nature, determinants, and implications for health and well-being*. Stockholm: Stockholm University.

Berntson, Erik and Staffan Marklund (2007), 'The relationship between perceived employability and subsequent health', *Work and Stress*, 21(3), 279–92.

Berntson, Erik, Magnus Sverke and Staffan Marklund (2006), 'Predicting perceived employability: Human capital or labour market opportunities?', *Economic and Industrial Democracy*, 27(2), 223–44.

Bloch, Susan and Terry Bates (1995), *Employability: How to get your career on the right track*. London: Kogan Page.

Bricout, John C. and Kia J. Bentley (2000), 'Disability status and perceptions of employability by employers', *Social Work Research*, 24(2), 87–94.

Conway, Neil and Rob B. Briner (2005), *Understanding Psychological Contracts at Work: A critical evaluation of theory and research*. New York, NY: Oxford University Press.

De Cuyper, Nele and Hans De Witte (2008), 'Job insecurity and employability among temporary workers: A theoretical approach based on the psychological contract', in Katharina Näswall, Johnny Hellgren and Magnus Sverke (eds), *The Individual in the Changing Working Life*. Cambridge: Cambridge University Press, pp. 88–107.

European Commission (1997), *Proposal for Guidelines for Member States Employment Policies 1998*. Brussels: European Commission.

European Commission (1999), *The Bologna Declaration*. Brussels: European Commission.

Finn, Dan (2000), 'From full employment to employability: A new deal for Britain's unemployed?', *International Journal of Manpower*, 21(5), 384–99.

Fugate, Mel, Angelo J. Kinicki and Blake E. Ashforth (2004), 'Employability: A psycho-social construct, its dimensions, and applications', *Journal of Vocational Behavior*, 65(1), 14–38.

Hall, Douglas T. (1996), 'Protean careers of the 21st century', *Academy of Management Executive*, 10(4), 8–16.

Hillage, Jim and Emma Pollard (1998), *Employability: Developing a framework for policy analysis*. London: Institute for Employment Studies.

Hind, David W.G. and Stuart Moss (2005), *Employability Skills*. Business Education Publishers.

Kanter, Rosabeth M. (1993) [1977], 'Afterword to the 1993 edition. How the global economy is reshaping corporate powers and careers', in Rosabeth M. Kanter (ed.), *Men and Women of the Corporation*. New York, NY: Basic Books.

Kluytmans, Frits and Marlies Ott (1999), 'The management of employability in the Netherlands', *European Journal of Work and Psychology*, 8(2), 261–72.

Knight, Peter and Mantz Yorke (2004), *Learning, Curriculum and Employability in Higher Education*. London: Routledge.

Kongshøj Madsen, Per (2002), '"Flexicurity" through labour market policies and institutions in Denmark', in Peter Auer and Sandrine Cazes (eds), *Employment Stability in an Age of Flexibility: Evidence from industrialized countries*. Geneva: International Labour Office, pp. 59–105.

Lazarus, Richard S. and Susan Folkman (1984), *Stress, Appraisal and Coping*. New York, NY: Springer Publishing Company.

Lefresne, Florence (1999), 'Employability at the heart of the European employment strategy', *Transfer*, 5(4), 460–80.

Magnusson, David (ed.) (1981), *Toward a Psychology of Situations: An interactional perspective*. Hillsdale, MI: Lawrence Erlbaum.

McLean Parks, Judy, Deborah L. Kidder and Daniel G. Gallagher (1998), 'Fitting square pegs into round holes: Mapping the domain of contingent work arrangements onto the psychological contract', *Journal of Organizational Behaviour*, 19(7), 697–730.

McQuaid, Ronald W. and Colin Lindsay (2005), 'The concept of employability', *Urban Studies*, 42(2), 197–219.

Meyer, John P. and Natalie J. Allen (1997), *Commitment in the Workplace: Theory, research, and application*. Thousand Oaks, CA: Sage.

Rousseau, Denise (1989), 'Psychological and implied constraints in organizations', *Employee Responsibilities and Rights Journal*, 2(2), 121–39.

Stockholm University (2007), *Långsiktig plan 2008–2012*. Stockholm: Stockholm University.

Sverke, Magnus, Hellgren, Johnny, and Katharina Näswall (2002), 'No security: A meta-analysis and review of job insecurity and its consequences', *Journal of Occupational Health Psychology*, 7(3), 242–64.

Van der Heijde, Claudia M. and Beatrice I.J.M. Van der Heijden (2005), 'The development and psychometric evaluation of a multi-dimensional measurement instrument of employability and the impact of aging', *International Congress Series*, 1280, 142–7.

Van der Heijde, Claudia M. and Beatrice I.J.M. Van der Heijden (2006), 'A competence-based and multidimensional operationalization and measurement of employability', *Human Resource Management*, 45(3), 449–76.

Weinert, Patricia, Michèle Baukens, Patrick Bollérot, Marina Pineschi-Gapènne and Ulrich Walwei (2001), *Employability. From Theory to Practice*. New Brunswick: Transaction Publishers.

# 9.   Home help work: balancing loyalties

## Marie Hjalmarsson

In home help work, many things are as they have always been. The main work tasks of caring for people in need of support and assistance remain the same. Important parts of the work similarly continue to be people-to-people relationships with elements of both joy and difficulty. The home help services in Sweden are still publicly funded, financed by taxes and organized by local councils. Private and for-profit agencies are a growing industry in Sweden, but the municipal responsibility for home health and home care still dominates. But much has also changed, and working in home help services in the 2000s is different than in the past. The reorganization of municipal home help services that really took off in the 1980s has had considerable consequences, not only for those who use home help but also for the staff's ability to perform their work. One of the arguments for the reorganization was based on economic consider-ations, where the vision was a welfare policy governed by an economic/instrumental rationality (see, for example, Drugge 2003; Eliasson 1992; Szebehely 1996). This has meant a rise in market thinking, where cost efficiency has been equated with care efficiency. This in turn has led to rationalization measures in the form of a downgrading of priorities and cuts to certain work tasks, above all household-related tasks such as cleaning. Another argument put forward was that it was a way to upgrade the value of home help work. In connection with this, demands on enhancing skills were also raised, where certain types of knowledge and skills were advocated over others.

   In the study described in this chapter, I looked at the consequences that ideas about economic and instrumental rationality have for home help workers.[1] Special focus has been placed on the introduction of handheld computers in the home help work, to record hours and register what is done during the workday, and how this tracking affects the home help workers' discretion to act, when only certain skills are made visible. The study shows how home help staff are forced to develop their *balancing skills* to continue to provide the care they do for the elderly. The far-reaching marketization and economization of home help services contribute to an intensification of loyalty conflicts in the daily work. The staff are forced to decide between the immediate needs and wishes of the care recipients, and formal and detailed rules on how the home help work is to be carried out. When handheld computers were introduced as an instrument to make visible and micro-manage work performance, the loyalty of home help workers in relation to various interests was put to the test, and the balancing intensified. Being able to *balance one's loyalty* to different stakeholders is therefore a skill that has increased in importance in home help services, as employees are expected to be responsible for both the quality of the work carried out and for the organization's reputation and welfare. Can this balancing act mean that human values in home help operations can be preserved despite rationalizations and increased bureaucracy (cf. Drugge 2003; Ellström, Ekholm and Ellström 2003)? One argument that speaks for this is that employees sometimes break the formal rules in order to get all of the elements of the work to function smoothly and to continue to provide quality services. The chapter is based on an ethnographic study that followed a group of home help workers in a Swedish municipality during the years 2003–2005 (Hjalmarsson 2009).

## INFLUENTIAL TENDENCIES

The following sections address two interacting politically directed tendencies and how they have affected (and continue to affect) home help services: economization and marketization in the welfare sector; and ideas about education initiatives, where certain knowledge and skills are made visible while others remain hidden.

### Micro-management – an Effect of Economization and Marketization

The idea of social solidarity with weaker members of society and those in need of help, which forms the basis of the welfare society, has taken on more and more elements of economic and instrumental rationality. Lundquist (1998: 135 ff.) describes the change in the welfare sector as an economization, concluding that it gives rise to an intensification of tensions between human interests and market economy principles. This economization is seen in, among other things, a change in language use. The words and concepts used to interpret the welfare task, with social justice as a fundamental human value, have increasingly been replaced by economic terms. Defining and evaluating activities according to economic principles when human values should take precedence has consequences – not only for those who are recipients in the welfare system, but also for those tasked with interpreting and providing the welfare professionally, on an everyday basis. The drive for cost efficiency also means that models for management and organization are borrowed from traditional industrial production contexts and tested in activities with completely different content and purposes (McKenzie 2001: 59–65). It is uncertain whether these borrowed attempts actually create the conditions for better efficiency, since it is more a question of ideal pictures that are applied rather than methods adapted to the activities themselves (Lundqvist 1998: 146). This also implies constraints in the employees' ability to act in the work situation (cf. Lundqvist 1998; McKenzie 2001; Rasmussen 2004; Star and Strauss 1999).

This overarching change shows up in the reorganization of the work in home help services. It means that the previous situation-adapted home help services that were regulated with respect to time, came to be regulated in terms of both time and content. Home help services that used to be carried out according to a mutual agreement between the person needing the care and assistance and the home help staff, became instead micro-managed tasks regulated by formal decisions regarding assistance. A care recipient, who earlier received a specific number of hours of help per week for services that he or she had mutually agreed upon with the home help staff, received instead access to a number of time-specified assistance activities. The responsibility for the daily planning of home help work was transferred from the home help staff to a supervisor. Gradually, the responsibility also became further redistributed. Care recipients and possible family members participated when a home care organizer made a formal assessment regarding the content and extent of the care recipient's need for assistance. The assistance assessment is still used as the formal guide, but much of the responsibility for the daily planning has now been transferred back to the home help staff. The process can be such that one or two people from each work group (sometimes according to a rotating schedule) take responsibility for the daily planning and distribution of tasks.

Detailed regulation of the work of home help staff in the form of specific sub-tasks that are carried out at a certain time during a home services visit has consequences for home help workers' ability to balance loyalties to their care recipients, employer and colleagues. The arguments put forward included the principle of fairness, in which the position of the care recipients should be strengthened. From having earlier been situation-adapted and directly user-guided to having become predetermined and governed by formal decisions regarding assistance, the new way of working also helped to make it possible to estimate costs and revenue of the services performed. The care recipient became a kind of customer who, in addition to contributing via taxes, also paid for the services that were delivered. These revenues were not sufficient to balance the costs of home help units, but were nevertheless a starting point when assessments were made of the (economic) efficiency of the activities and the staff (see, for example, National Board of Health and Welfare 2005).

The idea that care and assistance can be measured in units of time and assessed using economic measures has also meant that audits have been carried out (national as well as local) of the home help staff's work performance using the micro-management of home help services as a starting point. We may conclude that home help staff's work hours with associated costs for wages etc. (*working time*) are higher than the time-regulated home help work that users pay for (*client time*). The discrepancy between working time and client time that becomes apparent in this context is referred to as 'indefinable time'. This latitude in the work hours of home help workers is defined as an efficiency problem and the amount of *indefinable time* in home help services is a topic of debate both locally and nationally (Hjalmarsson 2009; National Board of Health and Welfare 2005).

It should be added that other personnel categories in health and social care are also the subject of similar audits. The work efforts of home help staff appear, however, to be especially intriguing to measure and control. As the employer, it is essential for the municipalities to create opportunities to utilize their personnel as economically as possible during work hours. Even for the municipalities as providers of welfare, with the National Board of Health and Welfare as their supervisory body, the performance of the home help workers is key to being able to establish user-related quality and productivity. The specific interest in measurement and control of home help staff's work performance is also enhanced by two actual conditions. Firstly, home help work is a mobile form of work partially carried out in public spaces: in stores, on streets and in squares, at medical clinics, pharmacies, etc. This public aspect creates occasions for the public to ponder how home help workers are performing their work when they are 'in town'. Secondly, the system for detailed categorization of home help services in accordance with assistance entitlements decisions, which also constitutes the basis for how home help work is organized, in itself creates the opportunity for some degree of auditing. The work that is performed and that can be divided into predetermined categories can be measured, in terms of time, and the content can be specified. The performance that fits into the categorization system, however, tends to be valued higher than that which is more difficult to define and categorize.

## EXPERIENCE-BASED KNOWLEDGE – A HIDDEN COMPETENCE

What employees need to know to be regarded as competent enough to be able to perform their jobs is influenced by the spirit of the times as well as by impactful economic and political ideas. Through the 1990s and beginning of the 2000s, we have seen how ideas about lifelong learning and knowledge enhancement have changed our view of what competence is and what competence is desirable (see Chapter 1 of this book). Caring work and support is sometimes described as people-intensive and therefore primarily not as knowledge-intensive (cf. Giertz 1999). When initiatives to boost knowledge are initialized in this type of work, the main focus has been scientifically accepted knowledge (often referred to as evidence-based), for example, medical knowledge. This has significance for what is considered necessary in order to stay current with respect to today's new working life. Here, there is a risk that this may lead to a cropped picture of many jobs' actual and potential core skills. Many jobs still contain 'old' work tasks that demand 'old' knowledge and capabilities (cf. Chapter 10). The experience-based knowledge used in many jobs is seldom regarded as formal competence, and there is a risk that its potential with respect to organizational development as well as personal development is underrated. When a need for renewed competences is defined by performance assessments or development initiatives, both local and national, there is a risk that experience-based knowledge and capabilities may be overlooked. Similarly, there are many jobs that succeed or fail on the employees' willingness and ability to pursue continual and day-to-day learning in work situations.

Health and social care is an occupational field that contains work processes where ethical, social, educational and psychological aspects form the basis of action and must be considered, often under extreme time constraints. These work elements involve knowledge and abilities that can be difficult to define in that they are taken for granted and constitute obvious requirements for performing the work. This applies to a particularly high degree in home help work. The experience-based knowledge and abilities required for these work elements is situation-bound and difficult to make visible. One of the requirements for being able to develop them is that opportunities be created in the home help work for continual learning, by allowing employees a fairly high degree of discretion to act in the work situation. When this is reduced through micro-management, it not only affects the quality of the care and support but also possibilities for learning in the work situation (cf. Drugge 2003; Eliasson 1992; Ellström, Ekholm and Ellström 2003; Rasmussen 2004).

The dominating content of home help work is the provision of social care and support. This means providing people who live in their own homes with the assistance, support and care they need to manage in their day-to-day lives. For home help workers, an important prerequisite for these work tasks is an ongoing acquisition of knowledge about the care recipients in order to meet their needs and wishes in a professional manner. Working in home help thus demands multifaceted competences. These should include a certain degree of knowledge about diagnoses, disease conditions and treatment, which is offered by way of secondary education for assistant nurse and/or professional development in the form of contract training programmes and one-day courses. It is also important that home help workers (as well as other professional groups with a relationship to clients, care recipients, students, etc.) have both the possibility and ability to develop experience-based knowledge in order to be able to act professionally in care relationships. This knowledge development can consist of testing and improving situation-adapted work methods for performing health and social care, as well as more general strategies to get the task of home help in its entirety to function smoothly. This competence base has both a collective and individual dimension. It has to do with coherent, collective experience-based knowledge complemented by individually developed and situation-adapted strategies for action.

## HANDHELD COMPUTERS MAKE SOME THINGS VISIBLE AND HIDE OTHERS

Within home help services, attempts have been made to streamline, in various ways, how the personnel work, and this has had an effect on the workers' ability to act as well as on the development of experience-based knowledge in home help work. On the initiative of municipal management, handheld computers were being tested in the work group I studied during the years 2003–2005 to make visible how home help staff used their work hours. The staff were expected to record the activities they performed during work hours in real time. With the aid of the handheld computers, they were to enter what they were doing and how long it took, all in accordance with the categorization system that forms the basis of the assistance granted to care recipients. The computer's menu allows the home help workers to select a category for a work task performed, and the amount of time the task takes is measured in real time by way of the computer's clocking function. The computers thus contain personal information about the care recipient and information about the services he or she has been granted. The introduction of handheld computers can be seen as an attempt to change the way home help staff work, from situation-adapted and recipient-oriented to a more strict adherence to home help services' rules for how the work should be carried out. However, the computers were not presented as an instrument of control in the first place, but as an opportunity for home help staff to show that they are doing their job in a professional manner. Professionally performed home help work is defined in this context as following the assistance decisions as a basis for the work to be done. The computers were also presented as something that could potentially raise the status of the home help services profession.

When handheld computers are introduced to measure and record home help staff's work performance, it is yet another in a series of examples of management's attempts to control employees' work performance. In this case, it means that the home help staff and their activities during work hours are questioned and audited. Monitoring employees' job performance is, however, neither uncommon nor new.[2] The attempts to audit the workday activities of home help personnel have, on the other hand, new elements in the 2000s. Auditing is made possible in new ways by developments in information and communications technology (ICT). Handheld computers are examples of how new tools can be used for old purposes.

From a learning perspective, the handheld computer project has an impact on knowledge development in home help work. One expects to find knowledge about care recipients and their needs in the computers by connecting to the municipality's central system for health and social care activities, which contains decisions regarding assistance. The development of knowledge related to care recipients and their needs has transferred earlier, with other professional groups (home care organizer and supervisors) taking over the responsibility. From having been an informal agreement in a care relationship, it became a formalized and regulated process with investigations and decisions carried out by a handling officer formally trained for the task. The handheld computers are manifesting this knowledge transfer. It is also strikingly visible in that the home help staff must have the computers with them throughout the entire workday and it is there that the information is processed.

The handheld computers are instruments of governance and control, and have an influence on the employee's discretion to act in the workplace. It is expected that the aspect of home help work's degree of freedom, referred to as indefinable time, can be identified and audited with the help of the computers. But the computers cannot make visible things that do not fit into the software's predetermined and limited categorization system. A significant part of the work done in home help services can be described as constantly ongoing 'background work' (Star and Strauss 1999: 20–21). Background work is work that is necessary in order to be able to perform the main work tasks. It is a part of all work, but is found to a higher degree in jobs where high demands are placed on accessibility, and where workers must be prepared for unexpected events, such as in home help work. Background work has an informal nature and is a prerequisite for workers being able to perform more formal work tasks. It is difficult to see the results of background work since it consists of constantly ongoing processes that enable the performance of work tasks where more visible results can be shown. It can be a matter of fairly concrete elements such as acquiring knowledge in order to be able to provide care, or to develop and use techniques (or 'tricks' as home help workers call them) that enable both the care and the planning and organization to function smoothly. A basic premise for this continual knowledge development is a loyal mindset: a will to make problem-solving smooth, and a desire to be helpful, responsible and trustworthy. In the next section, the background work of home help personnel is described. This involves knowledge and skills that are hidden in a system of categorizations and time measurements, but that nonetheless represent important work performance. What is it that takes time in home help work?

## THE HIDDEN COMPETENCE OF HOME HELP WORK

Home help workers interpret and carry out their work tasks in numerous different ways. As noted earlier, care situations have a large element of situation-adapted problem-solving, where continual knowledge development about the care recipients, their needs, expectations and wishes, is a necessary ingredient. There are individual as well as local and cultural variations in how home help work is performed, but within this variation a pattern still appears. *The home help worker strives to conduct him- or herself as someone you can depend on and who is ready to help out and manage the situation regardless of who or what is involved, and when.* They therefore have a *loyal attitude* in much of what they undertake during work hours. To whom or to what the loyalty of home help staff should be directed is something they weigh more or less consciously in the day-to-day work. One home help worker expressed the basic premise of this loyal mindset as: 'You make it work, no matter what ...'

They use techniques to remain flexible, both emotionally and with respect to knowledge and skills, in order to be reliable and responsible. Home help staff solve problems by fixing and arranging things so that barriers and difficulties are detected and can be eliminated before they become unsolvable. 'Fixing and arranging' is the home help workers' collective term for what they do to make home help work function smoothly. It can be a matter of quickly solving problems as they arise, at the same time as thinking strategically. This occurs daily and is an essential dimension of home help work. These problem-solving sessions are part of what homecare personnel call 'the endless planning', since it is repeated over and over again. For example, one person may offer a solution to an acute problem, another may have an alternative solution, and by talking it through they often agree on a compromise. These problem-solving sessions are creative and often transpire quickly and efficiently. There is a high level of flexibility with respect to new solutions and new ways of carrying out old tasks. There is also considerable adaptability to what co-workers want.

They coax and cajole care recipients to provide care even under difficult circumstances. The expression 'to cajole' (*lirka*) is also used when the employees tell each other about happenings in the day-to-day work and how they approached a situation, and when they discuss problematic situations encountered with care recipients. Everyone appears to agree on what the word means. The expression serves as a tool for developing and refining, together with one's workmates, their ability to coax and cajole care recipients. When I ask the home help personnel to explain what 'cajoling' involves, they tell me that playful joking is an important ingredient: '*Cajoling with people*, some people you need to *cajole*. With some care recipients who don't want to do certain things, you have to talk them into it and joke with them a little'. This joking that is required is adapted to the situation and the individual. Even here, one must tread lightly and test the waters, using one's knowledge about each individual to decide how to apply the joking. Situation-adapted joking and knowledge about each individual care recipient enables them to deal with the difficulty of helping a person who appears not to want that help:

> You can't just go in and say now you have to have a shower. If it's someone you know, then you learn to know after a while what you should say and how to take them, how you can joke them into it. Then they get into the shower

anyway. But it's really hard with a person you don't know; you can't go in and force them, but it takes a while.

They also cajole with colleagues, managers and other actors to make home help function smoothly. They develop an ability to 'adjust' emotionally in care situations, as well as in relation to other aspects and other actors in the work situation. The home help workers strongly emphasize that when you work in social care and support it is important to put a proper, pleasant and happy face forward, even if it is not always easy to be happy and pleasant. They highlight the importance of being able to adjust in relation to care recipients:

> You have to play a role sometimes, a lot of the time. You have to put on a mask. Then I think, okay, now I've got to go in and do this, and now I'm going to do this or that, and then I know that 45 minutes have gone by and now it's done. That's how it feels sometimes, because you're not always at your best. No-one is. And if you're not, this is a pretty tough job.

The home help workers also express a conflict between acting according to the formal rules for performing the work and being compassionate and emotionally flexible. When home help staff follow the formal rules for how home help work should be performed, it is sometimes seen as something that makes providing care more difficult. In one interview, a woman in the home help group talks about how she thinks home help workers should act:

> I don't mean that they should work a lot more, and give the person much more, but that they could just maybe open up a bit. Show some warmth, not everyone does that. It depends on their personality, some people have a harder time with that … Some just find it easier to deal with people than others. I really believe that. If you're strict like that, where everything has to be by the rules, it can be hard. Then it's more difficult to work in this job. You have to be a little, like, that you can solve things as they come up.

'Fixing and arranging', 'cajoling' and 'adjusting'[3] are difficult to define, but at the same time obvious elements of the work, and the home help workers describe them as central for the home help work to function smoothly. Some of the respondents in the study firmly claimed that they are preconditions for the work to function at all. The willingness and ability of home care staff to engage in continual learning make home help work possible. They 'learn by doing' (Dewey 1916/1997), where mistakes are made and the testing of alternative solutions and work methods is something that is ongoing. Fixing and arranging, cajoling and adjusting are elements of work performance that presuppose the integration of informal learning in the work.

Another important skill that is difficult to make visible is the balancing of loyalties. The loyal way of thinking and acting of home help workers are rooted in the care relationship. They are above all loyal in their daily meetings with care recipients, but also in the planning before these encounters. In actual care situations, being responsible, adaptable and reliable is a prerequisite for the provision of care. This means that their loyalty is, firstly, directed towards care recipients, but is also expressed in other situations and contexts. It exists in relation to colleagues in the day-to-day work, in contexts where the home help operations and their organization demand a loyal home help staff, or when the integrity of the professional role must be maintained. A loyal mindset is a rational action and functions as a fundamental value and goal for the actions of home help workers. One home help worker describes her thought process when it comes to doing extra work tasks, even when the care recipient is not entitled to them according to the formal assistance entitlement. She defends her actions on the basis of loyalty toward the care recipient:

> If someone needs to pick something up from the pharmacy, they've run out of it at home, and maybe don't have family, then you do it. Or if they need you to do some shopping, if they're out of milk on a Friday afternoon. Then you go and buy a litre of milk even if you're not supposed to. But that's so that everything works, to provide good care.

She goes on to explain to me the possible consequences if workers don't follow the rules, when they act out of loyalty to the care recipient:

> So, if you're somewhere [with a care recipient] and maybe you wash the windows, and then they ask the next person: *Why can't you wash the windows? She did.* Then it can get a little weird ... And then maybe that person does it, and then the next one gets asked: *Why don't you do it?* Then there can be a bit of conflict.

Washing windows for care recipients is not included in the home help work, but if someone does it anyway conflicts can arise in the work group, and this is not desirable. Loyalty towards the care recipient has its limits.

Consequently, performance of the home help work means that the staff sometimes bend the rules and act on their own decisions so that things function smoothly and a reasonable quality can be maintained. With the introduction of the handheld computers, however, more attention is paid to home help workers' loyalty to the organization and following its formal rules. The computers contribute to an intensification of loyalty conflicts, and it makes it harder for the workers to weigh the different interests against one another. A kind of 'balancing skill' acquires renewed importance in the home help work.

## A BALANCING ACT OF GROWING IMPORTANCE

Home help staff's balancing of loyalties is put to the test when the requirements and conditions of home help activities change. It is not always easy to know where to direct one's loyalty and this can sometimes mean that different interests conflict with one another. Home help workers often find themselves in situations where they have to decide which or whose interests to fulfil. In the day-to-day work, they weigh, more or less consciously, their loyalties towards care recipients, the service's organization and rules, and co-workers. These decisions have to do with the home help workers reflecting on where to direct their loyalty, but also on the strength of that loyalty. The loyalty towards care recipients can, for example, be affected by the response they get to their actions. The home help workers in my study say that it is easier to take more responsibility, engage, and adapt themselves, when the care recipients are appreciative and satisfied. This troublesome but commonly occurring balancing act usually means weighing what is best for the care recipient against following the organization's rules and norms. One home help worker describes the situation as follows:

> … sometimes I've done more than I should, and sometimes I've said no and tried to explain in a nice way. Often the person in question doesn't want to accept or understand. *How can the municipality not let me have help with this or that? Who's going to help me?* It can be both the assistance and the municipality as a whole that they're dissatisfied with, and then maybe I do a little more.

Home help workers are thus continually weighing the pros and cons of being loyal to care recipients in the here and now, and loyally adhering to the organization's rules regarding the performance of home help work. But such deliberation also occurs in cases where loyalty towards co-workers is important:

> … if Asta [a care recipient] hasn't been granted shopping, and then I go and do the shopping for her because she's out of milk or she doesn't have this or that. Then I do it even though she hasn't been granted that service. So next time, when Karin [a co-worker] goes in and Asta asks her to do it, then Asta won't to be very happy with Karin. So, I may seem really nice for doing these [extra] services, but I'm doing my co-workers a disservice by performing a bunch of tasks that haven't been granted. That's the danger when you start doing lots of things over and above what we're supposed to do.

The home help workers sometimes break the formal rules when they make choices like these. When they perform other and/or additional services for care recipients besides those that have been granted according to the assistance entitlement, they are acting in a situation-adapted manner with the care recipient's best interests in mind. They do what they believe should be done according to their interpretation of what it means to be a competent home help worker. The organization/management can then decide to look the other way with respect to the extra services home help workers are providing, or to initiate measures to change the home help staff's way of working. When home help workers' deviations from formal rules are not a disruptive activity, but are instead a subtle, sensitive balancing that does not change the nature of home help operations, management chooses to look the other way. Thus, the actions of home help workers are (re)interpreted by management such that they are not regarded as a breach of the rules but as something that makes operations function and allows them to maintain a certain level of quality. The actions of the organization's management can, however, appear inconsistent, since they actually initiated the handheld computer project in order to measure and control the way home help staff work in accordance with the service's/organization's formal rules. But the attempt to 'make *indefinable time* more visible' with the help of handheld computers is expressed more as a way of showing how much is done rather than questioning and changing it. The operating manager articulates it as follows:

> Our personnel are professional, they do this and this when they're not at the care recipient's home. We use every minute; we're not sitting back with our arms crossed. This [the handheld computers] is a way for me to show that. It feels extremely important in order for us to be credible.

The home help workers are put in a double bind (Bateson 1972) of sorts, as they are exposed to two conflicting messages, which creates uncertainty about what it is that applies. They are described as trustworthy and responsible, at the same time as their work performance becomes the subject of an audit. They are unable to question this auditing because they would then risk being seen as having something to hide.

The home help workers' balancing act with loyalties is an old, proven skill that receives new and increased importance with the reorganization of home help work. In step with rationalization and increased bureaucratization, home help workers are developing strategies to cope with the changing work conditions and new forms of governance they are faced with. As an employee, it is a matter today of not only taking the responsibility included in the concrete work tasks, but also shouldering an implicit responsibility for the service's/organization's best interests (this can apply to both the economics, and to the organizing and development of home help), and in home help services the employees do this by balancing loyalties. Taking care of the care recipients often comes first, but increasing responsibility for and adaptation to home help services as a market economy actor and as an organization with rules and norms, lead to an intensification of this balancing. In their choices, the workers take into account home help service's financial situation, the organization's culture, with formal and informal rules, and home help's reputation as a good provider of welfare. In addition to this, loyalty to one's colleagues – as co-workers, as representatives of the profession and as fellow human beings – is also a consideration.

It is likely that similar balancing acts occur also in other professions. In *triangle professions* (Szebehely 1995), where relations to (at least) three stakeholders are involved, the ability to balance different loyalties becomes an important skill. This can be a matter of professions involving relations to some type of user and to an organization/business, as well as to colleagues/a professional identity. This means that, in addition to relations to management and colleagues, these jobs include also relations to some form of user, for example, clients, patients, students or care recipients (see Figure 9.1). In addition to certain jobs in health and social care, teaching can also be seen as a triangle profession where balancing between loyalties is important.

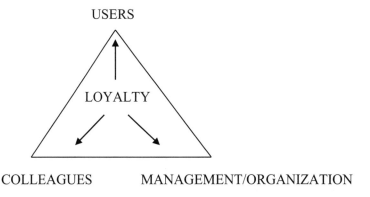

*Figure 9.1  Balancing loyalty*

The relationships to users in a triangle profession are long-term and characterized by continuity, and build on ideas of empathy for and a commitment to other people. These jobs are also often (though not always) driven by a desire to do good, to help and to be of service. A cautious assumption is that the higher degree of micro-management in a triangle profession, the higher the demands on the employees' ability to balance different interests. In jobs where profit is the main driving force for operations, but where the work content involves assisting, supporting and contributing to people's development, high demands are likely put on the balancing acts of employees.

## CONCLUDING DISCUSSION: BALANCING LOYALTIES

In health and social care activities where there is a tendency for economic values to receive increasing influence, management and organization methods are changing. Human values, flexible organizing and trust in the employees' ability to do a good job tend to be secondary to economic values, instrumental rationality and control. The ways of controlling and managing employees appear, however, to have a certain duality. While traditional disciplining attempts with elements of Taylorism are carried out to manage how the staff work so that formal rules are followed, certain breaches of the rules are *at the same time* accepted, since the quality of the health and social care becomes increasingly dependent on the employee's ability to bend the rules to perform the work. An old, proven care skill is put to use to meet new conditions, and the home help workers' balancing of loyalties enables them to keep up with a questionable change in work life. But they are also faced with mixed messages and conflicts of loyalty are becoming increasingly frequent and more difficult to handle.

Home help workers develop their balancing skills by continually using and refining their agility when faced with changing situations and circumstances in their work. This is true despite the fact that home help services are a field where such learning does not pay off in the form of formal qualifications or career opportunities. Neither does it affect wage increases or employability to any great extent. The seamless balancing that home help workers demonstrate is a way of responding to a newer form of governance by way of self-discipline (Foucault 1991). It is no longer merely a matter of, as an employee, adapting and being shaped, but of being creative by overstepping and testing the boundaries. These newer forms of management technologies in an increasingly marketized environment are also expressed in home help services (cf. Ball 2002, 2009; McKenzie 2001). Continually choosing between human values, market (economic) values and individual/collegial autonomy becomes an increasingly important skill in home help work. When employees in home help services develop and refine this skill in order to deal with changing work conditions, it is not something they do because they have been forced or even encouraged to do so. Home help workers act on their own, bend the rules, and do what they consider to be good work. They break the organization's rules because their loyalty towards the care recipients outweighs them. Stretching the limits of what is permitted in the workplace may be what makes performing the work tasks possible and enables problems to be solved in a seamless manner. Management overlooks the staff's actions precisely because these actions are what make operations function smoothly and enable good quality to be maintained.

In addition to self-discipline, there are other recognizable characteristics of this newer form of governance: there is a mobile exercising of power with no fixed address that is difficult to trace. It quietly slips in and is almost impossible to localize to one power centre. McKenzie (2001) calls this newer form of power 'nomadic'. For home help workers, this means that it is difficult to voice objections. When the handheld computer project is presented as a way of raising the status and quality of the work as well as strengthening the rights of care recipients, it is difficult for home help workers to object. They want to appear open to development, quality conscious and, above all, loyal to the care recipients. Even if the actions of home help workers have large elements of self-discipline and the nomadic power makes it difficult to object to, it does not mean a passive acceptance of the state of things. Home help workers stage an informal resistance of sorts when they balance loyalties (cf. Ackroyd and Thompson 1999; Scott 1985). This balancing can be regarded as subversive since it is in fact an action that disrupts power relations. Home help workers make their own interpretation of what good home help work is and diligently act accordingly – despite the fact that this sometimes conflicts with the norms of home help services and intentions of management, and despite that it also means that their work performance and skills may be questioned.

## NOTES

1. The research that this chapter is based on was made possible through a PhD position at the Learning In and For the New Working Life (*Lärande i och för det nya arbetslivet*, LINA) research centre at University West, and through the Graphical Component-based Architectures for the Future (GCAF) project and the LearnIT research programme, funded by the Knowledge Foundation (*KK-stiftelsen*) of Sweden.
2. Cf. F.W. Taylor's scientific management system for the division of labour, management and organizing for maximum utilization of staff. The fact that work is 'taylorized' can mean

rationalizing by way of regulating the time and content of work tasks for a more efficient performance of work elements (see, for example, Huzell 2005; Theliander 1999).
3. These are terms used by the home help workers themselves (in Swedish: *ordna och dona*, *lirka* and *ställa om sig*, respectively).

# REFERENCES

Ackroyd, Stephen and Paul Thompson (1999), *Organizational Misbehaviour*. London: Sage.

Ball, Stephen J. (2002), 'Performativity and fragmentation in "postmodern schooling"', in John Carter (ed.), *Postmodernity and the Fragmentation of Welfare*. London: Routledge, pp. 187–203.

Ball, Stephen J. (2009), 'Privatising education, privatising education policy, privatising educational research: Network governance and the "competition state"', *Journal of Education Policy*, 24(1), 83–99.

Bateson, Gregory (1972), *Steps to an Ecology of Mind: Collected essays in anthropology, psychiatry, evolution and epistemology*. Chicago, IL: University of Chicago Press.

Dewey, John (1916/1997), *Democracy and Education*. Gothenburg: Daidalos.

Drugge, Christina (2003), *Learning in the care of elderly people*. Doctoral thesis no. 2003. Department of Teacher Education. Luleå University of Technology.

Eliasson, Ros-Marie (ed.) (1992), *Egenheter och allmänheter. En antopologi om omsorg och omsorgens villkor*. Lund: Studentlitteratur.

Ellström, Eva, Bodil Ekholm and Per-Erik Ellström (2003), *Verksamhetskultur och lärande: om äldreomsorgen som lärandemiljö*. Lund: Studentlitteratur.

Foucault, Michel (1991), *Discipline and Punish: The birth of the prison*. Harmondsworth: Penguin.

Giertz, Eric (1999), *Kompetens för tillväxt – verksamhetsutveckling i praktiken*. Malmö: Celemiab International.

Hjalmarsson, Marie (2009), *Lojalitet och motstånd: anställdas agerande i ett föränderligt hemtjänstarbete*. Gothenburg: Acta Universatis Gothoburgensis no. 285.

Huzell, Henrietta (2005), *Management och motstånd. Offentlig sektor i omvandling – en fall studie*. Karlstad: Karlstad University Studies 2005:4.

Lundqvist, Lennart (1998), *Demokratins väktare: ämbetsmännen och vårt offentliga etos*. Lund: Studentlitteratur.

McKenzie, Jon (2001), *Perform or Else: From discipline to performance*. London and New York, NY: Routledge.

National Board of Health and Welfare (2005), *Tid för vård och omsorg – Hur använder personalen inom vården och omsorgen om äldre och funktionshindrade personer sin tid?* www.socialstyrelsen.se.

Rasmussen, Bente (2004), 'Between endless needs and limited resources: The gendered construction of a greedy organization', *Gender, Work and Organization*, 11(5), 506–24.

Scott, James C. (1985), *Weapons of the Weak: Everyday forms of peasant resistance*. New Haven, CT: Yale University Press.

Star, Susan Leigh and Anselm Strauss (1999), 'Layers of silence, arenas of voice: The ecology of visible and invisible work', *Computer Supported Cooperative Work*, 8, 9–30.

Szebehely, Marta (1995), *Vardagens Organisering. Om Vårdbiträden och Gamla i Hemtjänsten*. Stockholm: Arkiv.

Szebehely, Marta (1996), 'Från hemsamarit till vårdbiträde', in Ros-Marie Eliasson (ed.) *Omsorgens Skiftningar. Begreppet, Vardagen, Politiken, Forskningen*. Lund: Studentlitteratur, pp. 176–94.

Theliander, Jan (1999), *Studying the Transition of Capitalist Labour: Ure and Taylor in a pedagogical perspective*. Gothenburg: Acta Universatis Gothoburgensis no. 132.

# 10. In the name of evidence-based practice: managing social workers through science, standards and transparency

## Renita Thedvall

It is possible to order a starter package in evidence-based practice for social work from the Swedish government agency, the National Board of Health and Welfare. The package explains what evidence-based practice means in social work and gives examples of systematic, evidence-based methods that social workers can use in their daily work life. It explains the criteria set out by the National Board of Health and Welfare for what is to be considered evidence-based method. The criteria are based on a scale from 1 to 5, where 1 is optimal. A ranking of 1 refers to a randomized controlled trial (RCT), and preferably two trials showing the same results. In a randomized controlled trial, participants are randomly assigned to receive either an intervention or control treatment (often standard care services). This allows the effect of the intervention to be studied in groups of people who are: (1) the same at the outset, and (2) treated the same way, except for the intervention(s) being studied. The idea is then that any differences seen in the groups' outcomes can be attributed to the difference in treatment alone, and not to bias or chance. A ranking of 2 on the scale refers to non-randomized controlled trials with a placebo or untreated control group. A 3 refers to pre- and post-evaluations without a placebo or untreated control group, a 4 to correlation studies, and a 5 to expert opinion.

According to the National Board of Health and Welfare, the first two (a ranking of 1 or 2) are reliable since they include three important criteria.[1] First, the studies use a placebo, untreated group or standard treatment as a control, for comparison. Second, studies in the first category also use a randomized design, that is, who will get which treatment is chosen randomly. Third, it is possible to show statistical evidence that the methods work. The following three (rankings 3, 4 and 5) are not seen as credible, since they cannot be said to follow the three criteria noted. The idea of evidence-based practice is modelled on the medical profession's focus on evidence-based medicine (EBM) in that treatment of patients should be based on scientific evidence gained through randomized control trials. Evidence-based medicine certainly has its merits. Researchers have, however, pointed to problems with randomized control trials and evidence-based methods (Bergmark and Lundström 2006; Lakoff 2007; Petryna 2007; Ecks 2009; Sandler 2011).

There is also reason to believe that transferring a model from medicine into social work has its own problems in that people's psychological and/or substance abuse problems, inability to take care of their children or lack of means to support themselves have dimensions other than those involved in the treatment of stroke or heart failure (see Morago 2006). Some of these problems of translation from one context to another could have partly been solved when introducing evidence-based practice. It is possible to argue that evidence-based practice opens the way for professional analysis and a client perspective, not leaving all decision-making power in the hands of scientific evidence. In an article from 1999, Eileen Gambrill puts forward the idea of using evidence-based practice (EBP) in social work. She argues that social workers should undertake assessments in three stages. The first is to conduct their own professional analysis, the second, to consult evidence-based scientific research in the area that relates to the client, and the third and final stage is to take into account and weigh in the client's values and expectations (Gambrill 1999). This was also how EBP was launched by the Board of Health and Welfare's former director-general, Kerstin Wigzell, in her official government committee report in 2008 (SOU 2008:18).

In practice, however, the introduction of evidence-based practice in social work in Sweden has focused mainly on scientific evidence, in that social workers are to use evidence-based methods in their treatment of clients (National Board of Health and Welfare 2011). Professional assessments and the client perspective can only be taken into account within the framework of evidence-based methods. Furthermore, the professional assessment is also overridden by another organizational trend: the quest for standardization in the use of methods at social services offices in Sweden, also advocated by the National Board of Health and Welfare (see also Timmermans and Berg 2003). One solution has been to set up national guidelines for the assessment process, for example, for substance abuse (National Board of Health and Welfare 2007b) or mental illness (National Board of Health and Welfare 2007a). Another has been to advocate the use of evidence-based methods. This is further emphasized by another ongoing trend that guides government and municipal management of the public sector, which is the notion of *transparency*.

In the area of public policy it has become more important to make *transparent* the ways in which taxpayers' money is used and whether there is observable evidence in the methods used (see also Strathern 2000a; West and Sanders 2003; Garsten and Lindh de Montoya 2008; Thedvall 2006, 2012). Policy-makers see the advantages of certain methods being given the 'evidence based' stamp of approval. The idea is that the use of standardized evidence-based methods in social services will not only make social work scientific, it will also help to make social work easier to audit, since universal use of the same methods enables the measurement of success or failure in a controlled fashion (Power 1997; Strathern 2000b). The accounting firm PricewaterhouseCoopers (PwC) recommends, for example, in a 2009 evaluation of the social services office in focus in this chapter that the social workers should aim for uniformity and stringency in their evaluation methods with respect to substance abusers. PwC suggests that the office should implement the addiction severity index (ASI) advocated by the Board of Health and Welfare. ASI is a structured, evidence-based interview method developed in the US, which has been modified by the Board of Health and Welfare to suit Swedish conditions (National Board of Health and Welfare 2003). Though the social workers at the office had already been trained in this method, it was not being used as the office standard. In its 2011 evaluation, PwC confirmed the use of the ASI model as a standard at the social services office, making the standardization complete.

In many ways, this changes the social workers' individual decision-making power, since it is being moved from the social worker to researchers and laboratories, filtered through the National Board of Health and Welfare, the municipality and auditing firms. This development had already led to a change in how social workers are trained to do their work at the social services office studied, towards an increasing emphasis on formal, standardized training in evidence-based methods. This evokes interesting questions about how the introduction of standardized evidence-based methods is understood by the social workers. What knowledge and learning is valued? How does the organization of knowledge and learning into a standardized form change the work practices of social workers?

The chapter examines how the idea of knowledge based on scientific evidence contributes to a change in social workers' learning and work practices. Particular focus is placed on social workers at a social services office in a municipality in greater Stockholm. In a wider perspective, I discuss how evidence-based practice answers both to trust in scientific knowledge and to an increased scepticism in society with regard to the value of scientific knowledge, by advocating standardized, articulated and transparent knowledge that can be examined and evaluated.

In Sweden, social work is the legal responsibility of the municipalities and is governed by Swedish law, the Social Services Act (Swedish Code of Statutes 2001, SFS 2001:453). Some social work may be outsourced to private firms, but the investigation and assessment of clients, the so-called exercise of authority, has to be performed within the realms of the public sector. This study is based on documents and interviews.[2] An interview study was chosen since I was mainly interested in what knowledge and learning was valued by the management and staff, and how they viewed the introduction of evidence-based practice and standardized ways of performing client assessments. The interviews were conducted at a social services office (hereafter referred to as the Office) in a municipality in greater Stockholm. The documents were collected from the Swedish government, the National Board of Health and Welfare, conference material on evidence-based practice, municipal audit reports, and material from a research and development unit funded and shared by the municipality in question and with seven other municipalities. The social workers interviewed worked in three different units at the Office: social assistance; children and youth; and mental health and substance abuse. At the time of the study, a combined total of 116 people worked in the three units, of whom 12 were men. I conducted 23 interviews at the Office, which included interviews with the head of the Office and unit heads, as well as employees in each unit. Most of the people interviewed had a BA in social work in their educational background. In addition, one interview was conducted with the HR manager at the municipality, two at the National Board of Health and Welfare, one at the Union for Professionals (*Akademikerförbundet,* SSR), and one with a representative from the municipality's R&D unit mentioned above. The interviews were conducted in 2006 and 2007, and the collection of documents has been ongoing.

## EVIDENCE-BASED AS THIN DESCRIPTION

There has been a long and heated debate about whether the social worker's most important methods are based on senses, impressions, perceptions, social norms and values or on scientific knowledge. There are those who argue that social work is a personal skill, an art, that one acquires through learning by doing (England 1986; Nygren and Soydan 1997; Graybeal 2007), often referred to as tacit knowledge (Polanyi

1967). On the other side of the debate are those who believe that the most important methods of social work stem from scientific knowledge. Michael Polanyi (1967), who coined the concept of tacit knowledge, would argue that tacit knowledge is always involved in shaping scientific knowledge. In social work, there are also those who argue that there is no contradiction between the arts and sciences (Eliasson-Lappalainen 2007). During the last 16 years in Sweden, however, we have seen a shift in focus towards the sciences, but in a specific way. Professional or expert knowledge is often perceived as legitimate, since it is understood as based on both experience and the scientific knowledge gained through higher education. Still, knowledge claims made by professions have been increasingly questioned. We have seen a wave of different management techniques and processes to control and evaluate the knowledge used by professions in the form of, for example, audits, standardization of knowledge and evidence-based practice. These processes and techniques have thus changed the practice of medical doctors, nurses and social workers, to focus more on statistical evidence rather than what these practitioners observe and deduce from their experience (Ecks 2009).

This opens up for a discussion of what kind of knowledge we use to organize society. Knowledge based on statistical evidence has been referred to as thin description or thin simplification (Geertz 1973; Scott 1998) in that it is narrow in scope, yet it makes universal claims. Its scope is narrow in the sense that the outcomes are really only valid for those who take part in the randomized controlled trials themselves (Cartwright 2007). Still, evidence-based knowledge has universal claims in the sense that the results of randomized control trials are discussed in terms of evidence-based methods and used all over the globe. The contrast to thin description is thick description (Geertz 1973) or practical knowledge, or metis (Scott 1998), which refers to dense, specialized expert knowledge localized within a profession, field or place. This is knowledge that is based on many different observations, interactions and conversations, much like anthropological knowledge (Engelke 2009). It is based on evidence of a different form than the statistical, combining observations and experiences into standards of judgment for assessing what methods work (cf. Engelke 2009). This kind of evidence based on experience is, however, being devalued, and increasingly so. The use of evidence-based practice entails using methods in social work that have been scientifically proven to work, and the logic is then that they do actually work because they are proven. The social workers should not only rely on their art, but also on science. And the science should be based on standardized knowledge in the form of evidence-based practice, and, in the case of Sweden, preferably that recommended by the National Board of Health and Welfare.

At the centre of this transformation is what Brunsson (2006) calls *mechanisms of hope*, in that people continue to believe in the ideal of the objective and rational model that will solve all the problems of management. These ideal objective and rational management models often come in stable, standardized and reproducible forms (Miller and Rose 1990). Evidence-based practice is no exception. By managing social workers through evidence-based practice, the assessments and work practices are understood to be streamlined through the evidence-based methods recommended by the National Board of Health and Welfare. These standardizations of form rarely take place without negotiations and discrepancies, and they often produce unforeseen consequences (for example, Brunsson and Jacobsson 2000; Dunn 2003, 2004; Tamm Hallström 2004; Lampland and Star 2009). This signals a bureaucratization of processes focusing on the investment in form rather than content (Thevenot 1984).

## STANDARDIZING SOCIAL WORKERS' METHODS BY ORGANIZED LEARNING

The investment in form was evident at the Office where I conducted research. Over the last few years the focus of socials workers' skills development had been on organized courses that taught evidence-based methods. The aim was to standardize the evidence-based methods used so that the client assessments made by the social workers were performed in the same way. The traditional learning in social work, in the form of mentoring, gut feeling and learning by doing, was still part of the learning at the office, but the focus was on the scientific, in the form of research circles, seminars and standardized courses in evidence-based methods. This has changed both the education and training at the Office as well as the practices, in that the intention is that the methods taught should permeate practice at the Office.

### R&D Coffee Sessions, Seminars, Research Circles ...

The focus on social workers' skills development contributed to the organizing of (more or less voluntary) learning opportunities. For example, the Office did cooperate with the local R&D unit in the municipality. The joint R&D units were formed to create a venue for researchers and practitioners in the field of social work to meet. From 1996 to 2002, local and regional R&D units also received financial support from the National Board of Health and Welfare. Since then, the municipalities have been responsible for their funding. Many of the R&D units disappeared when the responsibility for their survival was transferred to the municipalities, but in the municipality where I did my study the R&D unit remained and was active at the Office. The R&D unit held seminars and lectures, and a number of social workers from the Office had also worked for a number of months at the R&D unit, for example, to study whether rehabilitative interventions to prevent further criminal activity for young offenders had worked, or projects relating to promoting children's reading. The social workers were also invited to so-called R&D coffee sessions, which involved morning coffee breaks with lectures. During the year of the current study, they had six such lectures. The lecturers varied, from R&D unit researchers who presented their recent studies, to social workers reporting on their findings from studies at the R&D unit and students from the Department of Social Work at Stockholm University who presented their bachelor's theses.

The Office had also initiated voluntary law interpretation groups. There were law interpretation groups in the children and youth unit, in the mental health and substance abuse unit, and a group was also about to be started for those working with legislation regarding support and services for people with disabilities (LSS). According to one member of management, these groups were extremely popular. The children and youth unit had also started with a research circle led by a researcher from the Department of Social Work at Stockholm University. All of these arenas for knowledge permeated the workplace. The staff were focused on taking part in and familiarizing themselves with recent scientific research. This was particularly visible in the range of courses the Office offered its employees.

## From Gut Feeling to Standardized Courses, Courses and More Courses

The employees interviewed had all participated in organized formal training in the form of courses at the Office. The National Board of Health and Welfare had, for example, advocated national uniformity in the investigations of children through the use of the integrated children's system (ICS), an investigation technique developed in Britain and adapted by the National Board of Health and Welfare for Swedish conditions. The staff at the child and youth unit had also been trained in ICS. The ICS method uses a triangular model to map out the needs of a child in relation to the ability of parents and other adults to meet those needs (National Board of Health and Welfare 2006). The model enabled a systematic documentation of the child's needs, and in turn made it 'clearer to the child and parents, what Social Services does, and clearer to Social Services what the child needs' (National Board of Health and Welfare 2006).

Social workers working in the mental health section had been trained in the CAN method. Similarly to ICS, CAN (Camberwell Assessment of Need) is an evidence-based method that puts the client at the centre and then evaluates the resources in her or his surroundings, such as institutions, health care providers and other people who can help to meet the assessed needs, and assigns a score on a so-called CAN-scale. The substance abuse section had been trained in a different evidence-based method, the Addiction Severity Index (ASI). ASI is a structured interview method developed in the US and adapted by the National Board of Health and Welfare for Swedish conditions (National Board of Health and Welfare 2003). ASI is used primarily as an assessment method for matching treatments for substance abuse (National Board of Health and Welfare 2003). At the time of the interviews, the entire office had also received training in motivational interviewing (MI). The MI method is also client-centred, with a focus on motivating the client to change through interview techniques (www.motivationalinterview.org).

All of these courses and arenas to make social work scientific required coordination. One member of management at the Office also worked full-time with skills development for the social workers. In line with the National Board of Health and Welfare's and the municipalities' ideas on an evidence-based practice, this person worked to find courses in methods based on the best scientific evidence available. Management also wanted to promote the use of a standardized approach at the Office, as illustrated by a young woman working at the mental health and substance abuse unit. She explained to me that when she came to work at the municipality she had already taken part in an ASI course in another municipality. The head of unit still thought it would be best for her to take part in the ASI course in this municipality, since she wanted everyone to have the same approach to ASI. The head of unit argued that different teachers taught differently. In other words, there was little room for individual solutions, and the learning was focused on standardized courses in evidence-based methods, preferably learned from the same teacher. But how did the social workers perceive the focus on standardized evidence-based methods, and what knowledge did they value?

## THE SOCIAL WORKERS' VIEW ON EVIDENCE-BASED METHODS

I sit in the client waiting room, waiting for my interviews. I have three interviews planned today, the first with a woman in the social assistance unit. The room has beige walls and floors and is furnished in typical institutional style made of hard-wearing beech and flame-resistant fabric, in this case green. There are several other people in the room, waiting to meet a social worker. I feel a bit out of place and am conscious of my own privileged position. After a relatively short wait, a woman in her early thirties calls my name. We move into her office and I notice that she also places herself in the chair closest to the door, as many other social workers I have interviewed have done. She explains that it is something she does so that she can easily escape if there are problems with a client. We talk about her work, what is needed to do a good job, and how she feels about the idea of evidence-based practice.

She, like most of the social workers, was interested in working with evidence-based methods. She saw great benefits in their knowledge being made scientific. She noted that she was accustomed to having her decisions and knowledge questioned, and the use of evidence-based methods would make her decisions credible and transparent. Timmermans and Berg (2003: 90) also point out that standardization of knowledge is a way for less established professions to formulate and outline their expertise. In another interview in an office with similar décor, but with different view of the municipality, a social worker, a woman in her forties working at the children and youth unit, explained:

> I think it's really, very important to have evidence-based knowledge and [in the municipality where the study was conducted] we do work with evidence-based practice. More than in many other municipalities where I've worked. And I feel it's much more professional. But, often, it may be at the expense of other knowledge and experience. In our working group, we have many, many years of collective experience of social work.[3]

Another social worker, a woman in her early thirties working at the children and youth unit, felt that the evidence-based methods were useful because they helped to make it clearer and more understandable for the client what social workers do. On the other hand, she said that it was not always easy to see what actually works. As she put it:

> Yes, I believe it's good to use evidence-based knowledge. I think that it can make it a bit easier to understand what we do and don't do. That it's not just our own opinions. But sometimes that doesn't work either. It's hard to know.

I imagine that in [evidence-based] medicine it's easier to check. So if you provide family therapy, or do preventive work, who can say what helped? That's more difficult.

A third social worker, a woman in her late thirties in the mental health and substance abuse unit, said that there are methods that are not evidence-based that she knows, from experience, have worked:

I know that there have been discussions at times about NADA [National Acupuncture Detoxification Association]. That's one example. It's acupuncture given in the ears to addicts to reduce cravings and such. There has been a lot of discussion about that. If we can continue to use it in the county and municipality, even if it's not evidence-based. But we've seen that it works. There, I feel: *Yes, but it's worked, we've seen results. Why should we care that it isn't evidence-based?* So I have to say it's a little bit of both there. Then it's probably always good if you can establish that it's evidence-based. But I don't think we should reject something just because it's not.

The social workers agreed that they should pursue evidence-based practices. They felt that it was more professional. When I asked the social workers what they needed to know to become good social workers they often, however, mentioned different types of knowledge, tacit and experience-based knowledge. Several social workers pointed out that the ability to like people, and to understand and have empathy for them was important. A number of social workers said that social work often involved working on their own prejudices. They had to reflect on why a particular client triggered particular emotions, both positive and negative, and how they had to try to put them aside in their decisions. This was something they learned through experience. The knowledge and qualities that social workers put forward as necessary for being a good social worker included knowledge of the law, good interviewing methodology, personal maturity, empathy, the ability to like people, and having humility. One social worker, a woman in her thirties working at the mental health and substance abuse unit, expressed this as:

Two things: the law is our framework. It's really, really important that we know the law. Then we must be able to see. We must be able to see people … not just as they appear to be, but as they are. And it sounds really vague, but not to be swayed by your own prejudices and preconceptions. And not be so sure that we know best, because we don't. It's obvious that we don't.

Another social worker, the woman in her early thirties working at the social assistance unit notes:

And you need to know a lot about how society works in general. Know something about our social security system. How to go about looking for an apartment. How to conduct yourself and what to do when looking for a job. Pretty basic stuff, but things that you may still need to help people with or advise them on. And then it's obviously an advantage if you find it easy talk to people. Not that you need to be a psychologist, but still be able to meet people in a respectful manner. This is the area that I've developed most since I started working.

Another skill they felt was important was being able to express themselves in writing. Many brought up the importance of writing in clear and plain language in the social services assessments reports. Several noted that this had become much more important in recent years. One social worker told me that she used to be able to write that a need 'can be met by other means'. Now she has to specify 'the other means' by which it can be met. Another social worker described how the assessment reports could earlier be one page long, but that now they were six pages. The written word had become much more important in the day-to-day work of social workers. They argued that the structured, evidence-based methods could be used for clarifying the basis for their decisions to their clients, both verbally and in writing.

When I asked how they learned these skills, most responded spontaneously that it was a matter of learning by doing. Most saw their university studies in social work as a foundation for doing their job, but the work and skills themselves were learned at the Office or came down to personality. One social worker, a woman in her late thirties working at the children and youth unit, explains:

In addition to my education, I think that it's really important to have an interest in people and to have humility. Knowing what your role entails. You are a government official. I also think it's important to be ... to play different roles. I speak in one way when I talk to young people and another when I talk to people in other professions. And yet another when I hold meetings or talk to parents. 'Matching' is what it's called in social work.

I asked more specifically what knowledge they found useful from their university training. One social worker, the woman in her thirties from the mental health and substance abuse unit, replied: 'There I'm a bit surprised [*laughs*]. No, but I've learned to think critically and look for information, to find information ... At my university, we studied law for a full semester, which is a bit more than in other social work programmes, and I'm grateful for that.'

She went on to say:

Yes, that's a little less clear, but there are naturally things that you take with you. But what are those things? Well, it's the theoretical knowledge. The basics in a way. But when you come out into the real world it's not like you learned in the theoretical courses at university. Reality is different. Yes, the theoretical basis, you might say. Some parts of the job you can only learn through experience.

Several people noted that client interviews were something they could only learn through experience. One social worker said that although they had had interview exercises in their courses at university, it was never the same as in real life. Social workers used the evidence-based methods as tools to both clarify for clients, and to build and create professionalism around their work. Still, when asked what they needed to know to become skilful social workers, most valued other skills. One of these was the so-called gut feeling. This gut feeling stood in contrast to what some social workers perceived as an over-emphasis on the use of evidence-based methods. Nevertheless, the introduction of standardized methods for performing social work at the office had already changed the social workers' practices towards the evidence-based, nudging gut instinct into the background.

## CONCLUSION: SCIENTIFIC, STANDARDIZED AND TRANSPARENT

During the past 16 years, the National Board of Health and Welfare has worked actively to make social work scientific through evidence-based practice. The evidence sought in evidence-based practice is scientific in a certain sense. It is not scientific in the sense of qualitative, interactive, experience-based evidence. It is scientific in the form of thin knowledge based on statistical evidence that is narrow in scope, but that has the capacity to move across the globe. This shift towards evidence-based practice takes place at a time when the sciences are being increasingly questioned. Professional knowledge is increasingly met with scepticism, which has led to increased control of these professions' professional knowledge through various administrative tools, such as standardization of knowledge and audits (Rose 1996; Power 1997). For social workers in the current study, this control is exercised in three ways. First, the National Board of Health and Welfare has developed several new standardized national guidelines that all social workers must follow. Second, the social workers were offered standardized courses in evidence-based methods that were not only for the whole local office, or for Sweden, but which originate from the UK, the US or other places. Third, the evidence-based methods are designed in such a way that they can be evaluated. They are standardized. This is in line with the increased demands on policy-makers to make transparent the ways in which tax revenues are used, and whether there is observable evidence in the methods used. There needs to be auditable evidence.

There remains, however, a contradiction in the way science is treated in that there is a trust in science. On one hand, the power to make decisions is moved from the social workers to researchers and laboratories that produce scientific evidence. On the other, policy-makers and government officials do not trust science when arguing for evidence-based methods. That is, they control which evidence-based methods are used through a standardization of knowledge via the National Board of Health and Welfare. This development has already led to a change in how social workers are trained to do their work at the social services office in the study, towards a greater emphasis on formal, standardized training in evidence-based methods. It has also changed the social workers' work practices in that decisions regarding what methods are to be used have been moved from the social worker to research laboratories, and filtered through the Swedish government via the National Board of Health and Welfare, and in this case also the municipality and the auditing firm PricewaterhouseCoopers. In this way, it changes the organization of the social workers' orders in the labour market. Evidence-based practice works as a technology of government (Miller and Rose 1990), managing social workers into performing social work in standardized, observable and comparable ways.

## NOTES

1. http://www.socialstyrelsen.se/fragorochsvar/evidensbaseradpraktik#anchor_1, accessed 2014–10–09.
2. This research was funded by the Swedish Research Council within the framework of *The politics and practices of capability: Lifelong learning for all in a knowledge-intense worklife?* project, led by Christina Garsten.

## REFERENCES

Bergmark, Anders and Tommy Lundström (2006), 'Mot en evidensbaserad praktik – Om färdriktningen i socialt arbete', *Socialvetenskaplig tidskrift*, 2, 99–113.
Brunsson, Nils (2006), *Mechanisms of Hope. Maintaining the dream of the rational organization*. Copenhagen: Copenhagen Business School Press.

Brunsson, Nils and Bengt Jacobsson (2000), *A World of Standards*. Oxford: Oxford University Press.

Cartwright, Nancy (2007), 'Are RCTs the gold standard?', *BioSocieties*, 2, 11–20.

Dunn, Elizabeth (2003), 'Trojan pig. Paradoxes of food safety regulation', *Environment and Planning A*, 35, 1493–1511.

Dunn, Elizabeth (2004), 'A steak is an outcome space. Travelling facts, negotiated meaning and the social construction of safe meat', in Caroline Baille, Elizabeth Dunn and Yi Zheng (eds), *Travelling Facts. The social construction, distribution and accumulation of knowledge*. New York, NY: Campus, pp. 27–43.

Ecks, Stefan (2009), 'Three propositions for an evidence-based medical anthropology', in Matthew Engelke (ed.), *The Objects of Evidence*. Oxford: Wiley-Blackwell, pp. 1–20.

Eliasson-Lappalainen, Rosmari (2007), 'Om olika vägar till kunskap', in Anna Meeuwisse, Sune Sunesson and Hans Swärd (eds), *Socialt arbete. En grundbok*. Stockholm: Natur & Kultur, pp. 319–33.

Engelke, Matthew (2009), *The Objects of Evidence*. Oxford: Wiley-Blackwell.

England, Hugh (1986), *Social Work as Art: Making sense for good practice*. London: Allen and Unwin.

Gambrill, Eileen (1999), 'Evidence-based practice: An alternative to authority-based practice', *Families in Society. The Journal of Contemporary Human Services*, 80(4), 341–50.

Garsten, Christina and Monica Lindh de Montoya (eds.) (2008), *Transparency in a New Global Order: Unveiling organizational visions*. Cheltenham and Northampton, MA: Edward Elgar.

Geertz, Clifford (1973), *The Interpretation of Cultures*. New York: Basic Books.

Graybeal, Clay T. (2007), 'Evidence for the art of social work', *Families in Society*, 88(4), 513–23.

Lakoff, Andrew (2007), 'The right patients for the drug: Managing the placebo effect in antidepressant trials', *BioSocieties*, 2, 57–71.

Lampland, Martha and Susan Leigh Star (eds) (2009), *Standards and Their Stories. How quantifying, classifying and formalizing practices shape everyday life*. London: Cornell University Press.

Miller, Peter and Nicholas Rose (1990), 'Governing Economic Life', *Economy and Society*, 19(1), 1–31.

Morago, Pedro (2006), 'Evidence-based practice: From medicine to social work', *Journal of Social Work*, 9(4), 461–77.

National Board of Health and Welfare (2003), *ASI – En strukturerad intervjumetod för bedömning av alkohol – och narkotikarelaterade problem*. Swedish National Board of Health and Welfare 2003-112-2.

National Board of Health and Welfare (2006), *Grundbok. Barns behov i centrum (BBIC)*. Swedish National Board of Health and Welfare 2006-110-7.

National Board of Health and Welfare (2007a), *Nationell strategi för evidensbaserad praktik för vuxna personer med psykisk sjukdom eller funktionshinder*. Swedish National Board of Health and Welfare 2007-107-25.

National Board of Health and Welfare (2007b), *Nationella riktlinjer för missbruks- och beroendevård*. Swedish National Board of Health and Welfare 2007-102-1.

National Board of Health and Welfare (2011), *Om evidensbaserad praktik.* Swedish National Board of Health and Welfare 2011-5-7.

Nygren, Lennart and Haluk Soydan (1997), 'Social work research and its dependence on practice', *Scandinavian Journal of Social Welfare*, 6(3), 217–24.

Petryna, Adriana (2007), 'Clinical trials offshored: On private sector science and public health', *BioSocieties*, 2, 21–40.

Polanyi, Michael (1967), *The Tacit Dimension.* London: Routledge.

Power, Michael (1997), *The Audit Society. Rituals of verification.* Oxford: Oxford University Press.

Rose, Nicolas (1996), '"The death of the social?" Refiguring the territory of government', *Economy and Society*, 25(3), 327–56.

Sandler, Jen (2011), 'Evangelists for truth as certainty. Evidence-based social policy in the United States'. Paper presented at the AAA in Montreal, Canada, 16–20 November 2011.

Scott, James (1998), *Seeing Like a State. How certain schemes to improve the human condition have failed.* London: Yale University Press.

SOU 2008:18, *Evidensbaserad praktik inom socialtjänsten – till nytta för brukaren.* Stockholm: Fritzes.

Strathern, Marilyn (2000a), 'The tyranny of transparency', *British Educational Research Journal*, 26(3), 309–21.

Strathern, Marilyn (ed.) (2000b), *Audit Cultures. Anthropological studies in accountability, ethics and the academy.* London: Routledge.

Swedish Code of Statutes (2001), Social Services Act. Ministry of Health and Social Affairs. SFS 2001:453.

Tamm Hallström, Kristina (2004), *Organizing International Standardization.* Cheltenham and Northampton, MA: Edward Elgar.

Thedvall, Renita (2006), *Eurocrats at Work. Negotiating transparency in post-national employment policy.* Dissertation, Stockholm University. Stockholm Studies in Social Anthropology, 58.

Thedvall, Renita (2012), 'Negotiating impartial indicators. To put transparency into practice in the EU', *Journal of the Royal Anthropological Institute*, 18(2), 311–29.

Thevenot, Laurant (1984), 'Rules and implements. Investment in forms', *Social Science Information*, 23(1), 1–45.

Timmermans, Stefan and Marc Berg (2003), *The Gold Standard. The challenge of evidence-based medicine and standardization in health care.* Philadelphia, PA: Temple University Press.

West, Harry G. and Todd Sanders (eds.) (2003), *Transparency and Conspiracy. Ethnographies of suspicion in the new world order.* Durham, NC: Duke University Press.

# 11. Skills development: an empty offer?

## Matilda Ardenfors and Jessica Lindvert

Few people question the benefits of skills training in working life. Research shows that skills development creates profitable workplaces and strengthens the health and well-being of employees (Ellström 1996; Holmer 2006: 23; Nilsson 1996; Rönnqvist and Thunborg 1996; Thång 2006). Access to skills development at different employers is mapped on a regular basis by quantitative compilations documenting which employees are offered training, and how access varies according to occupational group, gender and age group, and over time (Statistics Sweden). We know from these studies that those who already have good formal skills and knowledge tend to get more, while those with weaker formal competency get less. People with high education are given access more than low-educated people, public-sector employees participate more than employees in the private sector, and the proportion of women who take part is larger than the proportion of men (Ds 2002:47; Statistics Sweden 2007; SCB 2008; SOU 2000:115; Wikman 2001). In the chapter, we take the discussion one step further and show that *formal access* to skills development in working life and *actual ability* to participate in skills development are not always the same thing.[1]

The reasoning concerning actual ability is inspired by the work of Amartya Sen. Based on the concept of capabilities, Sen criticizes traditional economics' method of measuring economic and social development (1982, 1988, 1993). According to Sen, national economics has singly focused on the *resources* offered to people. He claims instead that people's *ability to transform* resources into actual ability is a more relevant measure because our possibilities of taking advantage of resources are very different. Central to Sen's argument is also the ability to refrain from utilizing those resources that are available. For example, he distinguishes between fasting and starving, where the former is self-chosen, and the latter not. The focus of his arguments is on the *actual* accessibility of resources, rather than the resources as such.

Using an inductive approach, our focus is on the issue of what hinders and what promotes the participation of employees in skills development.

And how do the various factors interact with one another in practice? The study is based on a total of 176 semi-structured interviews with employees, management, union representatives and local labour market actors, carried out in 2004–2007. We conducted a close study of four industries: the automotive industry, the food industry, the Swedish Police, and Social Services. The primary aim has not been to make comparisons between these sectors. The purpose of the broad approach is to identify different types of *hindrance* and how these are linked. In line with Sen, we want to examine what type of skills training people are offered and their ability to take advantage of it.

## LIFELONG LEARNING IN THE LABOUR MARKET

Skills development in working life is discussed here as part of *lifelong learning*.[2] There are many definitions of learning. Some describe it as a change in people's inner and outer behaviour, where their conceptions and knowledge are updated. Others describe learning as an activity of creating (Gustavsson 1996: 63), or a phenomenon that breaks routines (Ellström 1996: 163). Still others view it as a continual process, where learning is something constantly ongoing, from when we are born until we die (Ellström 1996: 167 ff.; Thång 2006: 70). What all of these definitions have in common is that they describe a change; when we learn something new, there is something in us that changes.

In academic contexts, education researchers were for a long time the only ones interested in learning, and then above all the learning of children in school settings (Gustavsson 1996: 50). Today, the interest in learning has expanded to other disciplines, such as political science and economics, sociology, psychology and anthropology. This development is most clearly expressed in the concept of lifelong learning. Lifelong learning implies that learning not only occurs in children but also in adults. The concept also links the formal learning of traditional learning institutions to the informal learning in daily life and work life (CEC 2001: 3 f.; Rubenson 1996: 30; SOU 1999:141, p. 51; SOU 2000:28, p. 38). Lifelong learning has gradually come to acquire more of a 'learning without borders' meaning, a learning outside formal institutions and fixed measuring instruments. The concept calls into question traditional education principles, rote learning, courses with a fixed beginning and end, and face-to-face teaching (Edwards and Usher 2001: 276; Garrick and Usher 2000).

The concept of lifelong learning not only has an academic prehistory, but also a political one. From an international standpoint, Swedish education policy has been a forerunner and worked to achieve a successively longer education in the lives of young people and adults. When the concept was introduced in the 1970s, a point was made to note that it was not only an education policy matter but also a matter of labour market policy. In 1965, Sweden was the first country in the world to adopt the International Labour Organization's Convention 122, regarding the drive to achieve, in the interest of both society and the individual 'full, productive and freely chosen employment' (Prop. 1966:52). In the 1970s, the concept of lifelong learning permeated the Social Democratic vision of levelling hierarchies, promoting democracy and creating opportunities for self-realization for the individual (Gustavsson 1996; Rubenson 2006). At the same time, a number of concrete measures such as advantageous student loans, free post-secondary education, opportunities for retraining and the right to take time off for studies were introduced.

It should be noted that skills development and learning in working life are areas that to a large extent lie outside the immediate responsibility of political decision-makers. In Sweden, the state and municipalities govern the terms and conditions for the basic education system, while matters like occupational development, skills training and transitions are regulated in cooperation with employers and unions (Lindvert 2006). However, this has not stopped political decision-makers from making certain targeted interventions. At the end of the 1980s, for example, a large-scale effort was launched to improve the work environment at workplaces through the Working-life Fund (*Arbetslivsfonden*). This was followed in the 1990s by a five-year adult education initiative (*Kunskapslyftet*) aimed at strengthening the knowledge and skills of people lacking secondary school equivalence and for employees with low education (SOU 1999:141). Thereafter, in the beginning of the 2000s, the Structural Funds programme was developed, where the Swedish state and the EU form regional partnerships to improve skills development in the workplace (Lindvert 2009). The following section presents the four types of work organizations in which the ability to participate in skills development and lifelong learning is investigated.

**The Automotive Industry. Plastal, Scania and Volvo**

The first industry studied, the automotive industry, represents a private-sector work organization that finds itself under extreme pressure today. The industry has to a very high degree experienced the effects of globalization at the national level, in the form of deregulation and international price competition. Production in the industry is organized to facilitate meeting short-term economic profit demands, inspired by the

Toyota Group's successes. Flexible production is viewed as a basic requirement for continued existence, and automotive industry employees today live under the constant threat of production being moved abroad.

The workplaces looked at in this study are Scania AB in Södertälje, Volvo Lastvagnar AB and Plastal AB[3] in Göteborg. A total of 90 semi-structured interviews were conducted with employees, management, union representatives and local labour market policy actors. Interviews have in addition been conducted with the management at three other automotive companies: SAAB Automobil, Volvo Cars Uddevalla and the US automotive supplier Lear.

The workplaces studied were all organized in a similar way – with a production organization and an administrative organization. On the production side were occupational titles like assembler, pre-assembler, and employees with team leader responsibilities (called operation managers at Scania and group representatives at Volvo). On the administrative side were occupational titles such as production manager, technician and production engineer, all of whom worked in proximity to assembly. Other administrative categories had a weaker connection to production.

The most common form of skills development at the workplaces was manufacturing-specific internal training. At Plastal, for example, there was an opportunity for training on the machinery, and at Scania workers who lacked upper secondary qualifications could attend a programme called 'the Scania technician'. At Volvo, there was something called 'production development training' that employees could take part in during work hours. The administrative staff at these companies could usually attend courses in leadership, languages and personal development, and take part in project training.

## The Food Industry. Factory Work in the New Labour Market

The food industry also belongs to the private sector. And, precisely as in the case of the automotive industry, it has suffered big cutbacks in recent years. Large parts of production have been moved abroad at the same time as new technology has been introduced. In contrast to the automotive industry, however, the food industry is dominated by female employees. A total of 36 interviews at three companies were conducted, with HR managers, production workers, administrative staff and union representatives. For reasons of privacy, the names of the food companies looked at in this study have been anonymized.[4]

Like the automotive industry, the workers are organized into two main groups: administrative staff and production personnel. The food companies included in the study have a high and a low season for their goods; some products sell better at Christmas, others during the summer. The fluctuation in production means there is great variation in the need for labour. The difference could vary by up to 100 workers between high and low season (in organizations with a workforce of between 450 to 1100 people). In order to manage these peaks, staffing agencies were often used.

At the time of the study, extensive restructuring was going on at the companies and, with this, also came redundancies. In order to handle the cutbacks, different solutions were used. Some employers handled the layoffs by trying to find other jobs for the employees and offering training, severance pay, or support for the employees to start their own business. Another solution was for a staffing firm to take over the people who had been let go and offer them a permanent position. The employees then received a re-employment guarantee in the event that the original employer needed to hire again. In this way, the employees' expertise was kept close to the company.

The production staff described the access to skills development above all in terms of manufacturing-specific internal training. This could be a matter of learning new data systems or other technology specifically linked to the day-to-day work. At one of the companies, for example, some of the employees were taught to use new machines and then passed this newly acquired knowledge on to their colleagues who were able to 'shadow' the trained employee. This form of skills training was carried out primarily during the low season when there was extra time. On the administrative side of the organization, employees participated in training on a regular basis, and specific management, leadership and specialist training programmes were arranged. The administrative staff at the companies studied were also given the opportunity to take part in courses that were not necessarily related to the company's specific core activities.

### The Swedish Police. Gothenburg Community Policing Districts

In Sweden, the police authority is a publicly run organization that operates under the Ministry of Justice, and whose central administrative body is the National Police Board (*Rikspolisstyrelsen,* RPS). As of 1998, police operations in Sweden are organized by county, forming 21 local police districts, each with its own county police commissioner. The police authority employs approximately 26 000 in total. Of these employees, two thirds are police officers and the rest civilian employees. The Swedish police force is predominantly male. At the time of the study, men made up 81 per cent of the workforce, though in recent years the force has actively worked to increase the proportion of women (polisen.se).

The police training programme includes two years of study at the National Police Academy, funded by student aid, and six months of paid cadet training at a police station. Passing one's cadet training makes one eligible to seek employment as a police officer. Other requirements include experience of working life, a valid driver's licence, and that the applicant is in good health. Body type is also important: the applicant must not be too short in stature or lacking in physical strength. Other qualities of importance include broad-mindedness, an even temper and stress tolerance, as well as a sound lifestyle and a good understanding of the law. Good language skills in Swedish are also required. Newly graduated police officers usually work on patrol for five years before they may apply for other positions within the organization.

The police organization is based on the professional bureaucratic model characterized by a decentralized structure where support and service units are established to assist a professional police corps that carries out the main activities. The county police authorities are responsible for policing at the local level, and since 1995 the local police work is organized according to the community policing model. The organizational principle means that individual police officers should have specific knowledge and skills in the area that they work in. Locally, there should also be ongoing cooperation with other public and private actors in order to reduce criminality (National Police Board 2001: 12).

For the current study, 22 interviews were conducted with employees, management and union representatives in eight of Gothenburg's community policing districts. The access to skills development in Gothenburg community policing districts for the first five-year period was above all comprised of shorter training programmes in computers and instructor training. Employees also had the possibility of taking part in internal training days every six weeks. On these occasions, employees were given the opportunity, for example, to acquire information about laws and regulations, and to participate in study visits or practical training such as marksmanship and self-defence.

## Social Services in a Suburb of Stockholm

Social Services are publicly managed organizations that fall under the National Board of Health and Welfare. It is, however, the municipalities that have the responsibility of carrying out the activities. Social Services work with individual and family social care for children and adults. This can involve financial assistance, introduction for new refugees, assistive devices for people with disabilities, or access to help with addiction or other social problems. To be eligible for employment within Social Services today requires a degree in social work (*socionom*). From earlier having been a profession that did not require an academic degree, the majority of employees now have a *socionom* degree, and most new recruits are graduates who come directly from a social worker programme. The Social Services are highly female-dominated organizations.

The study of the Social Services is based on 28 interviews with employees in individual and family care at a social services office in a Stockholm suburb, as well as staff employed by the National Board of Health and Welfare, the Union for Professionals, and representatives for R&D activities in the municipality. At the social services office, three departments that work with individual and family care were studied: children and youths, reception and financial assistance, and addictions and social psychiatry. Both managers and social workers were interviewed.[5]

At the social services office studied, skills development was seen as an obvious part of the work. The personnel had access to two training days per semester and so-called R&D coffee sessions were arranged on a regular basis. There was also a large selection of courses and seminars for the employees to participate in. The continual learning was explained as being important: social workers must constantly stay up to date with changes in regulations and new methods of practising social work.

## WHO ACTUALLY TAKES PART?

The review shows that, on paper, there is relatively good access to skills development for the personnel at the workplaces studied. In addition to this, however, our study shows a number of factors that hinder employees' possibilities of taking part in skills training when it really comes down to it.

The first of these factors is that it is of utmost importance to stay in the forefront, to make oneself visible, in order to be able to take part in skills development. On the administrative side in the automotive industry, there is, not surprisingly, talk about good opportunities for employees to pursue a management career if they show an interest. The interviewees explain that the responsibility rests on the individual to make him- or herself visible in order to make a career in the organization. The same applies to personnel in automotive production. One employee explains:

> I've taken on more work and more responsibility and stayed at the forefront and shown that I want to go somewhere ... A lot has happened in these seven years. I've friends who've worked here for 20 years and nothing, so to speak, has happened for them. Partly because they don't want it, and then because they don't even try.

There are at the same time others who attest to the difficulty of taking initiative themselves – they want to do the training, but maybe just do not dare to. One woman, a packer in the food industry, says that the employer should actively encourage employees to educate themselves:

> Maybe they should push a little, that is, women in general maybe have lower self-confidence and ... The jargon on the factory floor is a little, can be a little tough. So people don't always talk that nicely to each other, though it's not as bad as people from outside might think when they hear the language used. I do think the company could take more responsibility by forcing, quote-unquote, people to learn more.

There are also people who say that they actually do not want to take part in skills development. Here, there are employees who are content to do their job and then go home when the workday is finished. Employees in the food industry explain:

> I can stay here if they let me. People don't have the energy to engage and do something else and retrain. You know, when you're 40, you don't have the energy. It's like, you don't feel as engaged because you're happy here and you do your job. No, I'm satisfied with what I have.

> You've probably got to put yourself out there and go after what you want. So that they, in turn, can see if they can train you, and get to be a part of it and, like, there are people who want to get ahead. I think there are lots of people who don't want to. They just want them to leave them be, so you can't force someone.

One automotive industry employee makes a similar reflection: 'There are people who never take a course but then they probably don't want to either. And one department manager in Social Services adds: 'If someone is eager to take part in development of operations and such, then that will get things rolling. It's things like that we look at when we set wages.'

The police force, however, seems to differ to some degree here from the other three work organizations. There, the principle of equality is emphasized, where as many people as possible should take part in skills training, regardless of interest. A consequence of this is that it is not always the people who most want to participate in training that are given the opportunity. One manager says: 'We get a lot of training programmes today and then we sit here wondering: *Now who the hell did we send to training last time?* and *We sent him to that course, so, to keep things fair, then we should send someone there.*'

To stay in the forefront and make oneself visible in the workplace may sound like an obvious solution. But, as we will show below, the interviewees explain that this is not always easy.

## BEING LOYAL TO ONE'S COLLEAGUES

In practice, it is not always a given to show an interest in skills development, especially in a work organization based on work teams. Taking part in skills training during work hours can mean that an employee creates problems for his or her colleagues through his or her absence. In the work organizations studied, this is a problem specifically discussed in the automotive and food industries, and, in those cases, on the production side of the organization. One example comes from SAAB, where training for assemblers was drastically reduced in connection with the company's financial difficulties. An HR manager tells the story:

> Can it be a problem if, in a slimmed down organization, it's difficult to find time for training? Even if the company in principle wants you to attend? Yes. In principle the company wants it, but then in reality you have both the immediate manager and the employee him- or herself, who both feel that things will be tough if you go. So we don't bother.

Even at Volvo it is common for employees to refrain from training due to a shortage of personnel. This means that some people do not have the energy to engage in skills development when it really comes down to it:

> Yeah, it seems really hard to get it going, I think. There are training programmes and everything, but there's really just enough manpower as it is, so, like it doesn't, you don't have time to go ahead and apply for the courses and then go to them and all that.

The loyalty between co-workers is put to the test here. For many, loyalty to one's workmates is so strong that the thought of leaving one's team to take part in training is not seen as an option.

## BEING FLEXIBLE

The demand for flexibility is an additional barrier. A flexible production operation is usually held up as the way to organize work organizations for the future. For the employees (especially on the production side of the automotive and food industries), however, demands on flexibility have above all led to reduced influence on their work situation and work hours. Flexibility has brought increased demands on personal adaptability and has made the work more stressful. One assembler in the automotive industry tells about it:

> I'm 37 years old and I've worked here since 1994, and I see how incredibly fast those years have gone. I can't see myself standing on the line when I'm 50 years old. So I'm worried about what'll happen when I turn 50. Because no 50-year-old can cope with standing down there and assembling. It goes too fast!

At one of the food companies, a short time before the interview study was conducted, investments were made in an advanced manufacturing technology that uses robots to replace the heavy parts of the work. Our interviews with the employees show that these rationalizations have nevertheless meant an increased workload for many. One employee explains:

> We're going backwards in development. While many other industries are actually improving job rotation … I've read a lot about that, herring and herring plants, they're trying to make it humane. They rotate. They no longer sit there and clean fish for eight hours, but try to make it humane, you know. And then people last longer. And maybe there's a bit of job satisfaction then. So I can feel like it's a little frustrating now.

Demands for increased flexibility of work hours for the employees also make it difficult to participate in skills development *after* work, which means many people do not even try. As one employee in the food industry puts it:

> If you want to join a club or association or take part in something, a course or something like that, because it's … hard to make it work. Every second week you work evenings. And then, at pretty short notice, they can pull together, say four to five shifts, and things like that, and then you work weekends and nights.

The demand for a flexible workforce is also discussed within the police. For the first five years of intervention work, there is a high degree of irregularity, with a lot of evenings and weekend work. During this time, it is difficult for the personnel to take part in training activities either during or after work hours.

After the first five years, the employees can apply for other jobs in the organization and work as investigators, for example. Then they have the possibility of working days with the possibility of flexible hours, and can also participate more actively in the training offered within the framework of the workplace. One manager explains:

> I don't work weekends any more, because we work a lot of weekends, police work a lot of weekends, those who work shifts … Back then, there used to be only shifts for me, I couldn't imagine working days. But now that I've worked days for seven months and I'm starting to think about having to work shifts again, it gives me a pain in my stomach.

The feeling of not being able to get away and leave work, wanting to but not having the option, is also palpable for employees in the industrial sectors. One production worker in the automotive industry notes:

> You become more tied to standing and working for a certain amount of time. Here, it used to be more that we could plan it ourselves. So, if we do this and get this much done by 8 o'clock, then it's okay for us to take a longer break. But if it's a chassis line, all of a sudden we're dependent on what happens both before us and after us. You have to stand there and work no matter what. You can't take that extra 10-minute break that you could before.

At Social Services, the work hours are relatively fixed, with the possibility of flexible hours. Still, even if working overtime is not permitted (unless ordered by a manager), several of the interviewed workers tell how they sometimes do it to be able to get work done. Even the chief social services officer is aware of this and notes: 'This is a dedicated work group, I think, I'd venture to say, who like their jobs, and who you have to send home now and then. Yes, one of the problems is that we have to keep an eye on them so that they don't work too much.'

Even here, many explain that they would like to take part in the large selection of courses and seminars offered, but that they do not have the time because their work is so time-consuming.

## BEING A PARENT WITH YOUNG CHILDREN

Another factor that limits one's actual ability to take part in skills development is parental responsibilities. Having a supportive partner is often a requirement for being able to participate. One assembler, a single parent, explains how she wanted to seek further training for a long time but that it was not until her children got older that it became possible:

> Well, because the children are bigger now, I'm not needed as much at home so it's not a big deal if I work overtime or attend courses and such. So now I feel like I can do that. It was harder before when they were younger. Now you have more time for yourself. Because I've thought for a long time that I'd begin to study a little, maybe in the evenings and that, but it's a bit difficult when the kids are small. But now I have the time for it.

Another person describes how he made a deal with his spouse that he would stop going to night classes if the family suffered:

> When I took the step, that now I'm going to go back to school, I had to talk to my girlfriend first. Because I need to have the support if I'm going to start school, and we have one child and that takes quite a lot, and we have a house and that also demands a lot. But I got permission from my girlfriend [laughs] to start studying. She's promised to support me, but I did say that she should tell me if she feels that it's getting to be too much. Then I'll stop immediately, because I'm telling you that I've got it good already today, but it can be better. I'm doing this for myself and for my family, but if the family is affected I'll take a step back.

Combining the role of parenthood with gainful employment and skills development is not entirely easy. It can be even more difficult if the employer does not have a positive attitude towards time off. In the automotive industry, the feeling is that, formally, one is entitled to take time off when a child is sick, but that, in practice, this rarely happens because production workers are very dependent on one another. The industrial employees also perceived it as a problem that many people coming off parental leave want to work part-time, which makes it more difficult for the employer to plan shifts. At one of the food companies, the collective agreement stipulates that parents of young children cannot be expected to work four or five shifts in peak season, but in the end most agree to do it anyway. One union representative explains: 'Most of them try to shape their private lives around their work hours. It's almost the opposite of what was intended.'

Even the police profession is limited in this respect. The work schedule is drawn up by management without any greater possibility for employees to influence it. The people interviewed describe how this causes stress, fatigue and problems with adapting to childcare. This in turn means that it is almost impossible for parents with young children to fit in any skills training.

In social services, the majority of employees are women, and many describe how they also have the main responsibility for their families. There are lectures and seminars to go to, but they explain that it is difficult as an employee to do everything, and still have time for work and family. It is clear that the effort of combining work with the role of parent itself takes strength and energy. For many, adding skills training to the mix is not viewed as realistic and therefore receives no priority.

## GETTING AN EXCHANGE FOR ONE'S TRAINING

In the automotive and food industries, employees describe how training programmes that administrative staff take part in often lead to some type of formal certification, while workers out in production rarely receive any usable documentation of skills development. A packer in the food industry explains: 'We have those internal forklift operator licences, but they really only apply here, if you don't get a real forklift licence, because then it can be used somewhere else too. But mostly it's only internal programmes like those that apply here'.

An administrative employee who works in the food industry tells us:

> Out in production there are, they get different qualification ratings for having attended certain training programmes ... then it's more that the training isn't certified. But when it comes to administrative staff, then it's not like that. If you've taken management training or some form of project training then you get a diploma.

In the food industry, employees attest to how people have been let go for lacking the proper formal training. People who had worked at the same workplace for 20 years were all of a sudden no longer seen as having sufficient competency. This shows how the skills of the employees in the industry are valued differently: administrative staff are awarded explicit certifications, while documentation of the knowledge and skills that production workers acquire in the workplace is substandard at best. The experience-based learning remains tacit and difficult to describe.

A general observation is furthermore that many of the people interviewed, regardless of work organization, perceived the skills training they had received as highly industry-specific. It is difficult to translate and get an exchange for elsewhere in the labour market. It is only the administrative employees in the industries who appear to have access to more general and transferable knowledge. As in social services and home help services, more weight is put on formal, standardized training and education. Unless it can be made visible, compared and taught, the experience-based learning ends up in the background (cf. chapters 9 and 10).

## CONCLUDING DISCUSSION: SKILLS DEVELOPMENT AS ACTUAL ABILITY

In this chapter, we have met people in different work organizations. Through their stories, we describe some of the barriers that can prevent employees from participating in skills development. From the standpoint of the selection of training offered, this study confirms earlier findings that people who already have good formal skills and knowledge tend to get more, while those with weaker formal competency participate to a lower degree. The study clearly shows that employees at one and the same workplace (for example, in the automotive and food industries) are offered different types of skills development. The access to skills training is dependent on where in the organization one works, whether one is a production worker or an administrative employee. The professional groups whose jobs require post-secondary education (in the Swedish Police, Social Services, and administrative positions in the industries studied) have, as a whole, access to a wider selection of formal skills training in the workplace than others do.

A principal message is that there are a number of important factors that prevent employees from taking advantage of the programmes offered. Like Sen, we would like to draw attention to factors and circumstances that can prevent people from taking advantage of the resources formally offered. As discussed in the chapter, it is clearly of utmost importance for employees to make themselves visible and demonstrate an interest. But actual ability is not only about having the appropriate desire and commitment. In many work organizations, there are strong norms of collegiality and an unwillingness to disappoint the work team. A lack of influence over work hours and an inability to predict them also affects the real possibilities of participating in skills development. The same applies to the possibility of taking part in training outside regular work hours, a difficult equation not least for parents with young children. Many employees also have doubts about the ability of the skills training offered to strengthen their employability outside the work organization in question. Overall, skills development in the workplace appears to continue to be a resource primarily for employees who have already been given the key to lifelong learning and already, during their education years, learned to seek knowledge and learn new things. For others, the offer of skills development remains merely that – an offer.

## NOTES

1. This analysis was conducted with the aid of funding from the Swedish Research Council within the framework of *The politics and practices of capability: Lifelong learning for all in a knowledge-intense worklife?* project, led by Christina Garsten. The empirical data has been published previously in Jambren and Lindvert 2005 and Rossi and Thedvall 2009.
2. Only formal skills development is discussed here in the chapter, not the type of hidden, experiential learning that is integrated in working life.
3. Plastal AB filed for bankruptcy in March 2009.
4. Due to the extensive restructuring at the companies, it was also difficult to get permission to conduct the interviews.
5. This material also forms the basis for Chapter 10 in this volume.

## REFERENCES

CEC (2001), *Making a European Area of Lifelong Learning a Reality*. European Commission.

Ds 2002:47, *Kompetensförsörjning på arbetsmarknaden*. Stockholm: Ministry of Employment.

Edwards, Richard and Robin Usher (2001), 'Lifelong learning: A post-modern condition for education?', *Adult Education Quarterly*, 51(4), 273–87.

Ellström, Per-Erik (1996), 'Rutin och reflektion. Förutsättningar och hinder for lärande i dagligt arbete' in Per-Erik, Ellström, Bernt Gustavsson and Staffan Larsson (eds), *Livslångt lärande*. Lund: Studentlitteratur, pp. 142–79.

Garrick, John and Robin Usher, G. (2000), 'Flexible learning, contemporary work and enterprising selves', *Electronic Journal of Sociology*. Available at: http://www.sociology.org/content/vol005.001/garrick-usher.html, accessed 22 May 2013.

Gustavsson, Bernt (1996), *Bildning i vår tid: om bildningens möjligheter och villkor i det moderna samhället*. Stockholm: Wahlström & Widstrand.

Holmer, Jan (2006), 'Introduktion till arbetsvetenskapen', in Jan Holmer and Birger Simonson (eds), *Forskning om arbete*. Lund: Studentlitteratur.

Jambrén, Niklas and Jessica Lindvert (2005), *Landet lagom i 2000-talet: Arbete, lärande och socialt ansvar i politik och praktik*. Stockholm: Score Working Paper Series 2005:4.

Lindvert, Jessica (2006), *Ihålig arbetsmarknadspolitik? Organisering och legitimitet igår och idag*. Umeå: Boréa bokförlag.

Lindvert, Jessica (2009), 'EUs partnerskap på kollisionskurs med svensk partssamverkan', *Nordiske Organisasjonsstudier (NOS)*, 11(1), 50–68.

National Police Board (2001), *Polisen – A presentation of the Swedish Police Service*. Stockholm: Swedish National Police Board (RPS).

Nilsson, B. (1996), 'Företagsutbildning – anpassning och/eller utveckling?', in Per-Erik Ellström, Bernt Gustavsson and Staffan Larsson (eds), *Livslångt lärande*. Lund: Studentlitteratur.

Prop. 1966:52, Arbetsmarknadskungörelse.

Rossi, Nina and Renita Thedvall (2009), *Lärandets praktik inom socialtjänsten och livsmedelsindustrin*. Score Working Paper Series 2009:5.

Rönnqvist, Dan and Camilla Thunborg (1996), 'Personalutbildning – ett instrument för livslångt lärande?', in Per-Erik Ellström, Bernt Gustavsson and Staffan Larsson (eds), *Livslångt lärande*. Lund: Studentlitteratur, pp. 180–202.

Rubenson, Kjell (1996), 'Livslångt lärande: Mellan utopi och ekonomi', in Per-Erik Ellström, Bernt Gustavsson and Staffan Larsson (eds), *Livslångt lärande*. Lund: Studentlitteratur.

Rubenson, Kjell (2006), 'The Nordic model of lifelong learning', *Compare*, 36(3), 327–241.

SCB (2008), *Personalutbildning. Första halvåret 2008*. Stockholm: Statistics Sweden.

Sen, Amartya (1982), *Choice, Welfare and Measurement*. Cambridge: MIT Press.

Sen, Amartya (1988), 'Freedom of choice', *European Economic Review*, 32(2), 269–94.

Sen, Amartya (1993), 'Capability and well-being', in Martha Nussbaum and Amartya Sen (eds), *The Quality of Life*. Oxford: Clarendon Press, pp. 30–53.

SOU 1999:141, *Från kunskapslyftet till en strategi för livslångt lärande*. Swedish Government Official Reports. Stockholm: Swedish Ministry of Education and Research.

SOU 2000:115, *Aktuella trender inom kompetensutvecklingsområdet*. Swedish Government Official Reports. Stockholm: Nordstedts.

SOU 2000:28, *Kunskapsbygget 2000 – det livslånga lärandet*. Swedish Government Official Reports. Stockholm: Swedish Ministry of Education and Research.

Statistics Sweden (2007), *Education in Sweden 2007*. Statistics Sweden Education and Research report.

Thång, Per-Olof (2006), 'Arbetslivets pedagogik', in Jan Holmer and Birger Simonson (eds), *Forskning om arbete*. Lund: Studentlitteratur.

Wikman, Anders (2001), *Internationalisering, flexibilitet och förändrade företagsformer. En statistisk analys av arbetsställenas utveckling under 90-talet*. Stockholm: National Institute for Working Life.

# 12. The labour market as a market: exchangeability, measurability and accountability

## Christina Garsten

Our worlds of work are in sway. The transition from a society based mainly on industrial production to a society where the production of knowledge and services is in focus has meant big changes in the organizing of the labour market. From the 1990s onward, norms concerning work, employment and learning have become increasingly integrated with general economic policy and the development of the market. Many of the regulatory changes introduced have been motivated by factors that have no direct connection to the content of work or with the work contract itself but with reference to market development and state budgetary resources. Both the direction and scope of the regulatory changes implemented in the past two decades can be said to have followed broadly the economic development. Discussions about how responsibility for an equitable sharing of risks in the labour market should be organized have been lively.

This development may be understood in terms of the emergence of a new type of regulatory state and new forms of governance and control, with an emphasis on transparency and monitoring.[1] A number of researchers have analysed the transformation of the public sector in terms of the emergence of an 'audit society' where new ideas and norms for governance and control have been established (Power 1997; Strathern 2000). These norms point in the direction towards increased individual risk-taking and responsibility for decisions that affect planning of one's own life, increased emphasis on quantifiable forms of follow-up and control, and increased transparency with respect to how organizations and regulations are designed (Garsten and Lindh de Montoya 2008; Hood and Heald 2006). This trend is also evident in the norms and guidelines meant to guide individual people in making their skills and employability visible.

The content of labour market policy has undergone significant changes over the last decades. This has occurred not least through the deregulation of the state monopoly on Public Employment Services in 1993. This move opened up the market for other than state actors to mediate employment and fuelled a move towards temporary and project-based employment. The market aspects of labour market policy have also become more prominent through a focus on the so-called supply side. The matching activities of the Public Employment Service have been clearly accentuated, and jobseeker activities have been emphasized over training and practice. Clear economic incentives are expected to reduce social exclusion by making it profitable for an individual to work, in comparison to having one's livelihood met via insurance and assistance schemes. This is meant to occur through, among other things, reducing unemployment benefit levels, tougher controls of jobseekers and people on sick leave, and a new rehabilitation system. A recent important change is the increased attention paid to so-called weaker groups, with a dual labour market emerging, with 'regular' unemployed people having to fend for themselves, and weaker groups being subjected to tailor-made programmes. This new direction in labour market policy has received wide criticism, not least for being costly, and for its effects being uncertain and leading to a greater stratification of jobseekers and society at large.

'Employability' has secured its place as a central concept in both labour market policy and everyday working life. The concept indicates an increased emphasis on the ability to get and keep a job and to be able to adapt to fluctuations in the labour market. It is intended to signify a more dynamic view of the role and responsibility of people in getting employment and being able to move ahead in one's own working life, and is regarded as a requirement for a more dynamic and well-functioning labour market at a macro level (Berglund and Fejes 2009; Garsten and Jacobsson 2004; Gazier 2001). Via EU employment strategy, employability has become an important part of the national labour market policy. Nowadays, employability is not only a matter for labour market parties. Universities must also contribute to students' employability by clearly indicating possible areas of use for the knowledge acquired.

Employability as a policy concept does not stand in isolation, but is linked with numerous related concepts, of which each, both on its own and collectively, carries expectations and norms for how the relationship between employee and employer should be designed and what is expected of the individual person. To this conceptual assemblage belong also terms such as flexibility, work capability, lifelong learning and entrepreneurship (Nicoll 2008). In focus here is the strong connection to the conception of a competitive labour market, where people's skills and expertise compete for positions and better conditions. Although the labour market has always been associated with varying degrees of competition, the degree of this has been stressed differently under different political regimes. In the past decade, with the changes in policy that have been implemented, elements of competition and exchange have been emphasized as something desirable, above all in relation to conceptions of stagnation, structural barriers and inertia.

The conception of mobility itself has grown stronger in the conceptual assemblage of employability. People are expected to be prepared to physically move to where the jobs or training programmes are. They are expected to be prepared to bridge or transition between different types of work. We see this, for example, in the market for transition coaches that has grown considerably in recent years. People are expected to be flexible in relation to different work tasks, to be able to switch between different work tasks (commonly called functional flexibility). We are also expected to be prepared to be flexible from a time perspective, responsive to changes in relation to different rhythms and patterns of work, and to be prepared for short-term contracts (see, for example, Furåker et al. 2007).

The adjustments made to state labour market policy aim above all to create incentives for and to support people's mobility, adaptability and transitions. Initiatives in the area of learning and education, changes in security nets, and targeted initiatives for weak and vulnerable groups, aim to strengthen the work strategy and motivate people to work harder to find, keep or change jobs, and to hone their skills. The 'enabling state' (see, for example, Gilbert and Gilbert 1989) is another type of state than the 'caring state' (see, for example, Leira 1994). It is a coaching and supporting state, rather than a state that offers security and predictability. As jobseekers or employees, we are led to understand that today's knowledge and skills have a best-before date and must be continually updated and produced anew. We can therefore say that the exchange aspect of the labour market has increasingly moved into the foreground through the regulatory changes of recent years. Transactions between the supply and demand sides of labour have become central. The labour market is becoming more and more a market.

But what does it mean to say that the market aspects themselves have entered the foreground of the labour market? Which aspects is it that are being articulated and expressed? What are the implications of this for jobseekers and people in employment? Here, my interest is in the shift in norms, with an increased emphasis on exchangeability, measurability and accountability, which has taken place and is still occurring. In this chapter, I discuss the tendencies that contribute to an emphasis on making people's employability clearer and more visible. A step in learning to navigate the labour market today is not only learning what the relevant qualifications and skills are, but also learning to make these visible and legible to the world around us. Various obstacles to participating in the labour market are, in the process, clarified and made visible in an aim to increase the chances of a good matching process. The governing ideas and practices in the contemporary labour market are the focus of this closing chapter. The various aspects of the market logic that have been discussed throughout the book provide the basis for the discussion. The conceptions of measurability and efficiency articulated in today's labour market can be seen as an extension of a long-nourished dream of a rationally constructed welfare state. In this project, labour has had a distinctive position (see, for example, Furåker 1989).

A fruitful place to start when attempting to see the labour market as a market is to observe how workers are given value. What aspects of people are valued in a certain situation, which knowledge, skills and characteristics are desirable, and what does the process that makes this possible look like? Appadurai suggests that we should understand 'the social life of things' as a movement, a process, in which they can take on different types of value in different situations (Appadurai 1986). A 'thing' is not a commodity by definition, but is made into a commodity in a specific social and economic context. A thing campaigns for or has the potential of becoming a good or commodity (commodity candidacy). By studying how that thing moves between, beyond, in and out of the market, how it shifts between different types of values, we are able to get away from a fruitless dichotomization of commodities and other things. This perspective also entails a more proccessual view of how both commodities and markets come to be and change, and how goods or services are constituted as such in different contexts. A market pre-supposes movement, not only for those who act as buyers and sellers, but also for the commodities exchanged in the market. The good (or service) must be able to be moved from one context to another, from the buyer's context to the seller's. In this oscillating between different contexts, the commodity also takes on different values and is assigned different characteristics.

## A NEW INTERFACE

How labour market policy is designed has consequences for the relationship between employer and employee. Depending on how policy and guidelines are formulated, this relationship may be articulated in different ways. For example, in the temporary staffing industry, we see how employees are taught to be attentive to both the demands and expectations of the staffing firm, and to those that exist in the client organization. In the staffing industry, demands of malleability and flexibility towards the organization are especially evident (Garsten 2008). In an article on forms of public administration and labour market policy in the US, Emily Martin (1977) writes about the relationship as an 'interface zone' between the individual and her world. Martin uses this concept to help describe the cultural shaping that occurs in the relationship between organization and individual.

In the interface between the individual as a subject and the environment around her opens a world of possibilities for creating knowledge, for development, as well as for exercising power and influence. The interface is also the zone where reciprocal influence and formation of expectations and demands takes place. These may look different depending on the prevailing ideas and ideologies, practices and procedures of a given time point. Similar thoughts about the emergence of systems for diagnosis and interventions in the area of medicine have been put forward by, among others, Karin Johannisson (see, for example, 2004, 2009). Johannisson shows how diagnostic designations develop in a dynamic interplay between a number of actors and factors: doctors, insurance schemes, the media, the pharmaceutical industry, threat and risk profiles, globalization and market thinking. She also shows how these systems reflect time-bound conceptions and priorities. The templates and categories that organizations have developed to place individuals into under different time periods and political regimes are, as Johannisson also points out, not at all given or self-evident, but are products of specific ways of thinking and negotiations between standpoints and interests.

The matching that continually occurs in the labour market can be said to take place in this interface between individual and organization. It is also here that we can discern changes in the demands and expectations placed on potential employees. The increased emphasis on, in particular, matching activities in labour market policy is a clear expression of the importance of the interface and of the increased influence of market thinking. In his book on matching in staffing agencies, Lars Walter (2005) shows how matching occurs in a temporary staffing firm. Walter describes how the recruiting and sales work helps to construct and 'calibrate' the object to be matched, that is, the consultant who is contracted out, so that matching can occur. Above all, the study shows the importance of classification systems that lay the groundwork for and enable the calibration of the matching work. Walter demonstrates how the clients' and co-workers' intentions and interests are integrated into the construction of the matching object. This means an objectification, albeit a temporary one, of the individual. Construction and calibration of the individual also require his or her participation. In the process, the person to be contracted out becomes the object of a certain form of disciplining and control, but also contributes actively to the construction of the self as an outsourced consultant. The loose coupling between the matching and the work to be performed also means that the process occurs after the agreement is made and the contract is written. It presupposes that the outsourced person, in interaction with the client, actively contributes to constructing his or her identity as an outsourced consultant. In my own research on the social construction of employees in the temporary staffing business, I similarly found how staffing firm employees in Sweden, Britain and the US learn to see themselves through the eyes and yardsticks of the clients and the staffing firm, and are trained to adapt themselves to the demands of the market (Garsten 2004, 2008). This entails a disciplining of the self to the benefit of the demands and expectations that employers and client organizations have, and a reflexive attitude to one's own skills and abilities (Garsten and Haunschild 2014). To be evaluated and to measure one's value based on market demands is becoming a normalized element of their working lives.

In other words, it is in the interface between employer and employee, individual and organization, that the stage for demands and expectations is set. In a competitive labour market, where responsiveness to the market's demands is stressed, the interface becomes fluid. Needs and norms must constantly be constructed and reconstructed. For the individual, it is important to be seen as employable, as malleable and adaptable, in relation to the organization that might employ you.

## WORKERS AS A COMMODITY

A labour market policy that stresses competition and adaptation to demand also encourages the employee or jobseeker to see him- or herself as something of a commodity in the labour market. In contemporary discourses about 'how to succeed in the labour market', as we find them in popular science publications and books today, the trend towards exchangeability thinking is evident. Book titles like *You – A Brand* (*Du – ett varumärke*, Sandin and Frykman 2010) and *Your Personal Brand* (*Ditt personliga varumärke*, Werner Runebjörk 2006) encourage individuals to care for their image and their CV in the same way as companies groom and position their brands. We are encouraged to think about ourselves as goods in a market.

Another expression of this is the coaching market that has sprouted up to support transitions. Ilinca Benson describes in Chapter 7 of this book how people involved in transition programmes learn to maintain work routines, to identify their abilities and merits, and to adapt to the market. Benson's data shows that many jobseekers can be unwilling at first to take on the role they are encouraged to, and how they gradually acquire a market-oriented way of thinking. She points out that transition programs have a lot to do with framing an attractive and presentable offer based on the complexity of experience, relations and skills that the participant represents. To be 'coachable' means that one is receptive to the messages that course instructors convey, and that one is prepared to learn the approach described as enabling and successful. In other words, being coachable means that one adopts a special kind of reflexivity of the self and the possibilities it brings.

In the same spirit, in Chapter 3, Lars Walter describes how jobseekers learn to see themselves as a commodity in the labour market, training themselves to see and articulate their skills and expertise in a way that is assumed to be attractive to potential employers. In this context, the jobseeker has a 'commodity candidacy', to use Appadurai's wording. In connection with registration with the Public Employment Service, great importance is placed on informing jobseekers about the rules, demands and routines that apply to be eligible to receive unemployment insurance benefits: that they must actively seek work, that they must apply for the jobs they are referred to, that they must be accessible for contacts and meetings, and in other ways be at the disposal of the labour market and the Public Employment Service. But it is also a matter of the Public Employment Service's obligation to support the jobseekers. It must teach them how to look for work, how to write and develop appropriate application documents, how to use the job bank, and which recruiting and job sites can be used in their job search. Walter points out here that the registration entails a formalization of the unemployed person as a jobseeker. It means that the jobseeker must submit to the Public Employment Service's control and regulations, which is also a requirement for the jobseeker to qualify for unemployment insurance. The registration can be seen as an important step in the process that constitutes the jobseeker as a commodity in the labour market. The registration is a performative moment that defines the person in search of work as a 'jobseeker' in a formal sense.

Jobseekers and people who are about to change jobs learn to see themselves based on the demands and expectations set by the labour market. In the practice of job-seeking, one's own personality is negotiated in relation to what are perceived to be valuable skills and characteristics. This reflexive approach is especially evident in the art of CV writing. Marinette Fogde has written about the self-presentation in CV writing as a process that requires looking more closely at how one 'is' and identifying characteristics that can be constructed as positive for a prospective employer (Fogde 2009, IV:4). People actively contribute in the negotiation of demands and expectations so that they are reasonably consistent with each other. Fogde calls this reflexive negotiation 'selective conformity'. Being a job-seeking subject is a temporary position assumed in relation to an employer in a specific situation. Assuming this role means that the subject must reflect on and form his or her own personality in relation to specific discursive terms in the creation of him- or herself as a job-seeking subject (ibid.; cf. Krejsler 2007: 478). Fogde points out ambivalences and ambiguities in career counselling and the challenges that go along with constructing the self as 'marketable'.

Being attuned to the demands and expectations of the market, and exercising a reflexive approach to oneself, contributes to a special kind of subject taking form: *homo mercans* (Garsten and Hasselström 2004). The market-oriented person relates to the market and its demands and exercises a subtle and reflexive guiding of the self and how it is presented. In contrast to the neoclassical ideal of *homo economicus*, he or she is not governed by rational and calculating deliberations at every turn, but reflects on and negotiates contextually and with the demands of the market. Today's jobseekers operate in a competitive labour market that places a high value on the making visible of and marketing of products and certain expertise, skills, and ways of acting and thinking. As a market-oriented person, the jobseeker learns to think of him- or herself in valuative and evaluative terms, to value oneself as a commodity in the market and to make oneself auditable. The approach also includes learning to be independent, believing in one's own ability, and being disciplined. As this approach makes itself known and is normalized, it also becomes the template against which other approaches are valued (cf. Carrier 1997). In condensed form, we can say that it is possible, through education and training, labour market programmes and interventions, reward systems and incentives, to get people to accept and integrate the ways of the market as something given and as a starting point for their own actions. Market-oriented ways of thinking and acting thus become the normalized way to relate to a global and competitive labour market. And it is partly by way of such demands and expectations that new forms of power and governance are exercised:

The normalizing gaze ... establishes over individuals a visibility through which one differentiates them and judges them. (Foucault 1991 [1975]: 184)

A central point in dynamic theories about markets is that a 'thing' is only a commodity in a certain situation or a certain phase of a longer process (see, for example, Appadurai 1986: 13). This means that in order for us to understand how this thing is constructed as a commodity in a situation, we must follow the process over time. Appadurai describes this 'commodity situation' as 'the situation in which [an object's] exchangeability for some other thing is a socially relevant feature' (1986: 13). A similar point is expressed by Callon et al. (2002), who claim that goods or services exchanged in a market can only be temporarily specified. They qualify as goods and are given a value for a limited time, provisionally. In the transition programmes, the participants' attitudes and perceptions are calibrated and fine-tuned so that the participants become coachable and later employable again. When a jobseeker registers with the Public Employment Service, he or she learns the art of becoming a jobseeker and actively looking for job opportunities. An employee is similarly reconstructed to become an outsourced consultant by matching needs and expertise of client companies and staffing firms. Callon suggests that this type of qualifying, or framing, is necessary for a good or service to be able to be exchanged in a market (Forsell and Norén 2004: 80). Such framing occurs in many industries and it is not hard to find more examples of how people in the labour market are in certain situations constructed as a commodity with a certain value in the labour market. In service professions, this trend is perhaps especially obvious (see, for example, Ehrenreich and Hochschild 2003). For example, call centres have been noted for the intense micromanagement that the employees are subjected to and for the measuring methods that make each person's economic value visible (see, for example, Lindgren and Sederblad 2004).

Also those who work with matching people and occupations must learn how to assess the value of individuals in relation to a certain assignment. In Chapter 4 of this book, Julia Peralta shows how the job of the employment officers can be understood in terms of the different roles they perform: that of the 'broker' (placement officer) or the 'therapist' (counsellor). These roles reflect different larger trends in society, says Peralta – one towards market thinking and exchange relationships, and the other pointing towards interventions in individual people's lives in an aim to influence them in a particular direction. The reforming of the Public Employment Service carried out in the 1980s, which placed increased focus on 'employment-oriented' work methods and on finding suitable applicants for the job vacancies that arise, also meant an extensive reform with respect to staffing. The categories of job placement officer and employment counsellor were introduced. The work of the placement officers became oriented to the employer's needs and demands, to matching, and to creating a marketplace where workers and opportunities for work meet. The work of the counsellors was oriented instead towards job search and labour market training for people with special needs. The jobseekers that the placement officers deal with are assumed to be self-reliant and active individuals, easy to place in a competitive labour market.

It is interesting to note here how the Public Employment Service is organized to facilitate the matching and exchange of labour. That is, it is not only a matter of moulding the people who are the subject of exchanges in the labour market, but also, and to an equal extent, shaping the actors involved in the preparations for, and the evaluation of, the exchange itself. As a job placement officer, one must have good assessment abilities, writes Peralta. One must be able to distinguish between the various needs of the jobseeker for services and support, assess their abilities and competitiveness, their strengths and weaknesses. One must also be efficient in one's work. The actors who work with calibrating the workforce before the exchange, must also constantly hone this particular skill. To help them, they also have various types of manuals and tools. Standardized tests, CVs, process descriptions, inter- view forms and the like, are central tools in the organizing of the job market. As Ida Seing demonstrates in Chapter 5, with respect to the Public Employment Service's rehabilitation work with people with disabilities, calibration by way of tests and standardized assessments of work capacity are of particular importance when demand is low. In the work to assess and classify 'work ability', a series of specialists are involved, including occupational psychologists, occupational therapists and social counsellors.

In Chapter 6, Gunilla Olofsdotter shows that expertise in purchasing temporary staffing services is something that people acquire and not something that they possess automatically. Over time, the client com- panies, or more precisely the responsible managers at these companies, learn how the contracting of temporary employees works, what demands can and should be made, what they can expect as a client, and what the costs are. The purchasers of temporary staffing learn to specify which skills they are looking for and which work tasks are appropriate for temporary workers. The skill of staffing thus becomes visible and is made a required part of one's role in the company. When they have learnt the rules of the game, these buyers can also fully participate in the competition for the desirable consultants.

# MAKING KNOWLEDGE AND SKILLS VISIBLE

Contemporary labour market policy is oriented towards highlighting abilities, skills and possibilities. The current interpretation of the work strategy stresses the importance of seeing a person's ability to work, rather than barriers to employment. This point of departure, which has been the subject of heated debate with respect to the effects of applying such a policy for the people that it covers, builds on the assumption that relevant skills, experience and the like can be made visible and assessable with the help of standardized technologies. It also assumes that people's abilities are flexible and easily moulded, that they can be adapted to the requirements and demands of the labour market. Knowledge and skills must be verified and made visible in order to be converted into real value in the labour market. Professional practice has also been subjected to increased control by the implementation of various administrative tools, such as the standardization of knowledge, of procedures, and auditing (Power 1997; Rose 1996b).

Renita Thedvall (Chapter 10) demonstrates how the work of Social Services has come to be more and more oriented towards evidence-based practice, where scientific knowledge should ideally be the basis for activities and interventions. The work that social workers do is complex, as it contains elements of both bureaucratic rationality and compassion: it is both an exercise of authority and a 'form of art', as one social worker put it. Thedvall shows how the more everyday internal organizational learning in the form of advice and guidance, gut feeling and learning by doing – dimensions that have been of central importance in the profession – continues to live on, while the focus has shifted towards 'scientization' and evidence-based practice, aided by standardized guidelines for work, standardized work practices, and standardized courses in evidence-based methods. At the social services office where Thedvall's study was carried out, the most evident sign of this was that skills training and formal education were valued higher than everyday learning in practice. The idea is that, by making the service that social workers provide visible, by influencing which methods are used, it becomes easier to achieve the desired results. This development, says Thedvall, has led to a change in *how* people learn their jobs at the social services office, towards an increased emphasis on formal, standardized and evidence-based methods. It is therefore not just any learning or just any skills training that are offered to the employees at the social services office. The knowledge that is at a premium is knowledge that is formal, standardized, made visible and explicit, and that is founded on science. Experience-based learning, tacit knowledge and gut feeling must take a back seat.

Another assumption that permeates today's labour market is that it is possible, with the models and tools that the organizations provide, to actually define and articulate an individual's abilities in a way that can later serve as a starting point for interventions. In Chapter 5, Ida Seing shows how specialists at the Public Employment Service and its Work Rehab department strive to identify, categorize and sort their clients' capabilities and then match these to a suitable job. The Public Employment Service's work with 'work-related' rehabilitation involves numerous counselling, investigation and rehabilitation initiatives for people with various types of disabilities. There are also labour market policy support initiatives for jobseekers with disabilities linked to this, for example, wage subsidies, employment at Samhall (a company owned by the Swedish state aimed at providing development opportunities for people with disabilities through employment), publicly sheltered employment, and adaptation of the workplace. The aim of these initiatives is to compensate for the reduced work ability and to strengthen the jobseekers' possibilities of finding employment in the regular labour market. In order to do this, the specialists – occupational psychologists, occupational therapists and social counsellors – must categorize and sort the skills so that they can then form the basis for interventions. To assist them, there are a number of different tools: conversations and interviews are also complemented with different forms of occupational psychology tests and occupational therapy assessment instruments, aimed at providing a holistic assessment of the individual's ability in relation to the work environment and work tasks. The jobseeker is then assigned a code that enables him or her to gain access to the additional resources available for people with disabilities.

Seing makes clear that this work encompasses a host of difficult considerations and decisions. Coding a person's disability opens opportunities for assistance and resources, at the same time as it can contribute to stigmatizing and to screening and sorting people out (Garsten and Jacobsson 2013; Jacobsson and Seing 2013). The technologies that the specialists have at their disposal enable them to make people's abilities visible and to sort them in order to facilitate matching, but they are also tools that can normalize and idealize certain skills, and medicalize and stigmatize others (Holmqvist 2006). In other words, they are powerful tools in the hands of authority. With standardized tests and other tools, individuals can be made comparable and be referred to different forms of intervention.

One requirement is that individuals themselves take an active part in the process, that they agree to define themselves with the aid of the templates for making work abilities visible that are provided by the organization. People who undergo a disability assessment must also themselves accept the process and being assigned a certain code. Thus, also here a certain kind of reflexivity and a capacity for self-monitoring is needed in order for the process to work. From a critical standpoint, this can be seen as a subtle form of governance. It is a form of governance that presents itself in terms of freedom, rather than control, with the aim of empowering individuals. It works by appealing to people's free choice, as part of 'advanced liberal governance' (Miller and Rose 2008; Rose 1996a, 1999), empowering and activating certain forms of agency. Knights and Willmott (1989) have pointed out that our sense of subjectivity at work is especially receptive to such influences because they offer a way of attaining increased self-awareness, self-esteem and inclusion in a larger social context.

Preparing actors to exchange labour and skills for wages and other resources in a labour market does not happen at the wave of a hand but requires a good measure of work from all parties. The abilities of the workers must be made visible, classified and sorted in order to be matched to appropriate jobs and employers' expectations; knowledge and skills must be standardized and validated in order to be viable and comparable. Buyers of labour must learn to qualify their demands and desires. This process of qualifying and calibrating takes place on an ongoing basis in the labour market and contributes to making the exchange step explicit. It also contributes to a qualification of the labour as a commodity, with special characteristics and values, in a given situation.

## THE EXCHANGEABLE PERSON

A general principle is that products in a similar market, with a similar price level, are exchangeable. One pair of jeans from a manufacturer can be exchanged for another pair of jeans from another manufacturer. Here, the manufacturers strive, using brands and 'hard' marketing, to differentiate the products so that their jeans will stand out as more valuable than other jeans. The competition between companies drives a number of activities devoted to distinguishing one pair from the other. In the present-day labour market, it is becoming increasingly apparent that one person with certain professional skills and knowledge can be exchanged for another with the same skills and knowledge. The increased competition in the labour market means, for example, that one social worker with certain training and experience can relatively easily be replaced by another social worker with the same training and similar experience. The standardization of the documentation of completed training programmes, courses attended, and occupational experience makes it easier to measure one social worker against another, and to compare their value.

This particular trend towards standardization of knowledge and practice is easily discerned in the care of the elderly. Home help services have long been associated with a personal and flexible stance towards the care recipient. Professional qualifications have not been as important as the people-to-people caring element. The reorganization of municipal home help services launched in the 1980s was influenced by a welfare policy where economic, instrumental rationality had a big impact (see, for example, Drugge 2003; Eliasson 1992; Szebehely 1996). In the market thinking encompassed in this reorganization, the conflict between economic and human considerations becomes apparent. In Chapter 9, Marie Hjalmarsson shows how rationality measures have gone hand in hand with an attempt to raise the status of the home help profession. She describes the introduction of a management-initiated project to track time and register, with the help of handheld computers, what home help workers do during their workday. The tracking of time affects the workers' discretion to act in that micro-management of their work increases and draws more attention to work performance. Management justifies the project with talk about raising the status of the profession and making the work more efficient. The workers, on their end, react with different forms of resistance to what they perceive as a restriction of their freedom, integrity, and people-to-people relations with the care recipients (see also Hjalmarsson 2009). The work becomes chopped up into comparable units that are assumed to take a certain number of minutes. The care element is categorized and measured in an aim to standardize something that in itself is complex and variable. All of this is closely monitored with the aid of advanced technology.

Hjalmarsson demonstrates how, through breaking it down, measuring and monitoring it, the work is standardized and commodified. A job that is complex in its variety and socially multifaceted is transformed into a job with standardized and commodified elements. It is this very tension and oscillating between uniqueness and standardization, between singularization and commodification, that characterizes markets (cf. Appadurai 1986; Kopytoff 1986). The rationalization processes also contribute to the individual caregivers becoming more easily exchangeable. In home help work, a weighing of care recipient needs and employer regulations occurs every day. Loyalty conflicts and negotiations between the employer's wants and the care recipient's needs, as well as the interests of colleagues, are an inherent part of the day-to-day work. Different caregivers resolve this conflict in different ways, which is why their relationship to the care recipient has a personal and human character. Time-tracking and standardization are intended to reduce this variation. In this way, were it not for their resistance, each individual employee would become more easily exchangeable – a cog in the welfare machine.

In the temporary staffing industry, both the singular and unique, and the standardized and exchangeable aspects of the workforce stand out with particular clarity. In many ways, work in this industry demands a flexible adaptation to the client's special wishes, and it is only through one's unique combination of skills and experiences that one can become a successful consultant in the staffing industry. On the other hand, the staffing industry in turn is built completely on the fact that there is a high degree of competition in the labour market, that an individual consultant's work can be replaced by another consultant's, and that the work can be assigned a value using market tools and terms. The staffing industry can offer outsourced consultants 'with a guarantee', as one staffing firm expressed it in a marketing campaign. If clients are not satisfied with the performance, with a temporary consultant's attitude towards the work, or with his or her personal style, they can, at no extra cost to the client, exchange the consultant for another who better matches their wishes. The market for staffing services is based on the existence of competition between the people who are hired out, and of candidates being aware of this.

Employees in the staffing industry quickly accept the message about competition and exchangeability, and largely adapt their actions and expectations to this. In my own research (see, for example, Garsten 2008), I interviewed a number of people who had left the industry for the very reason that they felt that the competition and the feeling of being under continual review and appraisal put too much pressure on them. But most of the people I interviewed said that these circumstances – the market thinking, competition and evaluation – are something that they have embraced and that they now consider 'natural'. Many stated, however, that they prefer not to compete with the permanent employees that they replace or complement at the client company, since this can create problems in the internal organization and for the individual. Amanda, who at the time of the interview worked at a large staffing firm in Stockholm, explains:

> I'm in a bit of a sensitive situation because I'm replacing Jessica who is on sick leave. She's undergoing treatment, she's on sick leave. She's coming back. And she's one of the gang. I don't really want to replace her. So I try to keep my distance a little, so that they won't think I'm trying to take her place. It's also out of respect for her. So that she can feel that when she's here it's

really her job. So I try not to change too much. She says I can, but I know how it feels. If I move things around on her desk and that. It's clear that you feel it … And then it's important that I don't socialize too much with the others here [at the client company]. But on the other hand, it's important that you try to be a part of the gang, especially when you have a longer assignment.

Here the staffing industry also exhibits a characteristic feature of organizations: that every position is essentially independent of the person who holds it. As Göran Ahrne (1994: 18) expresses it: 'The recognition and identification of individual affiliates is indispensable for the running of an organization. Still, for the organization to last and survive no affiliate can be indispensable' (see also Selznick 1948: 25). Ahrne puts his finger on a (seemingly unsolvable) conflict between a person's endeavour to put a personal and unique stamp on his or her work, and the indifference of organizations and the market to these very unique and individual qualities. The labour market policies of different time periods and regimes have made various attempts to strike a balance on this theme, but no one has yet solved the inherent conflict.

In Chapter 8 of this book, Erik Berntson contends that employees' perception of their attractiveness in the labour market has a certain importance for how successful they are at getting a job and moving on in the labour market. Working life today is no longer characterized by someone having one job with one employer for his or her entire life. It has instead become a reality for many people to change workplaces, voluntarily or involuntarily, with some regularity. Thus, employability can have to do with holding onto one's current job or advancing within an organization, but also with being able to change jobs if necessary.

The *perception* of being able to change jobs can be an important resource in working life. Regardless of whether or not one actually does change jobs, the perception of having this option can provide a sense of control and security in an otherwise fluid working life. Berntson shows how perceiving oneself as employable affects a person's chances of getting a new job. In line with Berntson, we can argue that the content in the psychological contract between employer and employee has gradually changed over time, from being characterized by sustainability, loyalty and security, to having become more transactional in nature. The transactional aspect means that the employment relationship and the expectations placed on it have become more market-oriented in that the relationship is to a larger extent oriented to a market exchange between the parties. As Berntson expresses it, the employee has expertise that can be regarded as a saleable product and must continually be developed. The exchange between employer and employee takes place around this expertise – the employee delivers his or her knowledge and skills and receives in exchange the opportunity to constantly develop and improve them. Flexibility and exchange are central aspects in the new contract. We are, Berntson suggests, moving towards 'protean' career forms (Hall 1996) in which we, like the Greek god Proteus, are expected to be able to shift shapes when we want and need to.

The perception of employability also highlights the market element in working life. Competition and appraisal are accentuated, and a person who feels employable perceives him- or herself as a more or less attractive good. Perceiving oneself as employable can be described, in Appadurai's terminology, as sensing that one has considerable potential as a commodity in the labour market, a strong 'commodity candidacy'.

## CONCLUDING REMARKS: THE POLICY OF RESPONSIBILIZATION

In recent decades, labour market policy has entailed a shift in the relationship between employer and employee, such that the individual has to a greater extent become responsible for his or her career development. It has become increasingly evident that the individual is expected to take responsibility for acquiring the necessary knowledge and skills, to continually develop these, to get a job and to stay employable.

This development should, however, not be seen as merely aimed at the individual's responsibility. We also see that public policy includes many support measures in the form of special and targeted initiatives for particularly vulnerable groups. The general tendency, on the other hand, remains the same. This is a policy aimed at articulating and encouraging, but also demanding, the individual's own commitment, initiative and participation. We can talk about this as a policy of accountability or 'responsibilization'.

Accountability has in recent years been a hotly debated topic, above all in relation to employers' responsibility for maintaining good working conditions and for market actors' responsibility to keep within legal boundaries and adhere to ethical guidelines in market transactions (see, for example, Boström and Garsten 2008). It has also been discussed in relation to professional groups such as management consultants and others with mobile expert knowledge (see, for example, Grey 1997). The studies that this book is based on indicate that this responsibilization policy can be observed in the labour market as a whole. Jobseekers, people in rehabilitation programmes, people in transition programmes, and employees in the temporary staffing industry, as well as social workers and other specialists, are met with the message that they, like other individuals, must take responsibility for their own skills and career development. The practices that are intended to support and facilitate their job-seeking, transitions or learning are normative in their content, in that they also convey the message of how these people, as actors, should think and act in order to achieve success. They set the guidelines for how a market should be (re)formed and function, and refer to positive goals (see, for example, Brunsson and Olsen 1993; Czarniawska-Joerges 1988; Helgesson et al. 2004). Being flexible, coachable, willing to learn and relearn, and to work on one's employability, are some of the watchwords used. As a whole, a certain kind of reflexivity is also required, which means being able to see ourselves as others see us, and from the market's perspective, as well as being able to change and adapt according to what we see. In other words, it requires a subjectivity that is receptive and open to this form of 'soft' governance (Knights and Willmott 1989). These messages are in turn reinforced by incentives and conditions set. Thus, in order to be further matched to employment, a person who undergoes rehabilitation must, for example, be prepared to accept a disability code to gain access to the resources on offer. A person in a transition programme must demonstrate a certain receptiveness to the course instructor's assessment in order to move forward.

We suggest that these normalizing practices constitute a central aspect of how the labour market works today. We also suggest that they reinforce the message that the labour market is precisely that – a market – a place to exchange labour for wages and other resources. The normative practices contribute to constituting and qualifying people as labour and as goods in the labour market. They also contribute to constituting and qualifying the employers as buyers of labour. And they contribute to constituting and qualifying specialists, such as occupational psychologists and occupational therapists, as 'officials' who officiate the exchange itself. This is a constantly ongoing but non-linear process. It is instead the very oscillating between commodification and singularization, between stressing the person as a commodity and as a unique bearer of knowledge and skills, which characterizes the process (Appadurai 1986). The normative practices in themselves demonstrate this duality by alternately, and at times simultaneously, stressing people's exchange-ability and uniqueness in the labour market.

The new rules and incentives put into practice in labour market policy are put forward as novelties and innovations, as new approaches to old problems. The tendencies we see in today's labour market nevertheless give us reason to ask whether it might not in many ways have to do with an extension of the market's fundamental principles, trends that have characterized work and working life to varying degrees for many years, that are being tried again. The neoclassical market ideal presupposes a certain form of rationality in human action. It assumes a radical individualism combined with individual taking of responsibility in the quest for various forms of profitability and success. It also presupposes that it is possible, through education, incentives, reward systems and other structural arrangements, to get people to accept these as principles to guide their actions (Etzioni 1988; Ingelstam 2001).

As researchers, and as human beings, we should contribute to questioning existing concepts, definitions and established truths of our contemporary times, not least if we have reason to suspect that they are not working as intended, or if they prove to have obvious negative effects on society and people's living conditions. The dreams and visions that stake out major policies can have unforeseen and peculiar effects on the everyday lives of individuals. They can run contrary to learned cultural and social patterns in a way that counteracts their purposes. When labour market policy is formulated as a policy for a dynamic market, there is cause to critically examine, question and discuss what this approach, and the policy tools that come with it, entail. It is our hope that this book will provide inspiration and fuel for such a critical discussion.

## NOTES

1. The research that this chapter is based on was made possible by funding from the Swedish Research Council within the framework of the project *The politics and practices of capability: Lifelong learning for all in a knowledge-intense worklife?*, led by Christina Garsten. The research project LOCALISE (Local Worlds of Social Cohesion), coordinated by Martin Heidenreich and funded by the European Commission, also provided additional material and insight.

## REFERENCES

Ahrne, Göran (1994), *Social Organizations: Interaction inside, outside and between organizations*. London: Sage.
Appadurai, Arjun (ed.) (1986), *The Social Life of Things: Commodities in cultural perspective*. New York, NY: Cambridge University Press.
Berglund, Gun and Andreas Fejes (eds) (2009), *Anställningsbarhet. Perspektiv från utbildning och arbetsliv*. Lund: Studentlitteratur.
Boström, Magnus and Christina Garsten (eds) (2008), *Organizing Transnational Accountability*. Cheltenham and Northampton, MA: Edward Elgar Publishing.
Brunsson, Nils and Johan P. Olsen (1993), *The Reforming Organization*. London: Routledge.

Callon, Michel, Cécile Méadel and Vololona Rabehariosa (2002), 'The economy of qualities', *Economy and Society,* 31, 194–217.

Carrier, James G. (ed.) (1997), *Meanings of the Market: The free market in Western culture.* Oxford: Berg.

Czarniawska-Joerges, Barbara (1988), *Reformer och ideologier. Lokala nämnder på väg.* Lund: Doxa.

Drugge, Christina (2003), *Omsorgsinriktat lärande. En studie om lärande i hemtjänsten.* Luleå: Department of Teacher Education, Luleå University of Technology.

Ehrenreich, Barbara and Arlie Hochschild (eds) (2003), *Global Women: Nannies, maids and sex workers in the new economy.* New York, NY: Metropolitan Press.

Eliasson, Rosmarie (1992), 'Omsorg som lönearbete: Om taylorisering och professionalisering', in Ros-Marie Eliasson (ed.), *Egenheter och allmänheter. En antologi om omsorg och omsorgens villkor.* Stockholm: Arkiv, pp. 131–42.

Etzioni, Amitai (1988), *The Moral Dimension: Toward a new economics.* New York, NY: The Free Press.

Fogde, Mariette (2009), *The Work of Job Seeking: Studies on career advice for white-collar workers.* Örebro Studies in Media and Communication, 9. Örebro: Örebro University.

Forsell, Anders and Lars Norén (2004), 'Verktyg för offentlig upphandling', in Claes-Fredrik Helgesson, Hans Kjellberg and Anders Liljenberg (eds), *Den där marknaden: Om utbyten, normer och bilder.* Lund: Studentlitteratur.

Foucault, Michel (1991) [1975], *Discipline and Punish: The birth of the prison.* Harmondsworth: Penguin.

Furåker, Bengt (ed.) (1989), *Välfärdsstat och lönearbete.* Lund: Studentlitteratur.

Furåker, Bengt, Kristina Håkansson and Jan Ch. Karlsson (eds) (2007), *Flexibility and Stability in Working Life.* Basingstoke: Palgrave Macmillan.

Garsten, Christina (2004), '"Be a Gumby": The political technologies of employability in the temporary staffing business', in Christina Garsten and Kerstin Jacobsson (eds), *Learning to be Employable: New agendas on work, responsibility and learning in a globalizing world.* Basingstoke: Palgrave Macmillan, pp. 152–71.

Garsten, Christina (2008), *Workplace Vagabonds: Career and community in changing worlds of work.* Basingstoke: Palgrave Macmillan.

Garsten, Christina and Anna Hasselström (2004), 'Homo mercans and the fashioning of markets', in Christina Garsten and Monica Lindh de Montoya (eds), *Market Matters: Exploring cultural processes in the global marketplace.* Basingstoke: Palgrave Macmillan, pp. 209–32.

Garsten, Christina and Axel Haunschild (2014), 'Transient and flexible work lives: Liminal organizations and the reflexive habitus', in Bas Koene, Christina Garsten and Nathalie Galais (eds), *Management and Organization of Temporary Agency Work.* London: Routledge, pp. 26–37.

Garsten, Christina and Kerstin Jacobsson (eds) (2004), *Learning to be Employable: New agendas on work, responsibility and learning in a globalizing world.* Basingstoke: Palgrave Macmillan.

Garsten, Christina and Kerstin Jacobsson (2013), 'Sorting people in and out: The plasticity of the categories of employability, work capacity and disability as technologies of government', *Ephemera,* 13(4), 825–50.

Garsten, Christina and Monica Lindh de Montoya (eds) (2008), *Transparency in a New Global Order*. Cheltenham and Northampton, MA: Edward Elgar Publishing.

Gazier, Bernard (2001), 'Employability: The complexity of a policy notion', in Patricia Weinert et al. (eds), *Employability: From theory to practice*. London: Transaction Publishers, pp. 3–23.

Gilbert, Neil and Barbara Gilbert (1989), *The Enabling State: Modern welfare capitalism in America*. Oxford: Oxford University Press.

Grey, Chris (1997), 'Management as a technical practice: Professionalization or responsibilization?', *Systems Practice*, 10(6), 703–25.

Hall, Douglas T. (1996), 'Protean careers of the 21st century', *Academy of Management Journal*, 10(4), 8–16.

Helgesson, Claes-Fredrik, Hans Kjellberg and Anders Liljenberg (eds) (2004), *Den där marknaden: Om utbyten, normer och bilder*. Lund: Studentlitteratur.

Hjalmarsson, Marie (2009), *Lojalitet och motstånd: Anställdas agerande i ett föränderligt hemtjänstarbete*. Gothenburg Studies in Educational Sciences, 285. University of Gothenburg: Acta Universitatis Gothoburgensis.

Hochschild, Arlie Russell (2003) [1983], *The Managed Heart: The commercialization of human feeling*. Berkeley, CA: University of California Press.

Holmqvist, Mikael (2006), 'Medikalisering av arbetslöshet', in Mikael Holmqvist and Christian Maravelias (eds), *Hälsans styrning av arbetet*. Lund: Studentlitteratur, pp. 27–60.

Hood, Christopher and David Heald (eds) (2006), *Transparency: The key to better governance?* Oxford: Oxford University Press.

Ingelstam, Lars (2001), 'Introduktion: att rida på en tiger', in Geir Øygarden (ed.), *Vår tids ekonomism: En kritik av nationalekonomin*. Umeå: Boréa bokförlag, pp. 13–32.

Jacobsson, Kerstin and Ida Seing (2013), 'En möjliggörande arbetsmarknadspolitik? Arbetsförmedlingens utredning och klassificering av klienters arbetsförmåga, anställbarhet och funktionshinder', *Arbetsmarknad & Arbetsliv*, 1, 9–24.

Johannisson, Karin (2004), *Tecknen. Läkaren och konsten att läsa kroppar*. Stockholm: Norstedts.

Johannisson, Karin (2009), *Melankoliska rum. Om ångest, leda och sårbarhet i förfluten tid och nutid*. Stockholm: Bonniers.

Knights, David and Hugh Willmott (1989), 'Power and subjectivity at work: From degradation to subjugation in social relations', *Sociology*, 23(4), 535–58.

Kopytoff, Igor (1986), 'The cultural biography of things: Commoditization as process', in Arjun Appadurai (ed.), *The Social Life of Things: Commodities in cultural perspective*. New York, NY: Cambridge University Press, pp. 64–94.

Krejsler, John B. (2007), 'Discursive strategies that individualize: CVs and appraisal interviews', *International Journal of Qualitative Studies in Education*, 20(4), 473–90.

Leira, Arnlaug (1994), 'Concepts of caring: Loving, thinking, and doing', *Social Service Review*, 68(2), 185–201.

Lindgren, Antony and Per Sederblad (2004), 'Teamworking and emotional labour in call centres', Christina Garsten and Kerstin Jacobsson (eds), *Learning to be*

*Employable: New agendas on work, responsibility and learning in a globalizing world.* Basingstoke: Palgrave Macmillan, pp. 172–88.

Martin, Emily (1997), 'Managing Americans: Policy and changes in the meanings of work and self', in Cris Shore and Susan Wright (eds), *Anthropology of Policy.* London: Routledge, pp. 239–60.

Miller, Peter and Nikolas Rose (2008), *Governing the Present.* Cambridge: Polity.

Nicoll, Katherine (2008), *Flexibility and Lifelong Learning: Policy, discourse, politics.* London: Routledge.

Power, Michael (1997), *The Audit Society: Rituals of verification.* Oxford: Oxford University Press.

Rose, Nikolas (1996a), 'Governing "advanced" liberal democracies', in Andrew Barry, Thomas Osborne and Nicholas Rose (eds), *Foucault and Political Reason. Liberalism, neo-liberalism, and rationalities of government.* Chicago, IL: Chicago University Press, pp. 37–64.

Rose, Nikolas (1996b), 'The death of the social? Refiguring the territory of government', *Economy and Society,* 25(3), 327–56.

Rose, Nikolas (1999), *Powers of Freedom.* Cambridge: Cambridge University Press.

Sandin, Karin and Per Frykman (2010), *Du – ett varumärke.* Sweden: Addera.

Selznick, Philip (1948), 'Foundations of the theory of organization', *American Sociological Review,* 13(1), 25–35.

Strathern, Marilyn (2000), *Audit Culture: Anthropological studies in accountability, ethics and the academy.* London: Routledge.

Szebehely, Marta (1996), 'Från hemsamarit till vårdbiträde', in Rosmarie Eliasson (ed.), *Omsorgens skiftningar. Begreppet, vardagen, politiken, forskningen.* Lund: Studentlitteratur, pp. 176–94.

Walter, Lars (2005), *Som hand i handske: En studie av matchning i ett personaluthyrningsföretag.* Gothenburg: BAS. School of Business, Economics and Law, University of Gothenburg.

Werner Runebjörk, Isabel (2006), *Ditt personliga varumärke.* Malmö: Liber.

# Index